Teaching America

In *Teaching America*, Paul Carrese offers an intellectual justification for reviving a reflective and discursive approach to civic education. He explores why civic education is crucial for sustaining our democratic republic and explains how a sober, yet hopeful, civics is vital to both civic learning and perpetuating the American experiment. Blending gratitude for America with civil argument about what America means, Carrese implores educators to explore civics informed by rational patriotism. In this Tocquevillean approach, civil disagreement is a feature, not a failing, of our constitutional democracy. He argues that schools, colleges, and culture must develop citizens with the knowledge and virtues to operate our civic order, seeing self-government as crucial for the pursuit of happiness. Using a portrait of jazz as an American *e pluribus unum*, this compelling case provides a hopeful renewal of civics and civic friendship needed across formal learning and civic culture.

Paul O. Carrese is a professor in the School of Civic and Economic Thought and Leadership at Arizona State University. He founded the department on civic thought and leadership at Arizona State University that sparked a renewal of civics in public universities. A Rhodes Scholar, he taught for two decades at the US Air Force Academy. He serves on the Executive Council of the American Political Science Association.

Teaching America

*Reflective Patriotism
in Schools, College, and Culture*

PAUL O. CARRESE

CAMBRIDGE
UNIVERSITY PRESS

CAMBRIDGE
UNIVERSITY PRESS

Shaftesbury Road, Cambridge CB2 8EA, United Kingdom

One Liberty Plaza, 20th Floor, New York, NY 10006, USA

477 Williamstown Road, Port Melbourne, VIC 3207, Australia

314–321, 3rd Floor, Plot 3, Splendor Forum, Jasola District Centre,
New Delhi – 110025, India

Cambridge University Press is part of Cambridge University Press & Assessment,
a department of the University of Cambridge.

We share the University's mission to contribute to society through the pursuit of
education, learning and research at the highest international levels of excellence.

www.cambridge.org
Information on this title: www.cambridge.org/9781009746649
DOI: 10.1017/9781009746601

First published 2026

A catalogue record for this publication is available from the British Library

*A Cataloging-in-Publication data record for this book is available from the
Library of Congress*

ISBN 978-1-009-74663-2 Hardback
ISBN 978-1-009-74664-9 Paperback

Cambridge University Press & Assessment has no responsibility for the persistence
or accuracy of URLs for external or third-party internet websites referred to in this
publication and does not guarantee that any content on such websites is, or will
remain, accurate or appropriate.

For EU product safety concerns, contact us at Calle de José Abascal,
56, 1°, 28003 Madrid, Spain, or email eugpsr@cambridge.org.

To my teachers who offered me a liberal education and American civic education, and colleagues and students who have explored with me this duty and delight

It is substantially true that virtue or morality is a necessary spring of popular government. The rule, indeed, extends with more or less force to every species of free government. Who that is a sincere friend to it can look with indifference upon attempts to shake the foundation of the fabric?

Promote then, as an object of primary importance, institutions for the general diffusion of knowledge. In proportion as the structure of a government gives force to public opinion, it is essential that public opinion should be enlightened.

George Washington, Farewell Address, September 1796

Contents

Preface

Why is civic education crucial for sustaining our democratic republic? Serious preparation for citizenship is indispensable for the American idea: self-rule by *We the People* in a complex, constitutional politics. We must develop Americans with the civic knowledge and civic virtues required to operate our political and civic order, so that all citizens conceive self-government as crucial for their pursuit of happiness, whether unfolding in private life, civil society, or public affairs. Our founding principles entail self-government; *per* the Declaration of Independence, legitimate government rests upon consent of the governed as well as universal principles of justice. This implicitly calls for citizens to be active in registering consent or its absence, thus participating in the modes of government provided by existing forms. Partly because this chain of reasoning isn't natural, requiring a farsighted sense of one's self-interest in issues of justice, American political as well as educational leaders have held for nearly 400 years (Harvard was founded in 1636) that education in such citizenship is simply necessary. For the academic community this belief now presents an interesting philosophical question, at least among the relatively few who care about it in our day: why civics matters for a free people, whether it actually can work in some form, and whether it can be more than indoctrination or jingoism. Academia largely has been skeptical about citizenship education for the past sixty years and more, and given the widespread influence of academic thought in American culture, today we don't like the word civics, and we're not doing it well. We should look around at the current state of our civic health and grasp the reality that civics is now a matter of political survival.

This always has been so in America, and indeed America's leading founders wrote seriously and regularly about citizen education. Yet our deteriorating civic culture, together with the neglected, inadequate state of our programs of civic education in both schools and colleges, now makes this a matter of great urgency. One crucial component of a renewal of American civics, therefore, must be recovery of the *reflective patriotism* vital to both civic learning and to perpetuating the American experiment: a blending of gratitude for America with understanding of – and *civil disagreement* about – what America means, how we should self-govern, and how to improve. A reflective or considered patriotism is Alexis de Tocqueville's term in *Democracy in America* (1835, 1840) for the New World kind of public spirit he observes in the 1830s. He admires the American spirit of commitment to both liberty and equality, although he sees tensions between the ultimate aims of liberty and those of equality. He is concerned that a spirit of self-governing liberty and the discursive, reflective patriotism entwined with it will be difficult to sustain, given our egalitarian concern with material prosperity, in turn yielding a propensity for pragmatic and technological thinking. He does not quote the Declaration of Independence on the pursuit of happiness; nor the closing pledge by the Signers of their lives, fortunes, and "sacred Honor" staked in defense of the natural rights endowed by their Creator and embedded in the Laws of Nature and of Nature's God. Yet Tocqueville voices and praises all these principles, from the higher meaning of politics and the importance of honor among free, self-governing peoples to the American belief in a divine, metaphysical source of individual rights. Tocqueville would be dismayed yet not entirely surprised by the poor condition of our civic education nearly two centuries later and the low status of self-governing liberty for so many citizens, because he described America as a busy, dynamic place that tempts citizens to leave the work of governing to others. I suggest that anyone who enjoys the relative security, freedom, and equality of American life today should soberly assess the conditions of polarization and passivity that dominate our politics: angry and polarized partisans, especially in national politics, yet the passivity and civic apathy among so many citizens who've given up on the idea of genuine citizenship. That review should lead us to a Tocquevillean call for renewing a robust civic education, including a rational patriotism, in classrooms and beyond in order to save our self-government and the idea of America.

Indeed, we must ask: Is it too late for America? Our democratic republic commemorates in 2026 the 250th anniversary of its founding in 1776 with the Declaration. Are we now too fractured, too overwhelmed by extremes of anger and regular political violence at one end and civic apathy at the other, and generally too civically ignorant, to restore any consensus on renewing a patriotic, inclusive, and discursive civic education for all citizens and aspiring citizens? Compounding the question of errors in our philosophical approach to education and civic culture is the stark reality that digital technology now deeply shapes the souls as well as minds of Americans, particularly our younger generations, turning many citizens inward toward themselves and simulacra communities. Our technological advances tend to cut us off from the naturally human communities of family, local community, and civil society, let alone the reality of state and political communities. America is caught between an angry few who drive our further civic fracturing and a large population of the civically apathetic who are neither informed toward nor committed to citizenship, especially our youth. We have put ourselves into a perilous predicament. Is it too late to forge a consensus on teaching America about America, and for such teaching in schools, college, and culture to avert our self-destruction or our collapse if attacked by a foreign power or powers?

In 2019, I had the good fortune to be asked by fellow educators to join a national-consensus study adopting the premise that we had a civic duty to recognize American civic culture was in bad shape, but not hopeless. Our report on K-12 civics and history education fused center-left to center-right views among practitioners and scholars of citizenship preparation, seeking the best history and political science elements. It was released in 2021 as *Educating for American Democracy (EAD)*, aiming to foster "excellence in history and civics for all learners." The origin of this collaborative effort is itself a civic lesson, and an American tale. Danielle Allen and Jane Kamensky of Harvard University and Peter Levine of Tufts University were the most prominent center-left scholars who generated the national-consensus approach for the study, along with Louise Dubé, director of the education provider iCivics – and they deliberately reached out to flyover country to invite a constitutional conservative in Arizona as a coauthor. While both K-12 and higher education in America are dominated by liberal-progressive views on civics and history education, my *EAD* colleagues also welcomed contributions to the two-year study by other intellectual and academic conservatives. Our final report argued that K-12 citizenship education couldn't be repaired and renewed without also addressing higher education's failings in civics, nor without collaboration from civil society institutions and associations. Further, all such reassessment and renewal must be premised upon a reflective or discursive patriotism toward America, recommending a civics that embraces the American political project while embodying civil disagreement about both the larger meaning of America and particular issues.

What we learned as educators, fellow citizens, and civic friends in undertaking the *EAD* study across two years is an American tale because we chose to forge an *e pluribus unum* across philosophical, demographic, geographic, and institutional dimensions. This was the only way to help ourselves and the rising generations of citizens to understand America as the *E Pluribus Unum* of our national motto: out of many, one. To reinforce the principle that serious citizenship education and a reflective patriotism about America must occur beyond classrooms as well as within, it is useful to characterize the many meetings and arguments that produced the *EAD* report, ultimately involving over three hundred participants, as akin to jazz. Now in its second century, jazz is a globally appreciated art form while also a distinctly American invention and treasure. Only in America did it develop, and arguably it could have arisen only here: a musical blend of civilizational traditions, of the blues and Christian spirituals with black gospel music, of order and improvisation, altogether reflecting joy to sorrow, expressing and seeking truths about humanity and divinity. One could say the *EAD* coauthors are singing the blues about America, in the discursive mode of jazz, especially about the sorry state of our civic education and reflective patriotism. To borrow from the Duke Ellington classic, America's got it bad and that ain't good, but we're not giving up, so we've got a story to tell – all achieved through a blend of diverse backgrounds and voices, of group and solo efforts; a harmony comprising complexity. As the chapter on civic culture argues, the black Americans, such as Louis Armstrong and Ellington, who pioneered jazz, joined by white musicians, are exemplars of hope and amelioration in American history because they were builders of a popular and artistic *e pluribus unum* overcoming racial prejudice and barriers.

As many Americans have noted during our recent civic deterioration, hope is not optimism. We have grounds to hope America can recover, but few grounds for optimism. Anyone familiar with national polling in the past decade on views of those 18 to 35 about America, particularly their civic attachment and civic knowledge, is aware that America itself is deeply underwater among the rising generation. This is how we have prepared those whom we expect to take up political and civic leadership roles in the coming decades? That deplorable civic condition is not unrelated to the rise in tolerance for political violence, as well as strong markers of persistent civic distrust and animosity, across most age and demographic cohorts. As noted, all of these problems are amplified by the capture of American youth into a digital culture, which pulls them away from real, healthy human associations and politics. The inspiring jazz of the *EAD* report, with its recommendations for improving civic education in K-12 and beyond, has achieved some success since its 2021 release in spurring reform in K-12 schools. In a larger sense, however, it has been swamped by the culture of extremes suffocating the American idea: the polarized anger of a few, civic passivity and ignorance among too many.

Teaching America opens by arguing that the founders of our democratic constitutional republic knew civic education must be a priority because our form of politics is difficult to achieve and sustain; that America more or less heeded this lesson across its first two centuries, through the 1950s; and that in the name of reform and progress we largely have repudiated or neglected this crucial insight for sixty years or more. Alexis de Tocqueville, the great French political philosopher and observer of America and of the rise of modern democracy, informs my general approach to lessons we should draw and remedies to pursue. We must renew the civics of a democratic republic in formal schooling and also in civic culture if we are to shape the souls of our fellow citizens and aspiring citizens so that they care about the demanding yet fulfilling work of self-government, and are competent as to the knowledge and character needed. In schools, in colleges, and in civic culture, we need to assess our deficits. Through reasonable argument, we must then forge the compromises and plans of action necessary to restore a robust civic education and a healthier, happier civic culture.

We owe this to ourselves, as a matter of our own dignity and sacred honor, for as the Declaration argues, at stake are the equal natural rights endowed to all human beings. We also owe it to our forebears, including our great civic exemplars, and all those who made possible this extraordinary American experiment in constitutional liberty. Further, as the Preamble to our Constitution states, we owe to our posterity these efforts to secure the Blessings of Liberty. Our democratic republic is imperfect as all human things are, but worthy of gratitude and our renewed efforts to live up to her founding principles. The argument devotes more attention to those civic exemplars who were American reformers, from Elizabeth Cady Stanton and Frederick Douglass to Martin Luther King, Jr. They believed in the common ground of our founding documents and principles, but insist that serious reform was needed in laws or the Constitution to live up to our essential ideals of justice.

In the spirit of the national-consensus jazz that my coauthors and I negotiated and forged in the *EAD* report, I hope that *Teaching America* encourages consideration of a reflective, enlightened patriotism and civic learning as lifelong priorities for all American citizens and aspiring citizens. It seeks to do so by addressing five main questions, which readers can consider along with me: Can we sustain the American idea? (Introduction). What is American civics and why does it matter? (Chapter 1). Can reflective patriotism protect American civics from propaganda and partisanship? (Chapter 2). What should American schools teach? (Chapter 3). What should American colleges and universities teach? (Chapter 4). And how should civic culture sustain America's *e pluribus unum*? (Chapter 5). Chapter 6 proposes that reflective civics and civic friendship, the activities of discursive patriots and civic friends, is a delight as well as a duty for all ages of citizens and aspiring citizens.

Hope is not optimism. The grim reality of twenty-first century America is that two rival schools now dominate our political, educational, and media landscapes on civics, at least as to energy and prominence. In blunt but reasonable terms, the first can be summarized as an anti-patriotism emphasizing critique of America's founding principles and their historical unfolding; it is represented by *The 1619 Project of the New York Times* and its Pulitzer Center partners, first published in 2019. This view is widely present in K-12 and higher education, certainly among leading institutions and those with the most curricular influence. It appears either in its strong, explicit version made prominent decades earlier by Howard Zinn's *A People's History*, or in the weaker version of democracy education that disregards study of America's founding principles, their origins, and the unfolding story of 250 years of argument about how to live up to them – replaced by ideas about progress toward the perpetual self-invention of democracy, and engagement in policy advocacy. The rival school at the opposite pole can be summarized as a nostalgic-defensive patriotism reacting to the cynical or democracy-now view; it is represented by the 1776 Commission of the first Trump administration, carried in the interim by the National Association of Scholars among other advocates, and revived in the second Trump administration. There is some evidence that a large, less-vocal middle cares about civics, and in a less-polarized way; a majority that balances respect for America with appreciation for discussion of its failings and challenges. Yet the rival, polarized and polarizing schools of 1619 and 1776 dominate. Most teachers, schools, parents, academic units, and citizens holding a more reflective patriotism toward America have fewer voices, champions, and resources amid our civic decay. Of the polarized options, the effectively antipatriotic utopianism of the 1619 school is arguably the faster path toward America's self-destruction. Its hyper-critique is an unsustainable civic model that free rides on American liberty, prosperity, order, and relative equality while aggravating rather than redressing our polarization and civic decay. Yet the nostalgic-defensive patriotism of the 1776 school is not an adequate remedy, since it is not grounded in the American reality and spirit of *e pluribus unum*: our civic duty to hear out the arguments and complaints of American pluralism, constructively address them, and prepare citizens to find the sober patriotic balance of gratitude for our republic, civic honesty about our failures, and a spirit of reform. The common ground of America, our founding principles and institutions, includes debate and disagreement from the beginning. A reflective American civics must perpetually strike the balance between a focal regard for our distinctive ideals and disagreement about just what they mean and whether we are abiding by their full demands.

What the late US Supreme Court Justice Sandra Day O'Connor deemed, two decades ago, America's "quiet crisis" – the deplorable condition of civic education and reflective patriotism – is still a crisis, even if some progress has been made in provoking awareness about needed improvement, and some remedies have been undertaken. Further, the crisis is not quiet anymore. The heated contests of the past three decades over the content of US history and civics curricula in public schools have become only more heated and widespread. The concern arises that America has thrust herself into a doom-loop: undeniable evidence of civic ignorance among all ages of our citizenry, linked to widespread loss of confidence in all national institutions and professions – even the military – now combines with alarmingly low levels of patriotism toward America, especially among younger citizens, and an angry, polarized politics itself fed by civic ignorance and apathy among a vast proportion of citizens. We now are so polarized about what civics is, and how to improve its status and quality in schools and higher education, that our national civic culture might fully disintegrate before the long game of a renewed American civics can produce civic repair.

Teaching America proposes that a national-consensus view can develop, among educators and all serious citizens and aspiring citizens, bringing more reasonable debate and less polarization to consideration of crucial questions facing us: How to sustain the American idea; what a reflective patriotism and American civics is; how civics can avoid propaganda and partisanship; what our schools and colleges should teach to forge responsible, informed, discursive citizens; how our civic culture can sustain America's *e pluribus unum*; and why commitment to reflective civic learning and civic friendships, the activities of thoughtful patriots and civic friends, is a duty and delight for all ages. The ingredients today of a national consensus are readily evident, even regarding Tocqueville's peculiar philosophical phrase, a reflective patriotism. That great Broadway star, Alexander Hamilton, described America's duty in world history in terms similar to the quality Tocqueville later highlights about Americans: our capacity for reflection amid the tumult of our dynamic polity. In the first essay of *The Federalist*, published in 1787, Hamilton stated:

> It has been frequently remarked, that it seems to have been reserved to the people of this country, by their conduct and example, to decide the important question, whether societies of men are really capable or not, of establishing good government from reflection and choice, or whether they are forever destined to depend, for their political constitutions, on accident and force.

For my colleagues in higher education, and friends in K-12 schools, rediscovering and reprioritizing a reflective American civics should now be seen as enlightened self-interest. In 2025, the second Trump administration directed unprecedented pressure at elite universities to comply with antidiscrimination laws (to include prohibitions on antisemitism) and to correct what the administration deemed failure to act in the public interest, versus partisan interests, given the well-documented ideological skew of these institutions; at risk of losing huge sums of federal funding, even their nonprofit status. Harvard is a prominent target, as America's first and now wealthiest higher education institution, and among its most elite. Longtime faculty member Danielle Allen responded in *The Atlantic* that while the plummeting public confidence in higher education, which President Trump was exploiting, could not justify the unprecedented measures and threats being brandished, academia nonetheless needed to introspect. Higher education should propose for its own good a new social contract with America, beyond the one forged after World War II that gave universities public and private support of many kinds in exchange for producing technological innovation and advances in economic prosperity and competitiveness. Allen argues that both the public and academia allowed this social contract to neglect the core mission of educating citizens and citizen leaders for our constitutional democratic republic.

Allen's insight aligns with the brave argument made in recent years by Johns Hopkins president Ronald Daniels that universities had forgotten they owe to American democracy a higher education including civics for all college and university graduates. *Teaching America* pursues these insights to argue that the renewed bond between America and academia must place excellence in civic learning, in its fullest sense, on equal terms with excellence in science-technology-engineering-mathematics (STEM), and foundations for economic prosperity and physical health, as the main goals for successful graduates and successful universities and colleges. Further, regarding schools, we must apply the same logic, and the same convergence of institutional need with public need, to K-12 public education. Our schools should restore the main original mission of publicly funded or "common" schools: to provide an American civic education. They can thereby restore the public confidence lost in recent decades. Finally, for our culture, this renewed, high-priority civics in schools and colleges, and in lifelong learning beyond, must include discourse about the pursuit of happiness named in the Declaration as one of our natural, God-given rights. Discussion of these large ideas about humanity offers higher meaning to students in schools and colleges – including for students focusing on scientific and preprofessional study. Rediscovery of the pursuit of happiness in a sense that fits with civic duties and the sacred honor of defending self-government also offers meaning to an American civil society and culture that faces a crisis of despair, anomie, and alienation amid our general conditions of great wealth and security relative to the scope of human history, and most of the world still today.

The intersection of a reflective civics and serious discussion of the pursuit of happiness is evident in another of Tocqueville's evergreen insights from *Democracy in America*. Tocqueville suggests our democratic culture would tend to emphasize, most of the time and for most people, the practical and self-interested dimensions of human activities. Yet he was particularly concerned about the consequences of this democratic, egalitarian, and materialist spirit for education, and for civic participation in self-government. He counseled Americans to keep in balance the intrinsically worthy and higher dimensions of both education and civic participation on the one hand with the more utilitarian rationales for each. Today we should consider that this restoration of a primary place for a reflective, discursive civics in schools, colleges, and American culture is in our basic interest, as a matter of civic strength and health, while it also will help to renew the core, high-minded spirit that should animate our educational institutions and our culture: a spirit of truth-seeking, lively discourse, reasonable debate, and attention to the full human consequences of our theories, approaches, inventions, and technologies. Thus the renaissance effect from a genuine prioritizing of and investment in civics would orient us toward both the perpetuation of our republic and a deeper cause: that the activity of self-governing is intrinsically worthy for free human beings. Whether in resisting tyranny in 1776 or later crises, or in enjoying the more quotidian tasks and disagreements of self-government, we must perpetually recall that citizenship is a matter of sacred honor.

We should use the occasion of the 250th anniversary of our political founding in 1776, the Semiquincentennial commemorations beginning in 2026, to renew a rich civic education in our schools, colleges, and civic culture. Given the deep hole we are in, "America250" commemorations and the civic-learning opportunities they afford should extend, ideally, from commemorating the Declaration in 1776 through to at least the ratification of the Bill of Rights in 1791. That means a fifteen-year period of civic renewal, 2026 to 2041. Beyond our self-interest in repairing, perhaps saving, our damaged democratic republic this also would muster the appropriate honor and regard we should show to our founding achievements and founders, and to the centuries of freedom, equality, argument, and reform they made possible thus far – and that we should pass to our posterity.

Acknowledgments

Among several debts and notes of gratitude to register, *Teaching America* is dedicated to my teachers, colleagues, and students. In a Tocquevillean spirit I briefly thank my family, and the town and religious community, which reared me in upstate New York. In more formal modes of learning, my public-school teachers there prepared me for study with professors at Middlebury College, Oxford University, and Boston College. These mentors, along with academic mentors at institutions beyond, offered me a classical liberal education blended with an American civic education. I am indebted to them for introducing me to many of the philosophers, political figures, and ideas discussed in the book, and for setting me on the path of modeling their dedicated teaching and mentoring. I have been fortunate as a professor for over four decades – starting at the National University of Lesotho, thanks to my wife, Susan – in finding colleagues and students interested in studying these important ideas, questions, and debates; as both important in themselves and as a duty and delight for free human beings and citizens. I have learned from and been inspired by colleagues and students in Lesotho, Middlebury College, the US Air Force Academy, University of Delhi in India, Ashland University, and Arizona State University; along with visiting fellowships at Harvard University, Princeton University, and Stanford University.

After I began to build the School of Civic and Economic Thought and Leadership (SCETL) at Arizona State University in 2016, I realized more clearly that during my eighteen years as a civilian faculty member at the Air Force Academy (an Athenian in Sparta), I had been offering not so much a leadership education as a civic education to future officers and junior military colleagues. I learned deeply from civilian and military colleagues at the Academy, and again at SCETL, about America, citizenship, and civic education. While serving as Director of SCETL, I also collaborated with civic leaders in Arizona, and I am particularly grateful for the guidance and model offered by Senator Jon Kyl. Sean Beienburg at SCETL is owed special thanks, among many fine colleagues, for his supererogatory commitment to building and sustaining that new department, which in turn has yielded important national fruit.

The past decade has pulled me into a national community of educators devoted to American civics in schools and colleges. I am grateful for the conversation and camaraderie with the fellow deans and directors of the civic thought and leadership units at public universities. I also am indebted to colleagues at a range of other universities and institutions, including James Stoner, Robby George, Brad Wilson, James Ceaser, Josh Ober, Jenna Storey, Ben Storey, Yuval Levin, Peter Berkowitz, Bryan Garsten, Steven Smith, Dan Carpenter, Michael Poliakoff, Guy Burnett, Jeffry Morrison, Paul Ludwig, Phillip Muñoz, Danielle Allen, Louise Dubé, Jane Kamensky, and Peter Levine. The new community of educators in the Alliance for Civics in the Academy promises further conversation and learning. The visiting scholar position that Josh Ober arranged at the Hoover Institution and Stanford University in 2025, which allowed two immersions into the Stanford Civics Initiative and the new Center for Revitalizing American Institutions in Hoover, afforded rich conversations about the civics renewal in higher education and beyond. A particular thanks goes to my coauthors of the 2021 national study of K-12 history and civics education, *Educating for American Democracy* (*EAD*), as recounted throughout *Teaching America* – Danielle, Louise, Jane, Peter, as well as Kei Kawashima-Ginsburg and Tammy Waller. We forged an *e pluribus unum*, and I continue to learn about America and civics from that effort and its ongoing manifestations.

It has been an honor to work closely in recent years with Jack Miller, Michael Weiser, Hans Zeiger, and the team of professionals they have assembled in the Jack Miller Center for Teaching America's Founding Principles and History. More than two decades ago, before other institutions and voices began to focus on the abandonment of American citizenship education in schools and colleges, the JMC began laboring in the vineyards. Their commitment in our fractured era to renewing an understanding and appreciation of America's common ground – our founding principles, texts, ideals – is inspiring. I'm grateful they asked me to join their efforts in 2024 as Senior Fellow for Civic Thought and Leadership (CTL); and for their support of the CTL reform effort in public universities. They have supported, and patiently endured my conversations about, the project of *Teaching America*. I look forward to the great work the Jack Miller Center will undertake across the next two decades to mark America's Semiquincentennial, utilizing it as a moment for deepening the renaissance of American civic education.

In the final phase of writing the book, I had the happy surprise of reconnecting with Kara Buckley; we first met thirty years ago when she was a young professor of political science at Middlebury while I was visiting as an instructor. She volunteered to read the opening sections of *Teaching America*, and I am grateful for her fresh view and candid suggestions, which improved the final argument. Peter Minowitz helpfully reviewed the chapter on civic culture, which features jazz, bringing his experience as a political theory professor and a jazz pianist; affirming that my account wasn't too off-key.

My wife Susan has supported my work in civic education these many decades, including the writing of this book, and been my regular co-teacher and conversation partner – as well as a steady civic friend, even as we have disagreed about issues of theory, practice, and contemporary affairs. Our children, Hannah and Dominic, also have joined many conversations about or closely related to this project, as has my mother-in-law, Noeline. A special thanks goes to Noeline for providing a study in her house where I completed most of the drafting of the manuscript. Hannah also carefully reviewed the early sections of the completed manuscript with lawyerly attention to clarity and judicious regard for civic fairness and friendship, both of which yielded important improvements.

The various chapters of *Teaching America* draw upon and adapt several occasional essays and a recent journal article already published; I am thankful to the various publications and editors for granting permission to utilize these materials. I am indebted to Mike Sabo and Daniel Mahoney for asking me to write "Civic Education as a Duty and a Delight," for the American Civics portal of *RealClearPublicAffairs*, 1776 Series, August 25, 2021. I am grateful to Mike Sabo for asking S. Adam Seagrave and me to collaborate on writing essays explaining the main themes of the *EAD* "Roadmap" of curricular guidelines, as "Teacher Resources for American Civics," the American Civics portal of *RealClearPublicAffairs*, 2022. Chapter 1 adapts "Montesquieu's Call to Civic Education: Roots of and Remedies for America's Civic Crisis," in *American Citizenship and Constitutionalism in Principle and Practice*, eds. Steven Pittz and Joseph Postell (University of Oklahoma Press, 2022). Introduction and Chapter 3 draw upon "Civic Preparation of American Youth: Reflective

Patriotism and Our Constitutional Democracy," *The ANNALS of the American Academy of Political and Social Science*, 75(1), (January 2023): 39–52 (published November 2023). The Preface and Introduction draw upon "Civic Thought and Leadership: A Higher Civics to Sustain American Constitutional Democracy," *LAWS: Special Issue on Civic Engagement, Justice, and the Law in National and International Context*, 13(2), 19 (March 2024), MDPI open access. I draw throughout the book on "The Restoration of Higher Learning," lead essay in a Forum for *Law & Liberty*, September 3, 2024; and my final reply, "Restoring a Higher Civics in America's Universities," September 30, 2024. I am grateful to my conversants in that Forum – James Hankins, Michael Poliakoff, and J. Michael Hoffpauir.

The one image used in this book is the album cover of the Ray Charles 1972 album *A Message from the People*, in Chapter 5, when discussing jazz as an achievement of American hope. The source is a Wikipedia entry on the 1972 album; the album was released by Ray's own label, Tangerine/ABC.

Introduction

Can We Sustain the American Idea?

The disintegrating condition of America's civic culture today requires, for those who recognize it and seek to redress it, that we undertake a decades-long effort to commemorate America 250. This is the semiquincentennial of the founding of our polity in 1776 with the Declaration of Independence; and we should commemorate the great moments, texts, leaders, and debates that unfolded from 1776 to 1791, marking the ratification of the Bill of Rights as amendments to the 1787 Constitution. The point is not to make our founding the be-all and end-all. Yet as a polity distinctly founded on big ideas, we must know and debate these, so we can reasonably understand in turn how our ideas, institutions, and culture have developed over ensuing centuries; what constitutional revisions we have made and what new civic norms forged; and how well we have lived up to the founding ideals. A fifteen-year commemoration of national civic education, from 2026 to 2041, thus should renew the reflective patriotism vital to both civic learning and perpetuating the American experiment: blending gratitude for America with understanding of – including civil disagreement about – what America means, how we should self-govern, and how to improve.

A two-decade renewal of civics and civic culture would be the enlightened thing to do for the world's most prominent and successful democratic republic – and today it also is a desperate matter of self-interest. Aristotle, the founder of political science in the fourth century BC, grasped the philosophical importance of analyzing how to perpetuate a particular constitution of a free people, including the role of education in sustaining a polity.[1]

---

[1] *The Politics of Aristotle*, tr. and ed. Simpson, Book 4, chapters 14–17, and Book 5 (alternately Books 7 and 8 in the more conventional ordering of the books).

Throughout the twentieth century, however, the dominant view in elite American higher education held that we were smarter than this classical view; we didn't need to devote top scholars, departments, and institutions to considering citizenship education in terms of the challenge of sustaining our constitutional democratic republic, nor to educating undergraduate students on these topics. The priority, rather, should be critique of the polity and its foundations, either implicitly or explicitly; progress toward newer and more democratic vistas; and the utility of narrower policy and technological dimensions of political, economic, and social life.

The predominant kind of civics yielded by this confident progressive view, from John Dewey onward, was democracy-focused, emphasizing engagement among the current generation of Americans through elections and the policy-formation process. This democracy civics either took for granted or repudiated America's founding principles, and demoted or belittled the study of the founding and of the civilizational tradition that yielded America. Nor did democracy civics study the historical unfolding and development of America's principles across centuries, with its rich arguments, exemplars of reflective patriotism, and mixed record of advance toward fulfilling the promise of the Declaration. Democratic action now was the priority, based upon either neglect of America's distinctive principles – replaced by "democracy" – or explicit repudiation of America as mostly a fraud and a failure across three centuries and more.[2]

I suggest to my fellow professors and civics experts that this progressive view, in both its more moderate and radical modes, now must confront its own grave problems. This predominant neglect of our particular republic, its principles, its development, and its serious tradition of reforming American institutions and norms must be considered a cause of our current civic crisis. The only alternative is to admit that higher education and the leading lights of K-12 education so deeply shaped by academia are largely irrelevant to American civic life. There is a strong correlation between our increasingly progressive-democratic approach to civics and our trajectory of civic ignorance and disintegration; it is not

---

[2] Jonathan Zimmerman in *Whose America? Culture Wars in the Public Schools*, 2nd ed. (University of Chicago Press, 2022) investigates these developments from the 1920s, with greater sympathy to democratic and progressive education, yet noting the radical character of The 1619 Project and its forebears in Chapters 1, 3, 4, 9, and the Conclusion. Peter Levine advocates democracy education as civic engagement, yet with a Socratic moderation about its inherent tensions or problems, in *The Future of Democracy: Developing the Next Generation of American* Citizens (Tufts University Press, 2007), Chapters 1 and 2, with discussion of Dewey at 41–45.

plausible to think that the strong change in the approach and content of civic education is a minor or irrelevant factor in the new civic crisis. Indeed it has hardly been characteristic of American higher education across the past two centuries to diminish its ambitions and sense of influence on our national life. Given claims still made today by colleges and universities that they prepare leaders for American life, it would be odd to disclaim any role in or responsibility for the state of our civic health and strength. Higher education has either been doing the wrong thing for many decades, not enough of the right thing, or both.

Fortunately, there is now a cross-ideological, bipartisan view that we need to reprioritize civics in American higher education, to include the responsibility of colleges and universities *per se* for improving K-12 civics – rather than just pushing it off to their education schools or teachers' colleges, as occurred during the heyday of democracy civics. The 2021 report *Educating for American Democracy (EAD)* is one of those intellectually heterogeneous efforts.[3] I note earlier in the Preface that as an *EAD* coauthor, I see our two years of dialogue, debate, and consensus-forging as akin to that great American invention, jazz. (More on jazz in Chapter 5 on civic culture.) One of the foundational elements of jazz music from the early twentieth century is the blues. Yet blues music is not depressing; it expresses a spirit of persistence and resilience amid sadness. The *EAD* report was candid about the deplorable condition of American civic culture, civic knowledge, and civic attachment today; yet we argued national-consensus remedies were at hand if we would consider them. We had a sad tale to tell about America, but we were sticking together and not giving up.

If one thinks this approach puts too much blues in the mix, consider three dimensions of our common life today indicating an ever-deepening civic crisis. A sober consideration of teaching America about America, and how to do so in schools and colleges but also in our broader civic culture, must begin with the reality that it might indeed be very late in the day for our democratic republic.

The first dimension of our civic crisis is persisting negative polarization across party and philosophical lines, including the enduring appeal in recent decades of populist demagogues in both the Republican and Democratic parties. This is the spirit of Senator Bernie Sanders and his younger protégés,

---

[3] *Educating for American Democracy: Excellence in History and Civics for All Learners.* iCivics. www.educatingforamericandemocracy.org. I will refer to the report by its acronym, *EAD*.

and President Donald Trump and his protégés, each dominating their respective parties along with their associated media and intellectual communities.[4] Our politics is suffused with angry emotivism about the leading figures and ideas in the other party or faction, albeit with a largely apathetic middle not willing and able to break the pattern of rival extremes advocating radical measures to counter the odiousness of the rival party. Books expressing grave concern for the health and even survival of American constitutional democracy have been bestsellers for a decade, including *How Democracies Die* by two Harvard professors.[5] More telling is *The Bill of Obligations* by foreign policy expert Richard Haass, sounding the alarm about our civic disintegration because the lack of a healthy constitutional order and civic culture destroys the national consensus that policy makers need for crafting and sustaining American national security strategies and foreign policies.[6] Having served in presidential administrations of both parties and led the Council on Foreign Relations, Haass opens his call for emphasizing "habits of good citizens" by diagnosing "the crisis of our rights-based democracy" and our "democratic deterioration." When asked in recent years about the greatest threat we face, he has argued the "most urgent and significant threat to American security and stability stems not from abroad but from within, from political divisions that for only the second time in US history have raised questions about the future of American democracy and even the United States itself."

A second dimension of our civic crisis is that recent polling on confidence in our institutions and America itself – on the very legitimacy of our political-civic order – registers a steady decline into record low rankings. Only the military has above 50 percent support among national institutions in Gallup's annual surveys across recent decades, but its standing also has eroded.[7] Levels of patriotism have dropped; among

---

[4] One sign of the decay of American civic and constitutional culture is the fact that when Sanders and Trump contended for the nominations of the major parties in 2016, the former was not a Democrat and the latter not a Republican; parties are weak as organizations, even as we complain about too much partisanship. I briefly discuss in Chapter 6 why political parties can and should be seen as a positive element of American civic culture.

[5] Steven Levitsky and Daniel Ziblatt, *How Democracies Die* (Crown, 2018); also Yascha Mounk, *The People vs. Democracy: Why Our Freedom Is in Danger & How to Save It* (Harvard University Press, 2018).

[6] Richard Haass, *The Bill of Obligations: The Ten Habits of Good Citizens* (Penguin, 2023), Preface.

[7] Megan Brenan, "U.S. Confidence in Institutions Mostly Flat, but Police Up; Average confidence in institutions remains historically low, at 28%," *Gallup*, July 15, 2024, at www.news.gallup.com/poll/647303/confidence-institutions-mostly-flat-police.aspx.

young people they are alarming. Gallup recently found only 18 percent of respondents aged 18–29 were "extremely proud" to be American, down from over 40 percent in 2015 among an 18–34 cohort. America itself is deeply underwater with our younger citizenry. The civic spirit that rallied farmers and craftsmen to oppose the British army at Lexington and Concord in 1775 and ultimately win the Revolutionary War is hardly evident in these figures. Indeed, Gallup also found in a 2023 poll that only 41 percent of Americans are willing to fight if our country were invaded. A 2022 poll by Quinnipiac seemed to have better news, with a bare majority (55 percent) stating they would stay and fight, rather than flee, if our country was invaded as Vladimir Putin's Russia had just invaded Ukraine; yet among the 18–34 cohort in that poll, most would not fight: 48 percent would leave the country, 45 percent would stay and fight, and 6 percent didn't know or didn't answer. Such is our gravely diminished appreciation for the meaning and value of our freedom.[8]

A third and related dimension of our civic crisis is a sharp drop in confidence about higher education, which for a century has grown in prominence as an American civic institution; one indication being that college graduates constitute the great bulk of American political and civic leaders. Gallup and the Lumina Foundation registered in 2024 that only 36 percent of respondents held "a great deal" or "quite a lot" of confidence in American higher education, a 21 percent drop from nine years earlier. Roughly a third of respondents have only some confidence in higher education, and a third have very little to none. The concerns are not only about cost, degree completion, or the relevance of degree offerings to preparation for employment. Nor are the concerns simply partisan. Independents now join Republicans or conservatives in sharply declining trust in colleges and universities. The Gallup-Lumina survey found 41 percent rate colleges as "too liberal," trying to "indoctrinate" or "brainwash" students, or not allowing students to think for themselves. An American National Election Studies pilot survey found in 2024

[8] Megan Brenan, "American Pride Remains Near Record Low; Republicans continue to express more pride in the U.S. than Democrats and independents," *Gallup*, July 2, 2024, at www.news.gallup.com/poll/646655/american-pride-remains-near-record-low.aspx; Gallup International, "Fewer people are willing to fight for their country compared to ten years ago," March 25, 2024, at www.gallup-international.com/survey-results-and-news/survey-result/fewer-people-are-willing-to-fight-for-their-country-compared-to-ten-years-ago; Quinnipiac University Poll, "Vast Majority Of Americans Say Ban Russian Oil; Nearly 8 in 10 Support U.S. Military Response if Putin Attacks A NATO Country," March 7, 2022, at www.poll.qu.edu/poll-release?releaseid=3838.

that almost 60 percent responded "most colleges have a liberal bias in what they teach students," with only 26 percent approving of "how colleges and universities are run these days."[9]

There are several causes for these complex phenomena of deepening polarization and anger, sinking constitutional-civic legitimacy, and low confidence in higher education. The digital transformation of civilization has had liberating and empowering effects but also eroded face-to-face community from family and friendships to civil society and many institutions, with several grave effects on American political life. Counteracting the latter will require concerted efforts to restore human-scale civic and political community from the ground up. In this fractured and challenging moment of declining civic commitment and civic health, we can reasonably turn for guidance to the civic wisdom of Abraham Lincoln, still widely regarded by Americans 160 years after his death, and seriously studied by a diverse set of scholars. In 1838, the young lawyer (not yet thirty) diagnosed for fellow citizens in the town of Springfield, Illinois, at a Young Men's Lyceum meeting, that a failure of civic education was the main cause of our descent into violent division – opening a prospect of national "suicide."[10] Lincoln's prescience was confirmed by a ferocious civil war erupting two decades later. Yet a spirit of forewarning also informs a famous remark made fifty years earlier, during America's founding, by Benjamin Franklin. Eliza Powell, a Philadelphia civic leader, asked him in September 1787 at the close of the convention assembled to revise America's constitutional charter: What form of government has the convention recommended? "A republic" Franklin replied, "if you can keep it."[11]

---

[9] Jeffrey M. Jones, "U.S. Confidence in Higher Education Now Closely Divided," *Gallup*, July 8, 2024, at www.news.gallup.com/poll/646880/confidence-higher-education-closely-divided.aspx; American National Election Studies, 2024 Pilot Study, at www.election studies.org/data-center/2024-pilot-study/. Responses that these polling data are more ambiguous, thus less alarming for higher education, typically sidestep the issue of ideological bias; see, for example, Jessica Blake, "Have Americans Actually Lost Faith in Higher Education?," *Inside Higher Education*, September 24, 2024, at www.insidehighered.com/news/business/2024/09/24/report-nuance-needed-analysis-higher-ed-polls.

[10] Abraham Lincoln, "On the Perpetuation of Our Political Institutions," Springfield Lyceum Address, January 27, 1838; available in the new *ContextUS* collection at www.contextus.org/Abraham_Lincoln,_Lyceum_Address_(1838)?tab=contents.

[11] Brooke Manville and Josiah Ober open with this story in their analysis of prominent democracies and republics in human history, *The Civic Bargain: How Democracy Survives* (Princeton University Press, 2023), 1. Jeffrey Sikkenga and David Davenport take inspiration from this episode in their diagnosis of our civics deficit and remedies for it, *A Republic If You Can Teach It: Fixing America's Civic Education Crisis* (Republic Book Publishers, 2024).

1.1 FRANKLIN'S WARNING AND LINCOLN'S: AMERICA'S CRISIS AND OUR CIVICS FAILURE

Some 240 years after the Constitutional Convention, America has survived foreign wars and a civil war to become the most politically, militarily, and economically powerful republic in all of history. Franklin's sour note at our dawning thus might seem misplaced. Yet from where he stood as a statesman, he knew that the record of republics or democracies was checkered and leaning toward disastrous; these regimes were either too weak or internally divided to defend themselves against monarchies and empires, or, prone to destroy themselves in civil conflict. The brevity of Franklin's comment, adding no elaboration, also suggests he was reflecting a widespread concern among leading American minds about the inherent fragility of our form of self-government, given the fractious tendencies of human nature as well as a dangerous world still dominated by monarchies and despotisms. We further know that Franklin, like many leading founders, strongly recommended a priority for education as indispensable to sustaining our new republic. The most prominent institution to which he devoted his efforts became the University of Pennsylvania.[12]

Just as Franklin spoke for a widely held view of his era, it is noteworthy today that an echo of his concern, and of Lincoln's from a half-century later, arises not just from political or intellectual conservatives. Several prominent academics of the center and center-left have identified higher education's neglect of civic education as a cause of our polarization and declining civic health. Among the first was Derek Bok, former Harvard president, in his 2020 book *Higher Expectations* – which names the near-disappearance of civic education requirements as the foremost failing that twenty-first century-higher education must redress.[13] A bit more surprising is Ronald Daniels, the president of Johns Hopkins – America's first research university, designed to supersede the traditional liberal arts approach to educating civic and societal leaders. He argues with two coauthors in his 2021 book *What Universities Owe Democracy* that the near-disappearance of requirements for a serious civic education in most

---

[12] See generally Lorraine S. Pangle and Thomas L. Pangle, *The Learning of Liberty: The Educational Ideals of the American Founders* (Lawrence: University Press of Kansas, 1992), Introduction; chapter 4 analyzes Franklin's views and efforts on civic education in schools.

[13] *Higher Expectations: Can Colleges Teach Students What They Need to Know in the 21st Century?* (Princeton University Press, 2020).

colleges and universities is one cause of our angry moment of civic disintegration. An initial remedy is that at least one course in liberal arts knowledge about liberal democracy, and about American constitutional principles and ideals, should be required for every college and university graduate. Daniels and his coauthors further argue these institutions must provide students experiences of civic virtues such as civil disagreement and reasonable pluralism about important civic and political issues.[14]

Most recently, two leaders of Stanford University's efforts to restore the nexus of liberal arts and civic education – The Stanford Civics Initiative – argued in *The New York Times* that by "abandoning civics" in recent decades, American colleges and universities became a source of the civic ignorance and angry polarization undermining our civic culture.[15] In a similar spirit, Yale's Steven Smith has warned that "[c]olleges and universities were once considered the custodians of our most important civic values," that "[f]ields like history, political science, and literature once were thought of as a preparation for a life of national service" and had considered an enlightened American patriotism "not indoctrination into an ideology, but a component of an educated mind" – yet campuses now deride patriotism as jingoism and fail to provide any serious civic education.[16] Brook Manville and Josiah Ober in *The Civic Bargain: How Democracy Survives* even more strongly advocate for a renewed priority for civic education: It is one of the seven "essential conditions" of democracy, "necessary for citizen self-governance." The aim of civics, which the leaders and citizens of a democratic republic must commit to undertake, is to "provide civic learning and experiences for citizens, instilling the values and practices they need to keep ... self-governance" (4–5; also 38–40, 230–43). Haass similarly specifies, as Obligation IX among the ten obligations all American citizens should meet, "support the teaching of civics."

These voices deserve serious attention today because they revive the considered view of leading founders of our constitutional order, pointedly echoed by Lincoln in his 1838 address to that Young Men's Lyceum on "The Perpetuation of Our Political Institutions." The essays of *The*

---

[14] Ronald J. Daniels, with Grant Shreve and Phillip Spector, *What Universities Owe Democracy* (Johns Hopkins University Press, 2021).

[15] Debra Satz and Dan Edelstein, "By Abandoning Civics, Colleges Helped Create the Culture Wars," *New York Times*, September 3, 2023; at www.nytimes.com/2023/09/03/opinion/colleges-civics-core-curriculum-culture-wars.html.

[16] Steven B. Smith, *Reclaiming Patriotism in an Age of Extremes* (Yale University Press, 2021), pp. 7, 188–203.

Federalist, in 1787 and 1788, also repeatedly note the fragility of popular governments, whether democratic or republican. Yet after our constitutional order survived a civil war, and a century later had led an alliance of liberal democracies to victory in a global Cold War, elite American opinion seemingly concluded by the 1990s that our form of politics had locked in its success. A radical Enlightenment and late-modern confidence in rational progress, particularly the concept generated by the philosophers Kant and Hegel that "History" has a direction of itself – as the cumulative, irreversible human agency of rational progress toward liberal political and economic freedom and equality – was embodied in Francis Fukuyama's 1989 essay about the coming victory in the Cold War, extended in his 1992 book *The End of History and the Last Man*.

The rocky road since the 1990s gives grounds for reconsideration. America and the world have faced the growing presence of illiberal or antiliberal views in great and middling powers, and at home we have faced the rising presence of illiberal deeds and words on both left and right along with cratering confidence in most institutions of government. A few sober scholars thus have suggested that Lincoln's stark warning to his local Lyceum offers enduring wisdom about the fragile foundations of republican civic culture. (We also should note the Lyceum movement of the mid eighteenth century, named after Aristotle's school in ancient Athens, is just the kind of civil society association that itself has declined in America in the past half-century; and amazingly to us today, it was dedicated to self-directed civic education.) Two decades before civil war erupted in 1861, Lincoln warned of increasing political violence and lawlessness, both by opponents and advocates of slavery, as well as those animated by controversies from alcohol use to gambling. He predicted that if lawlessness deepened, a temptation would arise to seek refuge in authoritarian, demagogic figures who self-promote as restorers of order; citing Caesar arising from the Roman republic, and Napoleon from the nascent French republic. In recent years those alarmed by Donald Trump have cited this element of the Perpetuation Address. Yet elite American voices today less frequently recur to the major cause Lincoln identifies for this constitutional disintegration and civic crisis: A decline in civic education and particularly civic knowledge, most focally a rational, constitutionally informed patriotism. Ignorance of the laws and the Constitution and lack of patriotic devotion to observing their requirements was, he argued, the root of the lawless violence rising in America. Lincoln's remedy: A renewed emphasis on fundamental civic knowledge and reflective patriotism, grounded in both reverence for and rational study of the Declaration, the Constitution, and American law generally. America must prioritize efforts that induce *"general intelligence, sound morality, and in particular, a reverence for the constitution and laws."*[17]

Given skepticism of patriotism in our educational and elite intellectual culture today, we should note that Lincoln's remedy blends schooling in civic knowledge with broader and deeper forms of civic formation. It is true his core recommendation is to emphasize "sober reason" in studying the fundamental American texts and principles and the law, given that we cannot rely any longer on the "passion" of sentimental attachment to the heroes of '76, now dead. He also warns that populist passion without the ballast of civic knowledge is a growing threat: "Reason, cold, calculating, unimpassioned reason, must furnish all the materials for our future support and defence." Yet shortly after these lines, Lincoln movingly invokes, in closing, a reverence for "our WASHINGTON" as America's great founder, then for Christianity as a pillar of our free polity – "the only greater institution" than our republic. Also largely overlooked today in references to the Perpetuation Address is Lincoln's strong charge, earlier in his analysis, that if the American republic fails, it would not be by foreign conquest, but rather due to our own failings and consequent disintegration: "If destruction be our lot, we must ourselves be its author and finisher. As a nation of freemen, we must live through all time, or die by suicide."

The charge of impending civic suicide, caused by reckless carelessness, did not seem hyperbolic in an era that deemed constitutional self-government a fragile achievement; all the more so in a world clearly dangerous for the few republics existing. The perilous decline of American civic health in our time, coupled with cratering confidence in higher education, suggests we reconsider Lincoln's remedy: To prioritize a reflective patriotism and civic education in American constitutionalism and civic knowledge, including the civic virtues required for citizens and leaders to operate our constitutional order – and thrive – in a still-dangerous world. Democracy education per se, without grounding in our constitutional principles and the Declaration informing them, has left us too open to passion and demagoguery, thus destructive polarization. Indeed, the civic amnesia yielded by the past century of emphasis on abstract aims of democracy, participation, and progress has cut off most Americans from the reality that our Constitution was designed to address the endemic problem of factional disagreement in republics and democracies. Democracy education also means, in effect, amnesia about the greater

---

[17] Emphasis in original. See Smith's discussion in *Patriotism*, 103–5, 201.

success achieved by our constitutionalism compared to any other form of politics in fostering effective self-government amid perpetual disagreement – all while eventually producing ample progress in expanding participation, equality, and liberty.[18]

The national-consensus effort of the *EAD* study on K-12 schooling is one effort to diagnose the danger facing us, and then recommend constructive responses. It is encouraging that Manville and Ober in *The Civic Bargain* cite the *EAD* study in their argument for renewed civic education. The *EAD* study produced a "Roadmap" with guidance on improving state and local standards, curricula, and teaching – a content framework of civics and history education to be adapted in different ways by different localities, in the spirit of American federalism. The *EAD* report itself, subtitled "Excellence in History and Civics for All Learners," provides the analysis and fundamental rationale informing the Roadmap. The concept of civic education employed in the *EAD* consensus approach is useful for assessing the presence, and adequacy, of civics in both schools and colleges today, and indeed the report calls for renewal of civics in the entire K-16 ecosystem:

A self-governing people must constantly attend to historical and civic education: to the process by which the rising generation owns the past, takes the helm, and charts a course toward the future. The United States is the longest-lived constitutional democracy in the world, approaching its 250th anniversary in 2026, an occasion that calls for both celebration and fresh commitment to the cause of self-government for free and equal citizens in a diverse society.

Education in civics and history equips members of a democratic society to understand, appreciate, nurture, and, where necessary, improve their political system and civil society: to make our union "more perfect", as the U.S. Constitution says. This education must be designed to enable and enhance the capacity for self-government from the level of the individual, the family, and the neighborhood to the state, the nation, and even the world.

The word "civic" denotes the virtues, assets, and activities that a free people need to govern themselves well. When civic education succeeds, all people are prepared and motivated to participate effectively in civic life. They acquire and share the knowledge, skills, and dispositions necessary for effective participation. (*EAD* Report, 9)

Leaders in American higher education, along with all citizens and aspiring citizens concerned by our civic crisis, should consider the

---

[18] Two recent excellent contributions to recovering appreciation for the Constitution are Yuval Levin, *American Covenant: How the Constitution Unified Our Nation – And Could Again* (Basic Books, 2024), and Dennis Hale and Marc Landy, *Keeping the Republic: A Defense of American Constitutionalism* (University Press of Kansas, 2024).

nonideological calls from Bok and Daniels, Manville and Ober, Haass and Smith, and this recent report focused on K-12 civics. Too many educators and leaders have neglected the American idea: A self-governing people patriotically holding the truths in the Declaration and appreciating that these inherently call for education, argument, and civil disagreement to sustain the constitutional order that secures our ideals. We also could restore hope in this dark time by learning from exemplars of reflective patriotism who loved America yet saw failures to secure or live up to its ideas, thus undertook debate and proposed reforms to improve our *e pluribus unum*. As discussed later, George Washington is the first reformer-patriot; other greats we should rediscover and feature include Frederick Douglass, Lincoln, Elizabeth Cady Stanton, Susan B. Anthony, and the Rev. Dr. Martin Luther King, Jr.

In 2016, I was called to do my part by Arizona State University to bring to America's largest university my experience from the U.S. Air Force Academy as a civilian professor offering a reflective civics to future officers. I was asked to be the founding director of an ASU school on "civic thought and leadership"; in effect, a department of civics. Other public universities then adopted this idea, to blend liberal arts education and American civic education in university courses and degrees, along with public civics programming. The reform is now in at least twelve states, on seventeen public university campuses, including two public ivies – University of Texas at Austin and University of North Carolina at Chapel Hill – as well as University of Florida and Ohio State University.[19] This is just one dimension of a nascent national reform in American higher education to establish new departments, colleges, or centers focused on a higher civics, and to establish new graduation requirements in the study of American civics or democracy.[20] A few private universities, most

---

[19] My overview of the origins and rationale is "A New Birth of Freedom in Higher Education: Civic Institutes at Public Universities," *American Enterprise Institute*, January 2023, at www.aei.org/research-products/report/a-new-birth-of-freedom-in-higher-education-civic-institutes-at-public-universities. See also Benjamin and Jenna Silber Storey, "Civic Thought: A Proposal for University-Level Civic Education," *American Enterprise Institute*, December 2023, at www.aei.org/research-products/report/civic-thought-a-proposal-for-university-level-civic-education/, and John Murawski, "These Upstart Classes Hold a Woeful Lack of Civics Education to Be Self-Evident," *RealClearInvestigations*, December 3, 2024, at www.realclearinvestigations.com/articles/2024/12/03/these_upstart_classes_hold_a_woeful_lack_of_civics_education_to_be_self-evident_1075532.html.

[20] Heterodox Academy recently produced a brief overview of the national scale of civic education and "civil discourse" initiatives across public and private institutions; Shiri Spitz Siddiqi and Michael Regnier, "The New Landscape of 'Civics Centers' in Higher

notably Stanford University and Johns Hopkins, have moved to establish a civics or democracy education requirement for all undergraduates; and Yale University has just launched a Center for Civic Thought. These diverse efforts mark a restoration of the traditional liberal arts spirit in the modern research university, and also the spirit of the nineteenth-century Lyceum model, the occasion for Lincoln's prophetic warning – a movement, to use Tocquevillian terms, to form associations in civil society dedicated to self-improvement of Americans as self-governing citizens. The Stanford Civics Initiative recently developed a course on "Citizenship in the 21st Century" which Stanford faculty and leaders have approved as a requirement for at least two-thirds of all undergraduates. The SNF Agora Institute at Johns Hopkins University has established a minor in Civic Life, and led the effort – as advocated by President Daniels – to establish the new democracy education requirement for all Hopkins students.[21]

A leader of the Stanford Civics Initiative, Joshiah Ober, also has led the effort to launch a new association in higher education for those committed to promoting national-consensus, nonpolarized civic education: the Alliance for Civics in the Academy. While Alliance members are "highly diverse in our value commitments and pedagogic materials and methods," and hail from a range of higher education institutions, they "broadly agree" on some basic principles:

Preparing students with civic skills, knowledge, and experience relevant to understanding and exercising the rights and duties of citizenship in a self-governing republic is a basic responsibility of American colleges and universities. Faculty must intentionally engage with historically significant competing arguments on contested questions of civic life, oppose indoctrination, and model the democratic values of open inquiry and freedom of expression. Civic education should be a shared intellectual activity, grounded in texts, aimed at building a practical capacity for listening to and acting together with others, including those of differing beliefs.[22]

Efforts like these in private and public universities also are necessary for renewing and improving civics in K-12 schools and our broader civic

---

Education: An Analysis of Missions, Structures, and Legislative Origins Across U.S. Colleges and Universities" (December 2025).

[21] See Stanford Civics Initiative, Stanford University, at www.civics.stanford.edu; and SNF Agora Institute, Johns Hopkins University, at www.snfagora.jhu.edu/civic-life-minor/.

[22] www.hoover.org/research-teams/alliance-civics-academy. The center-right Hoover Institution, part of Stanford University, has stepped up to sponsor the Alliance; and in 2025, cosponsored with iCivics the Civic Learning Week National Forum on the Stanford campus.

culture. If a subject is not seriously encountered or required in higher education, it will not be taken seriously in schools; and it has long been true that most teachers, administrators, and school board members in our public schools, as well as leading figures in our media and cultural life, are college graduates.

These signs of renewed alertness to and action about our civic crisis are heartening, but the basic reality remains that American civic education is mostly in disastrous shape. There are excellent and dedicated teachers, professors, and leaders working to remedy this, but for too many Americans today, at least those still generally patriotic, "civics" is akin to dental hygiene: We know we should do it, and teach the young about it, but we avoid it if possible. To our great detriment, the ethic of dental care now probably has higher priority than our commitment to perpetuating the American experiment by learning to be informed, responsible, tolerant, patriotic, and self-governing citizens of our republic.

Our country increasingly chose the path of avoidance and ignorance across the past sixty years, demoting civics in schools and universities. The evasion or apathy arguably began in higher education; scholars like me (a professor of political science) deemed civics an unserious, low, or less-important endeavor – appropriate for schools, if at all. The news from the U.S. Department of Education on the 2022 scores in civics and in history by 8th graders in the National Assessment of Educational Progress ("the nation's report card") was not surprising to advocates for civics, but still alarming: The already-low performance of recent decades dropped, with only 20 percent of students reaching "proficiency." This is another piece of the plentiful evidence that the cost of our de facto policy of civic ignorance, of deprioritizing civic education, has been disastrous for America; for our civic culture and politics, educational institutions, and prospects for national survival. As noted when considering the low regard among those under thirty-five for America itself – as measured in views of patriotism, the importance of self-government, willingness to fight for one's country, and participation in elections as well as civil society associations – we face an urgent necessity to rediscover and rebuild the golden loop between understanding and appreciating the American ideal.[23]

---

[23] Lindsey Cormack recounts the poor state of civic and constitutional literacy and its strong correlations with lack of civic trust, low participation in voting and other forms of self-government, and vulnerability to manipulation and civic disengagement, in *How to Raise a Citizen (And Why It's Up to You to Do It)* (Jossey-Bass/Wiley, 2024), 19–36.

Eighty years ago, in 1954, the National Education Association issued a volume on *Educating for American Citizenship*, which showed the influence of Dewey's conception of democracy education, critical thinking, and participation – yet blended this into the original American approach of a democratic-republic civics. The NEA, then and now, is the nation's largest teachers and school workers union. The first two pillars of the recommended "program of citizenship education" are civic knowledge and understanding, and "attitudes of loyalty to American ideals"; followed by skills in civic thinking and "problem solving," and "practiced ability to work with others for the general welfare." The report devotes an early chapter to "ideals we live by," especially commitment to the Declaration and individual rights, the rule of law, and the Constitution and Bill of Rights particularly, to include equality regardless of race, status, or religion. It emphasizes that the "first concern" of civics is "a clear understanding" of these "ideals of the American democratic tradition" – and "a deep emotional commitment to them." A prefatory statement "to the reader" asks for "the devoted consecration of each citizen to the basic ideals and values of American life," echoing Lincoln's call in the Lyceum Address for reverence of the Constitution, and his language of consecration in the Gettysburg Address. The separate chapter on ideals includes among these "the right to be different," which encompasses the free market of ideas, the right of dissent, and the balance of unity and diversity.[24] The 1954 NEA report also made a priority of understanding the threat of international communism; clearly indicating that its entire approach was shaped by the Cold War consensus of a grave external threat to the American republic.

As we now mark America 250, we should not dismiss this balanced, comprehensive approach as merely historical information, or as propagandistic. Indeed as the *EAD* report argued in 2021, America today needs to adapt the response to Sputnik in 1957, when the Soviet Union beat us in launching the first satellite into space (*EAD* Report, 10). Immediately post-Sputnik, the 1958 National Defense Education Act prioritized and invested in education, including K-12 schools, as the long game for redressing a national security threat. Regrettably, for the remaining decades of the Cold War and up to the present, the concerns about national security – then from the 1980s onward about economic competitiveness arising under globalization – have led to prioritizing science and technology education, and funding, both in higher education and for

---

[24] National Education Association, *Educating for American Citizenship*, Thirty-Second Yearbook (Washington, DC, 1954), 21, 23, and chapter 3 generally (51–66).

schools; along with basic testing of and funding for reading, math, and science in schools; all at the expense of civics and history education. As Chapter 3 on colleges discusses, Danielle Allen has helpfully argued that after many decades of higher education also deprioritizing civics because our political culture (and federal funding) sought an educational focus on technology and science studies, along with support for economic prosperity and competitiveness, we now need to reset the social contract between higher education and America. Citizenship education should join "STEM" and preprofessional studies, and the advancement of economic prosperity, as primary missions for our universities and colleges.[25]

The threat America faces now is, primarily, ourselves; our inability to understand, appreciate, and sustain our republic. Foreign adversaries also are exploiting this weakness and fracturing of our civic culture through social media and other efforts. A Sputnik-like response today must emphasize, given our massive civic deficits, the need that the National Education Association had already perceived in 1954: The motivation among young citizens and aspiring citizens to care about civics in the first place.

I.2 REDISCOVERING AMERICA'S REFLECTIVE, DISCURSIVE PATRIOTISM

The lead authors of the *EAD* report decided in early 2021 that various declining measures of civic knowledge, health, and strength required that we open and close the main *EAD* report by invoking a distinctively American conception of patriotism as essential for excellent civics and history education in schools and beyond. We already had featured the concept in our draft analysis of, and recommended guidelines for, an improved American civics, but we decided to underline the point after the shock of the January 6, 2021, mob attacking the U.S. Capitol to disrupt the constitutional procedure of formalizing the Electoral College votes in the 2020 presidential election. The violation of the civic norm and tradition of an orderly, peaceful transfer of power after a national election, nearly unbroken in our history, called for this explicit response.

The United States stands at a crossroads of peril and possibility. A healthy constitutional democracy always demands reflective patriotism. In times of crisis, it

---

[25] Danielle Allen, "America and Its Universities Need a New Social Contract," *The Atlantic*, April 13, 2025; Allen continued the argument for higher education reform in "Trump's Imperfect Compact Is a Perfect Opportunity," *Chronicle of Higher Education*, October 6, 2025.

is especially important that We the People unite love of country with clear-eyed wisdom about our successes and failures in order to chart our forward path. (*EAD* Report, Executive Summary, 8)

Passing on a love and understanding of American constitutional democracy to future generations is an urgent civic necessity. We are all responsible for cultivating in ourselves and the young the reflective patriotism needed to navigate the dangerous shoals we now face as we chart a course between cynicism and nostalgia. To those who believe in America's principles and promise, what we have inherited is painfully imperfect. It is our task not to abandon but to improve it. (*EAD* Report, Conclusion, 22)

Reflective patriotism is itself a term capturing a dynamic tension between positive sentiment and the discursive, critical capacities of reason. The *EAD* Report sought to define and defend several such balances regarding an appropriate understanding of America and citizenship education. We were spurred to do so by the reality that as of early 2021 the rival, polar-opposite schools in the contentious public debates about civic education, each single-minded in its own way, had planted their flags. As Danielle Allen and I framed it in a *Washington Post* essay marking the report's release, we were watching "polarization consume efforts to renew history and civic learning" in "the debates over the *New York Times'* 1619 Project and the Trump administration's 1776 Commission … each approach insisting on achieving a definitive account of how to narrate the country's founding."[26] *EAD* notes this reality, and signals an intent to seek a higher, more reasonable middle path, in a section arguing that an effective civics renewal will require avoiding and overcoming "dysfunctional controversy about content" – in which we refer to The 1619 Report. This is followed by a section arguing that "history and civics must reflect the best scholarship" – in which we refer neither to the 1619 polemic nor its 1776 Commission polar opposite.

American leaders, educators, and committed citizens today should consider that the longstanding demotion of civics and reflective patriotism, because of higher priority for the technological and skills-based demands of national security and economic competitiveness, is only half of our problem. The other half is that these polarized views about America and civics – the critical-utopian and the defensive-nostalgic – have reinforced the urge to avoid civics, while also filling the vacuum of ignorance that has grown across the past half-century. A significant set of educators in schools and higher education either actively or

---

[26] Danielle Allen and Paul Carrese, "Our Democracy Is Ailing. Civics Education Has to Be Part of the Cure." *The Washington Post*, March 2, 2021.

passively hold the view made prominent by The 1619 Project, deeming America a fraudulent project grounded in racism, inequality, and imperialism at home and abroad. Stanford University education professor Sam Wineburg argued a decade ago that the forerunner to the 1619 polemic, Howard Zinn's transparently radical high school textbook *A People's History of the United States*, "has arguably had a greater influence on how Americans understand their past than any other book."[27] A smaller set of educators hold, in reaction, that celebration of 1776 and its lasting legacy must be inculcated, with minor attention to any failings to live up to the Declaration's principles of the equal natural rights of all humans to life, liberty, and the pursuit of happiness.

I believe the latter view is, of the two, generally the more historically accurate and educationally sound; yet in its partiality it fails to prepare twenty-first century Americans for the essentially American realities of *e pluribus unum*. The idea of America, of We the People, always has been a complex blend of ideas, principles, peoples, and traditions; and of triumphs and failings. It therefore always has been an argument. The *EAD* report clearly recommends that the degree of discursiveness and debate in history and civics education should be appropriate to student grade levels; graduating up toward the higher civics in colleges and universities which can and should accommodate the most discursive examination of American's principles, achievements, and failings. The general principle is that American citizens and aspiring citizens must always strive to learn how to discuss, argue, and compromise about the complexity of ideas and viewpoints we must forge into a unity; not least because the alternatives are ignorance, or, splintering and coming to blows. Both of these are paths to national suicide.[28]

---

[27] Sam Wineburg, "Undue Certainty: Where Howard Zinn's *A People's History* Falls Short," *American Educator* (Winter 2012–2013): 26–34, cited in Sikkenga and Davenport, *A Republic If You Can Teach It*, 15–17; Zimmerman also discusses Zinn's project in *Whose Country?*, xiv, 239, 252–55.

[28] The severe critique of The 1619 Project by historian David Hackett Fischer, in his encyclopedic study of the achievements of enslaved, escaped, and manumitted Africans in America across three centuries, should be noted by supporters of the Pulitzer Center and *New York Times* effort to distribute a K-12 curriculum to schools as if the Project is serious scholarship: "In public discourse during the twenty-first century we have seen a growing disregard for truth, and a cultivated carelessness of fact and evidence. More extreme … are deliberate falsehoods, actively concocted and widely deployed in new forms of rhetoric and communication." "[T]o condemn the United States as a racist society is fundamentally false. It misses the successful efforts of twelve generations of Americans, and especially the role of Africans born in slavery, and the children of slaves, in enlarging fundamental American rights … throughout the United States during the

An informed, considered, enlightened patriotism embodies this tension constructively. The *EAD* Report, and its recommended Roadmap guidelines for curricular improvement, argue that this distinctly American kind of discursive patriotism, a "reflective patriotism," must be rediscovered in formal education and civic culture. This is the term coined by the great French observer of America, Alexis de Tocqueville, after his visit in the 1830s. In *Democracy in America* (1835, 1840) he recounts that Americans displayed a patriotism unknown in the Old World. Yes, we showed gratitude and affection for our country, as patriots of all countries do; but because America was grounded in principles and ideals, we blended sentiment with argument and questioning – pointed toward both government and fellow citizens.[29] A crucial element of the bipartisan, national-consensus effort of the *EAD* study is to echo Tocqueville's insight by invoking the need for education in several "civic virtues" – to include *civil disagreement* across political and philosophical views; *civic friendship* among Americans across partisan and political differences; and *reflective patriotism*, in classrooms and beyond. We defined this last as "appreciation of the ideals of our political order, candid reckoning with the country's failures to live up to those ideals, motivation to take responsibility for self-government, and deliberative skill to debate the challenges that face us in the present and future" (*EAD*, 12).

Other recent observers of our civic education deficits include these civic virtues in their recommended reforms. Manville and Ober argue in *The Civic Bargain* that civic friendship is one of the seven essential conditions necessary to sustain a democratic republic (36–38, 220–21, 240–43). They identify other "civic virtues," including patriotism, that should be promoted in a civic education that encompasses not only classrooms but civic rituals (10, 89–91, 172, 231–32, 235, 240). Haass argues in *The Bill of Obligations* that we must prioritize ten habits and duties of good citizens – mirroring the ten sets of rights captured in the Bill of Rights – to balance a civic culture that has overemphasized individual rights; the tenth and overriding one is "Put Country First" (Obligation X, 147–53). We have a duty to "put the country and American democracy

eighteenth and nineteenth centuries. To overstate the negatives in American history is to miss its positive achievements and its central dynamic." *African Founders: How Enslaved People Expanded American Ideals* (Simon & Schuster, 2022) at 4, 720. I discuss the book in Chapter 5 on civic culture, in relation to jazz.

[29] Alexis de Tocqueville, *Democracy in America*, ed. and tr. Harvey Mansfield and Delba Winthrop (University of Chicago Press, 2000), Volume One, Part Two, Chapter 6, pp. 225–27.

before party and person," as an obligation forming "a thread that helps bind the fabric of this country and is an essential element in patriotism."

The *EAD* approach, then, is one of several recent works on civics encompassing center-left to center-right views that prioritizes civic and historical knowledge as prior to, because necessary for informing, constructive civic engagement or civic participation with its needed skills and dispositions. The analyses of Bok, of Daniels and his coauthors, and of Manville and Ober all argue that civic knowledge, while not exhaustive of what a sound citizenship education requires, must take priority over the democracy-education elements of participation or agency. Haass defines Obligation IX, Support the Teaching of Civics, in terms of fundamental ideas and texts from our founding and subsequent political development; study of "the country's political structures and traditions along with what is owed to and expected of its citizens" (Haass, 133–43). He notes that his appendix on "Where to Go For More" could be retitled "How to Become and Remain an Informed Citizen" – emphasizing major primary texts and sources from the Declaration, Constitution, and *The Federalist* onward, along with widely recognized secondary sources, and current political literacy. Yet Haass also argues for the importance of "experience" beyond reading, viewing, and hearing prepared materials, to include visiting presidential libraries, the National Archives, battlefields, and observing government bodies in action (167–75). Further, amid his account of the duty to support civics, he endorses President Ronald Reagan's counsel in his farewell address in 1989 that the "new patriotism" of "national pride" which Reagan had encouraged "won't count for much ... unless it's grounded in thoughtfulness and knowledge. An informed patriotism is what we want" (Haass, 135). This is very similar in spirit to the *EAD* argument that civic knowledge – constitutional and historical understanding about the American experiment of the last four centuries – is incomplete without civic virtues.

Indeed, students need study of, and encouragement to develop, the demanding civic habits and graces necessary to sustain the *e pluribus unum* of America. The social scientific language which education scholars use about civic (or democratic) attitudes and dispositions is not fully accurate; it does not capture the reality of the civic challenge of sustaining our republic and the demanding qualities this requires. As Chapter 3 discusses, the *EAD* report and *Roadmap* particularly emphasize three civic virtues, weaving them throughout the main content themes and principles we propose for a sound civics: The trio of civil disagreement, civic friendship, and reflective patriotism. The effort and continual practice required to form these higher habits is captured by the traditional term for moral excellence, virtues, which calls us to a higher plane of human choice and action. Even a generally progressive institution like the American Bar Association, in its *Human Rights* magazine, has recently recognized the need for democratic citizens to rise above minimum levels of civic responsibility toward the higher capacities denoted by "civic virtues" if American politics is to restore its civic health.[30]

Tocqueville praises Americans for their distinctively reflective, considered patriotism in contrast to the Old World patriotism of sentiment and mythic history, focused upon emotional bonds to blood and soil. As Chapter 1 discusses, Tocqueville finds Americans fiercely proud of America and thin-skinned about any criticisms from a foreigner, but he also discerns that the basis of that pride is only partly sentiment and bonds of fellow-feeling. The pragmatic American spirit moves from the founding ideals about natural rights of individuals to a realization that one's self-interest can only be secured through exercise of civic duties and the activity of self-government. The American citizen regularly calculates that civic participation, and the health of America's political system, directly benefit one's own family and friends. This discussion of reflective patriotism occurs in Volume One of *Democracy*, while in Volume Two Tocqueville deems the American utilitarian attitude toward civic participation and duties an "enlightened self-interest." In that later, fuller discussion of the complicated psychology of the new democratic citizen he notes that while the Americans claim to act only on rational, self-interested grounds, in fact they undertake "disinterested and unreflective" acts of magnanimous, altruistic conduct (Volume Two, Part 2, ch. 8, 502). Tocqueville's full picture thus sees Americans as blending a rational orientation of demand for results – from government, fellow citizens, and the entire political order – with love of country and commitment to civic duty.

The civic virtue of a rational, reflective patriotism is in a sense fundamental for the other two virtues in our *EAD* set. A free, rational people who believe their politics is founded on self-evident truths will love their polity and be grateful for it yet also be discursive and even argumentative about it; needing to develop the virtue of civil disagreement. In their freedom they will disagree about what their fundamental principles mean or require, and about the meaning of their history. Such a people thus

---

[30] Christopher A. Callaway, "Civic Duties, Civic Virtues, and the Barriers to Effective Citizenship," *Human Rights Magazine* 43 no. 2 (2018), The American Bar Association.

also will need an Aristotelian kind of civic friendship across philosophical and partisan divisions if they are to sustain an *e pluribus unum*, a polity unified enough to sustain itself and their argumentative freedom. As Chapters 5 and 6 will discuss, seeds of civic friendship can be planted through formal studies but must be nurtured in civic culture and civic practice. Further, the need for such civic friendship in turn is intertwined with the third civic virtue in our *EAD* set: civil disagreement. Only fellow American patriots, sharing this basis for civic friendship, can blend gratitude for America and its ideals with perpetual yet civil argument about what those ideals mean, how they fit together, and how we can live up to them.

As Chapter 1 discusses, Tocqueville's complete account of reflective patriotism reveals its roots in America's broader civic culture; and he identifies Christianity as the single greatest source of and influence upon that culture. Yet he also sees Christian belief being undermined by the relentless democratic quest for material security and prosperity, as well as by the increasing influence of modern science and materialism. His considered judgment is that these more modern, rationalist elements won't sustain a healthy civic culture that in turn is necessary for supporting a reflective patriotism and healthy spirit of self-governance. In our era, Robert Putnam's neo-Tocquevillean studies about the decline of "social capital," of self-starting and self-organized associations in American civil society not directly related to politics and government, have revived consideration of the importance of civic culture. Less widely appreciated is that Putnam's first sequel to *Bowling Alone*, with coauthor David Campbell, focused upon the importance of yet declining presence of religious belief and practice in American civil society.[31]

The Tocquevillean insight which has stood the test of two centuries is that formal schooling, knowledge of institutions, and even knowledge of the importance of civic virtues and civic participation are necessary but insufficient. Even experiential learning grounded in civic knowledge and civic virtues will not succeed absent a civic culture encouraging commitment to moral principles about justice, equal rights, and the importance of liberty. Tocqueville, drawing on his French philosophic predecessor Montesquieu, finds Christianity the crucial source for this civic culture of liberty, equality, and self-government. Tocqueville also identifies it as

---

[31] Robert D. Putnam, *Bowling Alone: The Collapse and Revival of American Community* (Simon & Schuster, 2000); Robert D. Putnam and David E. Campbell, *American Grace: How Religion Divides and Unites Us* (Simon & Schuster, 2010).

the source of America's characteristic hopefulness, spurring the view that effort expended now will yield larger and better prospects arising to one's own benefit and one's posterity as well. All of this noted, Chapter 5 will include the American tradition of religious liberty as a great achievement of our *e pluribus unum*; a liberty that includes atheists, agnostics, and believers in metaphysical and spiritual realities from more traditional religions and institutions to more personal beliefs. Americans now are more spiritual than religious in the traditional sense of organized belief communities with regular religious services. A question facing American civic culture is whether this more diffuse, pluralist religious-spiritual life can sustain the civic virtues, and motivation to undertake civic learning and a citizenship of dedication to self-government, that Tocqueville admired as the foundation for our successful democratic-republican polity.

Indeed, today's civic culture defined largely by angry polarization and civic apathy yields low confidence in national institutions and each other, and has little hopefulness. This is one reason theorists and practitioners of American civics should rediscover the importance of exemplars of the civic virtues, who offer real instances of civic duty and honor, hope and reform. Turning to these exemplars requires transcending the opposing academic poles of narrow rationalism and skepticism at one end, and critical ideology at the other, long predominant in the humanities and "soft" social sciences disciplines. Study of civic exemplars is a method philosophically appropriate for the distinct realities of civic life, not a flawed reliance on "great man" agency in human affairs. Study of biographies is also crucial for fulfilling the practical need to offer students meaning and motivation about subjects of learning, without veering into ideology or fervor. Further, since all humans are fallible, and most political and civic situations are complex, we can learn to appreciate the difficult decisions a great figure had to make, assessing whether we might have decided any better in the circumstances; all of which yields empathy toward such historic figures but also toward our fellow citizens today holding views divergent from our own.

I.3 AMERICAN HOPEFULNESS AND EXEMPLARS SUSTAINING THE REPUBLIC

The *EAD* report proposes that debate and disagreement about the meaning of America's civic principles is very American, and debate and disagreement about the meaning of our history is very American. A robust K-12 education can balance core knowledge of civic and constitutional principles, and core knowledge of historical moments and achievements, with questioning, debate, even strong disagreement. This balance of knowledge and discussion within a civic culture of considered, discursive patriotism then can be deepened in college or lifelong study. This is not a bug or failing of America and an education in thoughtful, engaged citizenship. It is a feature of American self-government and mature citizenship. Study of several great American statesmen and stateswomen can reinforce this balance. Exemplars such as Frederick Douglass, Abraham Lincoln, Elizabeth Cady Stanton, Susan B. Anthony, and Martin Luther King, Jr., can promote critical reflection about the American experiment by balancing belief in our founding principles with criticism about our failure to live up to these high ideals, thus their demands for reform. Nearest to our own time is King's "I Have a Dream" address, delivered on the National Mall in Washington, D.C. in 1963. King balances demand for improvements in civil rights and racial justice with his praise for "the architects of our republic" and the "magnificent words" of the Declaration of Independence and the Constitution.[32]

King affirmed and deployed the then-national consensus which held in high regard America's framers and our founding documents. He sought to build a national, constitutional majority on that basis for landmark national civil rights legislation that would bring America into alignment with her ideals and foundational laws. The event organizers including King chose to stand at the Lincoln Memorial, a century after the great achievement of the Emancipation Proclamation and also Lincoln's pledge in the Gettysburg Address that America would have "a new birth of freedom" by righting the wrong of slavery. This new civil rights effort should stand in what King called the "symbolic shadow" of the great reformer.

We can renew a reflective civics today by recalling that Lincoln in turn looked to the Founding Fathers as reformers, for having introduced into human history the bold truth that all persons are created equal, endowed by their Creator with rights to life, liberty, property, the pursuit of happiness, and government based upon consent. Further, we should recall that in Lincoln's lifetime many of the abolitionist opponents of America's persistent slavery also advocated equal political rights for women. Frederick Douglass, among the most famous and accomplished escaped slaves of the nineteenth century, was a close ally of Elizabeth Cady Stanton and later Susan B. Anthony in the cause of women's suffrage. Thus a

---

[32] Delivered August 28, 1963, at the Lincoln Memorial, Washington, DC, available at American Rhetoric, www.americanrhetoric.com/speeches/mlkihaveadream.htm.

twenty-first century reflective patriotism should consider a chain of civic exemplars of American reform, from those who forged the 1787 Constitution and then achieved the major constitutional amendments redressing slavery and women's suffrage in the latter nineteenth and early twentieth centuries, on to King's achievement of quasi-constitutional legislation in the Civil Rights Act of 1964 and Voting Rights Act of 1965. Though of course there are other great reformers and civic exemplars in the story of America – at the beginning, we must note John Adams and Thomas Jefferson as most responsible for achieving the Declaration of Independence – we could bolster our civic recovery by studying the Founding Father singularly crucial for securing both independence and the new Constitution, George Washington; then Douglass and Lincoln in forging the national coalition that eventually defeats slavery and secures the Civil War Amendments; on to Elizabeth Cady Stanton and Susan B. Anthony securing the national coalition that eventually achieves the 19th Amendment; then King's extraordinary reform effort.

Given the predominant concern in academia for a century that any traditional American civics must be a kind of jingoism or propaganda masquerading as education, Chapter 2 discusses how a genuine civics can avoid any proximity to ideology or partisanship by incorporating study of these civic exemplars of reflective patriotism. The focus there will be Douglass and Lincoln, Stanton and Anthony, and King, so a brief appreciation of Washington as reformer is fitting here.

To the extent that our civic culture and educational institutions today give any positive attention to George Washington, we think of him as the embodiment of solidity – as the establishment, so to speak. Yes, he was a revolutionary, the commanding general of the American forces, but he is more The Founding Father, the single most important of the founders from 1776 to his voluntary retirement from public life in 1796 after two terms as first president under the new Constitution. The Washington Memorial is fitting: massive, solid, pointing upward, but not, in popular imagination, as symbol of reform. Yet a reformer he was. A splendid recent biography is Richard Brookhiser's character study of Washington, consciously written in the tradition of the Hellenic philosopher Plutarch, whose studies of great Greek and Roman statesmen were widely consulted in the founding generation. Brookhiser recounts that Washington arrived at the Second Continental Congress in 1775 in Philadelphia, not long after the fighting at Lexington and Concord, in his Virginia colonel uniform from the French and Indian War (as Americans called it). He signaled that more than words would be needed given British deeds, and their repudiation of American petitions.[33] Granting Lincoln's view that the principles of the Declaration, and Washington's fight for them, mark a great reform in human history, we should more generally appreciate that Washington's entire career undertakes and largely achieves a series of reforms, improvements, and ameliorations of American affairs through to his death in 1799.

An often-overlooked triumph of the American revolutionary struggle is Washington's repudiation of the traditional view among conquering generals that they deserve to usurp all authority – even in the name of republics, as embodied in the famous types of Julius Caesar, Oliver Cromwell, and (shortly after Washington) Napoleon. This dark ambition plagues politics to this day. When an American colonel wrote to Washington, after the victory at Yorktown in 1781 which effectively meant victory in the war, proposing he should become a king given the obvious dysfunction of the Confederation Congress, Washington emphatically rebuked the idea in a written response. A mutiny against Congress formed among the officers in 1783 after the British conceded defeat, because Congress hadn't paid the officers; Washington again adamantly rebuked any idea of a military junta against lawful civilian government, and that Newburgh Address is still studied by American military officers today. Once the peace treaty was official he resigned his commission in late 1783, in a ceremony with Congress, stating his commitment to retirement from public affairs to become an ordinary citizen in a free republic. He did return to public life when recruited for the Philadelphia convention in 1787 considering reforms to the Articles of Confederation; but after two terms as president he insisted upon declaring in 1796 his refusal to serve a third term; he had intended to do so at the close of his first, but accepted the widespread response that his service still was crucial for the nascent government under the new Constitution. When in 1796 he really did retire from public life for a second time, laying down a very powerful office, King George III – his adversary in the war for independence – deemed Washington "the greatest character of the age."

We rightly honor James Madison as "father of the Constitution" given his extraordinary preparation for the 1787 Convention, his initial

---

[33] My highlights of Washington's career draw from Brookhiser, *Founding Father: Rediscovering George Washington* (Free Press, 1996). A comprehensive modern biography is Ron Chernow, *Washington: A Life* (Penguin Books, 2011). I study his statesmanship in "Washington's Harmony: The Balance of Traditions in the American Founding," in *Democracy in Moderation: Montesquieu, Tocqueville, and Sustainable Liberalism* (Cambridge University Press, 2016).

drafting of a new constitution to replace the ineffective Articles, his leading role in the convention debates, and, eventually, for the extraordinary records of the convention's secret deliberations which he published decades later. A great reformer, indeed. Yet we almost entirely overlook Washington's role in making possible the bold plan to not merely amend but rather replace America's first constitution. The fact that he agreed to attend the convention (along with Franklin, the other possible candidate for most famous American); that he was unanimously elected president of the assembly on the opening day; that his admonitions and example kept the convention at work every day (except Sundays) for nearly four months until a new Constitution was produced; that he did so without commandeering the deliberations toward his own preference for a much stronger federal government but rather by letting that path unfold in open debate (while undertaking private efforts at persuasion in Philadelphia's taverns at night); that he joined with Franklin on the final day in deftly gaining as may signatures as possible for the final draft; and that he wrote and signed the transmittal letter to the Confederation Congress recommending their approval of a ratification procedure to move toward possible replacement of the Articles – all of this points toward Washington as the hand behind the Constitution, through a blend of private and public efforts. Further, a private intervention by Washington was crucial for producing the Virginia Plan which Madison drafted before the convention began and which contained the outlines of the new Constitution. Having agreed to attend the convention, Washington wrote to Madison in March 1787 declaring "a thorough reform of the present system is indispensable," and his hope the convention would undertake just that. He stated his preference for a plan of government providing capacities for "energy" as well as "that secrecy and dispatch … which is characteristic of good government" – and posed that formulating such a political system "indeed will require thought." Just in case Madison missed the point, he further stated his "wish" that "the Convention may adopt no temporizing expedient, but probe the defects of the [current] constitution to the bottom and *provide radical cures.*"[34]

Washington's final act of reform was ostensibly private, but by the time he drafted his final will in 1799, he knew it would be a public document – and it is reasonable to think he hoped the third item might set

---

[34] Washington to Madison, March 31, 1787, in *The Political Writings of George Washington*, Volume I: 1754–1788, ed. Carson Holloway and Bradford P. Wilson (Cambridge University Press, 2023), 572–73, emphasis added.

an example. There, he emancipated or manumitted all the slaves he fully owned, effective upon the death of his wife Martha. One reason to delay this way was the fact that slaves from the Custis estate (of Martha's deceased first husband) had married with slaves from the Washington estate; and while Washington could manumit (the legal term) the latter, neither he nor Martha could emancipate the "dowager" slaves because they were the property of the Custis family. This is but one indication of the complex legal realities of slavery in Virginia during the founding, with most laws by the late 1790s working against manumission.[35] Most who today sit in judgment of Washington's decision are critical; they see it as coming too late, made decades after he stated his opposition to slave holding, after long violating the principles of the Declaration, and with delayed effectuation of even this long-delayed effort. We might consider, however, this striking fact: of the eleven US presidents who held slaves before the Civil War, George Washington was the only one to manumit all of his slaves.[36] It is tempting to look away from this dimension of his life, accepting a diminished regard for him today given his flawed record on slave owning. Educators, students, and everyday citizens instead should tackle this difficult episode as not only part of a sober appreciation of Washington but as a larger lesson about the civic empathy we regularly should extend to people of differing views, experiences, backgrounds from our own. The practice of considering where someone is coming from, so to speak, is a crucial part of the civic work of discussing differing views and perhaps arriving at workable compromises to disagree constructively and move forward together.

The culture and institution of slavery was so dominant that twelve of the first eighteen US presidents owned slaves. William B. Allen argues that Washington's exceptional commitment to reforming his own practice of

---

[35] Mary Thompson, "George Washington's Journey to Emancipation," *George Washington's Mount Vernon*, at www.mountvernon.org/george-washington/slavery/george-washington-and-slavery/journey-to-emancipation; more fully in Thompson, *The Only Unavoidable Subject of Regret: George Washington, Slavery, and the Enslaved Community at Mount Vernon* (University of Virginia Press, 2019). For Washington's will see *Political Writings*, Vol. II, ed. Holloway and Wilson (Cambridge University Press, 2024), 636–69.

[36] Gautham Rao, "US Presidents and Slavery: 12 of the first 18 American presidents owned slaves," Miller Center, University of Virginia, at www.millercenter.org/us-presidents-and-slavery. Ulysses S. Grant might be included with Washington in this exceptional status; but while Washington inherited many slaves, and the slave population at Mount Vernon grew upon his marriage, making for hundreds of slaves freed when Martha manumitted them in 1801 (before her death), Grant owned one male slave, for about a year, manumitting him in 1859. See Ron Chernow, *Grant* (Penguin Press, 2017).

slave holding, and his hope of setting an example to encourage the gradual emancipation by legislation which he had advocated since the close of the Revolutionary War, is evident in the long planning and effort which allowed him to amass enough wealth to make the manumission plausible.[37] Not only was he freeing 123 of his own slaves; the will also stipulates that those slaves deemed infirm or ill, and the very young, should be provided for as pensioners, taught to read and write, and trained for an occupation. Washington in fact had encouraged literacy and marriage in the Washington-Custis slave population, and had transitioned the Mount Vernon estate and outlying farms away from staple production (cotton, tobacco) to crops for making finished products (wheat for flour, hemp for rope) and thus had been training slaves for useful occupations as free people. If his final reform gesture of manumission seems imperfect and incomplete to us, it nonetheless was the product of long, careful planning; and committed his estate to substantial expenditure of wealth. This arguably is why it was entirely exceptional among the slaveholding presidents prior to 1861. Further, the terms of the will indicate full awareness that his effort would be read with skepticism and resistance by the Custis family and any court of law. Washington reiterates that these directives are his "will and desire," he "expressly forbid[s]" any evasion of these terms, and in summary states "I do, moreover, most pointedly and most solemnly enjoin it upon my executors hereafter named ... to see that this clause respecting slaves, and every part thereof, be religiously fulfilled ... without evasion, neglect, or delay."

The historian Annette Gordon-Reed, noted for her scholarship on Thomas Jefferson and his relations with his slave Sally Hemings, provides a model of civic empathy when observing in her memoir about growing up in segregated Texas that looking back required an effort of "striking the right balance" – to write about a place she loves with a "clear-eyed assessment" of its "strengths and weaknesses." Such love and balance, she argues, includes the patriotism toward America shown even by those so unjustly treated: "Almost from the very beginning of their time in North America, Blacks have shown their deep patriotic attachment to the country they helped to build"; evincing the paradox for descendants of slaves "of loving a place that was deeply oppressive to their ancestors."

---

[37] William B. Allen, "George Washington: Slaveholder and Liberator," in *George Washington: America's First Progressive* (Peter Lang, 2008); Allen had edited the first new one-volume collection of Washington's essential political and moral writings to appear in many decades, coinciding with the bicentennial of the Constitution, in *George Washington: A Collection* (Liberty Fund, 1988).

The challenge she poses to herself as historian, seemingly to her fellow citizens also, is "achiev[ing] the proper equilibrium." The history of Texas, and of the early American republic, are moments "when triumph and tragedy were inexorably intertwined." A serious citizenship requires this finding of balance. "As painful as it may be, recognizing – though not dwelling on – tragedy and the role it plays in our individual lives, and in the life of a state or nation, is, I think, a sign of maturity."[38]

Another prominent descendent of slaves, the musician Ray Charles, shows this balanced and empathetic view of America in the reflective patriotism that infuses his distinctive rendition of "America the Beautiful." He first recorded it in 1972 shortly before the bicentennial celebrations of 1776, and his version became so popular that he regularly performed it for the remaining thirty years of his life. Ray's building up of America's civic culture was an extension of the hopefulness in the face of injustice embodied in jazz, as discussed in Chapter 5. Ray's striking version takes the traditional third verse of the Katharine Lee Bates hymn-poem and places it first, so that he opens by praising the beauty of "heroes proved/ in liberating strife." This move celebrates the great moment of civic reform in the Civil War, which for the Union soldiers clearly became a fight to exterminate slavery. These heroes not only loved "country" more than self; these mostly white soldiers loved "mercy" more than their own lives. Ray's blend of hope, high standards, and sober appreciation for America is a model that a reflective civics should emulate.

[38] Annette Gordon-Reed, *On Juneteenth* (Liveright Publishing/Norton, 2021), 29, 98, 141.

I

What Is American Civics and Why Does It Matter?

"One cannot doubt that in the United States the instruction of the people serves powerfully to maintain a democratic republic." Alexis de Tocqueville's classic study of the new American experiment in self-government provides many such evergreen insights, which is why it is consulted 190 years after this observation was published in 1835. Yet it is a challenging work blending philosophical and historical analysis, both praising and warning America about our complex politics – a *democratic* (government by the people) *constitutional* (via carefully structured forms and institutions of separated powers and federalism) *republic* (government largely by representatives of the people). Several cautionary notes thus follow this praise for educating a broad population, which Tocqueville offers when summing up the first volume of *Democracy in America*.

Principally, Tocqueville cautions that this salutary effect of schooling will occur "everywhere that the instruction which enlightens the mind is not separated from the education that regulates mores," meaning moral principles and norms. He thus challenges the view then-current in Europe that one need only teach people basic literacy "to make them citizens immediately." Indeed, "genuine enlightenment" in a citizenry arises not only from "literary knowledge" of political principles and mores but also from practice with institutions, laws, and procedures of self-government. Observing the Americans, whom he praises for their "good sense" in civic affairs, confirms that while "books" and "literary education" do "prepare" committed, active citizens to develop "practical knowledge" about rights, laws, and administration, it is the exercise of self-governing that actually provides such knowledge.[1] He thus counsels

---

[1] Alexis de Tocqueville, *Democracy in America*, ed. and tr. Harvey Mansfield and Delba Winthrop (University of Chicago Press, 2000), Volume One, Part Two, Chapter 9, 291.

fundamental attention to civic education and citizen formation broadly understood; for the same reason so many of America's founders wrote and spoke about education for the new republic's citizens – and undertook efforts to advance it. The Founders, Tocqueville, and Lincoln all urge us to prize a blend of formal schooling in civic knowledge and civic virtues, to be completed by development of practical knowledge and a full civic character through participation in self-government.

After reviewing Tocqueville's observations and counsel about an American civic education, it will be helpful to then consult a main philosophical source for the views articulated by both the American founders and Tocqueville about our constitutional democratic republic, and the proper civics for it. The French philosopher Montesquieu, largely neglected in our discourse today, is indispensable for understanding our political order, civic culture, and initial approach to civics. Indeed, we might ask whether our current civic crisis and poor condition of civic education are partly a consequence of cutting ourselves off from Montesquieu's moderate liberal philosophy. Even a brief reacquaintance allows us to understand a proper American civics as a distinctive mix of civic knowledge, civic virtues, and civic participation – and to see the consequences of our long-term neglect of this democratic-republican approach.

1.1 TOCQUEVILLE'S AFFIRMATION OF AMERICAN CIVIC EDUCATION

In the Introduction to *Democracy in America* Tocqueville tells us he is interested in America for its own sake and for larger reasons, given the "great democratic revolution" unfolding in Europe and North and South America, challenging humankind's near-universal history of rule by monarchs, emperors, chieftains, and despots. "I confess that in America I saw more than America; I sought there an image of democracy itself, of its penchants, its character, its prejudices ... to know at least what we ought to hope or fear from it" (Introduction, 3, 13). Two momentous revolutions for popular rule and equal rights in recent times, the American and the French, had fomented other struggles for popular liberation. Yet in his homeland the revolution turned extreme; within a decade of 1789, it had destroyed a monarchy yet yielded Napoleon as First Consul, who crowned himself Emperor a few years thereafter. America's record has been more successful so far. This history likely informs Tocqueville's subsequent remark on civic education which praises the Americans while raising a warning for fellow Europeans: "In the United States, the sum of men's education is directed toward politics," toward informed and committed citizenship; whereas "in Europe, its principal goal is to prepare for private life" not for "civic affairs" (I.2.9, 291–92).

This is one of many moments in the work where Tocqueville judges the American experiment, thus far, to be exceptional. It does not indicate any view, however, that continued success is assured. He seeks to grasp what we can hope for and what we should fear about the democratic revolution. He discerns deep problems facing America in the 1830s, not dissimilar in scope and gravity to those that tested the prospects for democracy in Europe and South America. He traveled America for nine months in 1831–32 during the transformative moment of Jacksonian democracy, launched by Americans electing in 1828 the first president neither of the founding generation nor, like John Quincy Adams, directly a descendent of them. This opened a vista of rising passion and anger in politics, about slavery but also economic and moral questions. There already had been talk of civil war given the alarms set off in the Missouri crisis of 1820 over slavery's westward expansion, hardly calmed by Jackson's sympathy for both slavery and expansion. Tocqueville's observations on the indispensability of a complex civic education arise in a chapter, "On the Principal Causes Tending to Maintain a Democratic Republic in the United States," which summarizes his study in the first volume of *Democracy* of the political institutions and basic political character of our democratic republic. This emphasis on sustaining or maintaining shares the spirit of Franklin's 1787 admonition, and of Lincoln's Lyceum address just a few years ahead: America has successfully launched a republic, but can we keep it?

Within this telling chapter, the subchapter focused on civic education and formation is "How the Enlightenment, The Habits, and the Practical Experience of the Americans Contribute to the Success of Democratic Institutions." This optimistic title is an interlude in a more foreboding view of the American project. Shortly thereafter, in the actual closing chapter of this first volume of *Democracy*, Tocqueville addresses "The Three Races" in America and the "Probable Future" of each. This longest chapter across the two volumes includes a subchapter asking, "What Are the Chances That the American Union Will Last? What Dangers Threaten It?" (I.2.10, 302–96; see 348). Tocqueville sees race-based chattel slavery, with its effects on political character and policy, casting a shadow over our growing commercial power across the globe and our territorial expansion to the Rocky Mountains and beyond. He discusses several times the prospect of civil war caused by the differing interests and political cultures of the northern and southern states, with slavery the root issue. To be sure, he predicts that our egalitarian, rational, scientific, technological, and commercial power is destined to conquer all the temperate part of North America from Atlantic to Pacific, and our "commercial greatness" points toward becoming "the first maritime power on the globe" (eclipsing Great Britain) – for just as "the Romans were [driven] to conquer the world" so the Americans "are driven to gain control of the seas" (I.2.10, 363, 368, 390). Yet there is more warning here than first appears. How did that drive for martial conquest work out for the Romans?[2] How might the American drive work out for a democratic republic growing in wealth, power, and territory if it cannot resolve the moral failings of racism and slavery, and of nearly exterminating the native peoples in the Anglo-American march across the continent? It turns out our democratic republic survived civil war by 1865, but just barely. Tocqueville counsels in 1835 that if our republic is to avoid self-ruin, we need more of the complex civic education blending book-learning about ideals and laws with inculcation of civic virtues, then developed into a citizen's practical knowledge through participation in self-government. Less democracy, more civic knowledge and virtue, and a more self-disciplined republic.

Diana Schaub argues in her recent study that Lincoln's three greatest speeches are the 1838 Lyceum address on the need for civic education and recommitment to the Constitution and laws; the 1863 Gettysburg Address on the need for recommitment to the Declaration of Independence and for a new birth of freedom; and the 1865 Second Inaugural on the Biblical spirit of atonement needed from all Americans for the legacy of 1619, even on the verge of Union victory, to include malice toward none and charity for all. Across the three, our great common-man president echoes George Washington's calls for a civic character in America, blending moral and intellectual foundations for sustaining self-government.[3] We have no indication that Lincoln read *Democracy in America*; but we

---

[2] The subchapter on America's growing commercial and maritime power plays on the title of Montesquieu's *Considerations on the Causes of the Greatness of the Romans and Their Decline* (1732); Tocqueville's title is "Some Considerations on the Causes of the Commercial Greatness of the United States" (I.2.10, 384). The moral of Montesquieu's story is the Roman failure to moderate their drive for martial conquest and glory; leading to self-destruction first in civil wars (producing Julius Caesar) and then ultimately the loss of the republic to the empire.

[3] Diana Schaub, *His Greatest Speeches: How Lincoln Moved the Nation* (St. Martin's Press, 2021).

do know of Tocqueville's praise of Washington and Lincoln's admiration for Washington, and we see echoes of Washington's 1796 Farewell Address and other writings evident in Lincoln's three greatest teachings on our civic education and civic character. And Tocqueville, too, was a statesman-thinker: he was a magistrate in the French government when he visited America; by the 12th printing of *Democracy in America*, in 1848, he had served in the national assembly and as foreign minister. The consensus of these three great spirits and minds should give us pause today. In the past century, America's educational and intellectual elites, and political class, clearly turned away from the democratic-republican wisdom of these statesmen-thinkers.

We might dismiss such views as ancient history; irrelevant given the vast technological, democratic, demographic, and global changes shaping America in the 160 years since Lincoln's Second Inaugural, arguably the summative statement of the Washington-Tocqueville-Lincoln teaching on civic culture and civics. Yet we should consider the testimony of Richard Haass's recent book on the renewal of the civic character and education America needs to save itself from self-destruction, for it echoes this democratic-republican civic wisdom after we had long repudiated it. A statesman-thinker in his own right having served in several presidential administrations and as president of the Council on Foreign Relations, and prior to *The Bill of Obligations* not easily considered an intellectual or political conservative, Haass's culminating Tenth Obligation, Put Country First, includes a statement of American civic character that shows the imprint of these predecessors (all of whom he cites in the book). Having affirmed as Obligation IX – Support the Teaching of Civics – the necessity of education in civic knowledge and virtues, including civil disagreement and an informed patriotism, his final call to "put the country and American democracy before party and person" argues this duty is "an essential element of patriotism." Such a duty and patriotism always has been a national necessity, and now urgently is so:

[this] is the only way to preserve and, better yet, improve a United States of America that for any and all of its shortcomings and flaws is still the most successful political experiment in human history and the one with the greatest potential. As he did so often, Abraham Lincoln said it best: "We shall nobly save, or meanly lose, the last best hope of earth."[4]

---

[4] Richard Haass, *The Bill of Obligations: The Ten Habits of Good Citizens* (Penguin Press, 2023), p. 148; for Lincoln's phrase, see the close of his 1862 Address to Congress.

The sections that follow address Montesquieu's philosophy of civic education, and then the views of the American founders on civics; with the help of a few recent academic voices who have argued for recovering the philosophy and practice of citizenship education by blending civic knowledge, civic virtues, and the development of practical judgment. Studies of the educational writings and efforts of the American founders persist amid the predominance of the democracy education approach. Educational theorist E.D. Hirsch, Jr. recently assessed the failures of generic democracy education across the past century, arguing that American civics needs grounding in our own institutions, principles, history, and civic culture. Educational theorists in the twentieth century "had become optimistic about America. They no longer worried that the very stability and peace of the Republic hinged on diffusing shared knowledge and preparing virtuous, loyal citizens who would subordinate private aims to the good of the whole."[5] We now have grounds to doubt this rejection of American civic wisdom. I extend Hirsch's approach by turning to Montesquieu to help us grasp the complexity, balance, and subtlety of the consensus view of our founders regarding civics, given his deep influence on the American mind from 1760 to 1800. Among other dimensions Montesquieu illuminates, we can see how the Declaration itself implicitly calls for a citizenship education not only in individual rights but also in the source of those rights in a divine creator and natural law, and in the English constitutional tradition that shaped American political thinking – as well as in civic virtues, including a duty to fight for the right to self-government if needed. Only by consulting Montesquieu will we understand the Declaration's closing oath, the pledge of not just lives and fortunes but "sacred Honor" to defend justice. His analysis of civic education turns out to be particularly hospitable for Americans given his praise for the American colonial leader William Penn as a model founder and civic educator. Study of Montesquieu also better prepares us to appreciate the insights of his greatest protégé, Tocqueville.

1.2 MONTESQUIEU'S PHILOSOPHY OF A MODERN AND MODERATE CIVICS

Given a paradox from our founding era, perhaps I should be less critical of educational theorists and practitioners who from John Dewey forward

---

[5] E. D. Hirsch, Jr., *The Making of Americans: Democracy and Our Schools* (Yale University Press, 2009), 31.

have discarded the original American consensus on a civics blending constitutional knowledge and civic character in favor of progressive projects of democratic self-creation through civic engagement. For it was not clearly settled in 1776 just what an American civic education should be. Leading Enlightenment philosophers provided clear principles and guidelines on forming a new kind of constitutional republic, but offered our founders no similarly clear guidance on the companion civic education needed to perpetuate and operate such a polity. Hints and suggestions are scattered across several philosophical works; and arguably Montesquieu provides better general guidance for modern republican statesmen and leading civic thinkers than any other source. He emphasizes the necessity of civic education amid his main work on the politics and constitutionalism of moderation and liberty, *The Spirit of Laws* (1748) – rather than addressing it separately from his main work of political philosophy, as did John Locke and other philosophers. This is good news for Americans concerned with civic education, since Montesquieu shaped the formation of our constitutional order more than any other philosopher. Yet *Spirit of Laws* ultimately provides no specific guidance on citizenship education for the complex constitutional polity Montesquieu recommends as best providing for liberty, the very model our framers most consulted. All American civic thinkers, from the civic-minded political leaders of the founding era and beyond to recent academics and political scientists, inherit this original paradox. We are more at liberty to ignore or bungle the civics needed to sustain our intellectual and political liberty in part because the chapter on civic education in the owner's manual of our constitutionalism was demarcated as essential by our architectonic guide, yet left unfinished.[6]

American intellectual culture had long deemed development of the right American civics a high priority, and civic duty, for perpetuating our constitutionalism. Great intellectual and civic figures from the founding era and beyond noted this gap and sought to fill it. Until the recent renewal of American civics, too many leading scholars, civic thinkers, and political figures across the past century had spurned or neglected this legacy. The dominant intellectual and academic view became a civics of democratic progress, or a complete neglect of civics. In effect this was deficit-spending the principles and culture that sustain our peculiar

---

[6] This section abbreviates my analysis in "Montesquieu's Call to Civic Education: Roots of and Remedies for America's Civic Crisis," in *American Citizenship and Constitutionalism in Principle and Practice*, ed. Pittz and Postell (University of Oklahoma Press, 2022).

polity, taking for granted the liberty and prosperity that allows the pursuit of projects for progress and greater equality.

Those who perceive that the bill long since has come due should turn to Montesquieu for helpful indications about what civic education is, and why it is an integral, indispensable element of constitutionalism. This includes his basic call to thoughtful citizens regarding an intellectual and civic duty to formulate the right civic education for a particular polity. For American scholars and educators, the call to civic education tasks us with discerning what content and modes of education would best perpetuate our constitutional order and culture of liberty, as well as providing capacities for refinement of our law and culture.

Recent discourse on civic education and the American founding occasionally refers to the affirmation, early in *Spirit of Laws*, of the fundamental importance of this topic for our kind of politics: "It is in republican government that the full power of education is needed."[7] This declaration makes it a bit puzzling that, when Montesquieu later recommends the English constitution devoted to liberty – which he defines as a unique blend of republic and monarchy – he provides no further comment on what kind of civic education would be needed for this constitutionalism.[8] Deeper study of his full discussion of civic education, and of clues later in *Spirit of Laws* about the constitution of liberty he praises, can provide ideas for addressing this paradox from our founding and for taking up the call to civic education in his philosophy.

1.2.1 Montesquieu, Moderation, and the Idea of America

The Spirit of Laws was the work of political science most influential for John Adams, James Madison, Alexander Hamilton, the early Thomas Jefferson, and other framers of the new American state constitutions,

---

[7] Charles de Montesquieu, *The Spirit of the Laws*, ed. Anne M. Cohler, Basia Miller, and Harold Stone (Cambridge University Press, 1989 [1748]), Book 4, Chapter 5, 35. Subsequent references are parenthetical, citing the book and chapter of *Spirit* and the page in this edition. I occasionally revise the Cohler translation. See Lorraine S. Pangle and Thomas L. Pangle, *The Learning of Liberty: The Educational Ideals of the American Founders* (University Press of Kansas, 1992), 132; Walter Berns, *Making Patriots* (University of Chicago Press, 2001), 66; and George Thomas, *The Founders and the Idea of a National University: Constituting the American Mind* (Cambridge University Press, 2014), 2.

[8] Montesquieu describes England in Book 5 as "a nation where the republic hides under the form of monarchy" and confirms this in his second long chapter devoted to England: one often sees there "the form of an absolute government over the foundation of a free government" (*Spirit of Laws* 5.19, 70; 29.27, 330). His famous study of "The Constitution of England" as unique in its direct devotion to liberty is in 11.6 (156–66).

the 1787 Constitution, and the Bill of Rights. The constitutional debates of our founding era invoked Montesquieu more than any of the philosophers of radical enlightenment such as Hobbes, Locke, or Rousseau. The relative scholarly neglect of Montesquieu in the past century thus is an unfortunate trait of recent American political theory and political science, impeding our understanding of our constitutionalism, whether to criticize or endorse.[9] Our intellectual preferences no longer favor the complexity, coupled with concern for governing in particular regimes, that defines his political philosophy; we instead prefer clear doctrines or bold theoretical provocations. Montesquieu's philosophy seeks to discern the "spirit" of laws, their comprehensive, multifarious meaning beyond any one doctrine or principle. This approach of complexity reflects the principle of philosophical moderation or equilibrium he sought to embody in his masterwork. Thus today only a few scholars address his declaration that the key to his political philosophy is moderation – defined as avoiding extremes and finding the political good in the middle (29.1). It is a necessary challenge for us first to grasp that architectonic principle and then explore his application of it to civic education within his philosophy.

The few elements of *Spirit of Laws* still recognized in America today, including a complex constitutionalism of separated powers and the principle of federalism as forging a republic of republics, are instances of moderation. The political good is not found through singular ideas or powers, but by reconciling and balancing, in just the right way, several ideas or elements in specific circumstances – whether of human nature, or political reality, or legal forms. *The Spirit of Laws* propounds both a philosophical method and a view of justice defined by this balancing and reconciliation of multiple principles. After the more radically modern, single-minded philosophies of Hobbes, Spinoza, and Locke, Montesquieu seeks to improve liberalism by restoring elements of classical and medieval philosophy that appreciate the multifarious reality,

---

[9] See, for example, Donald Lutz, "The Relative Influence of European Writers on Late Eighteenth-Century American Political Thought," *American Political Science Review* 78 (1984): 189–97. I discuss Montesquieu's political philosophy and why it matters more than ever for America in *Democracy in Moderation: Montesquieu, Tocqueville, and Sustainable Liberalism* (Cambridge University Press, 2016). Sharon R. Krause argues in *Politics of Liberty: Essays on Montesquieu* (Bloomsbury Academic, 2025) that both critics and defenders of liberalism today would benefit from encountering Montesquieu's complex, moderate account of this political philosophy; citing an array of recent Montesquieu scholarship mining this moderate spirit.

and higher dimensions, of humanity and politics. Near the end of his massive work, he finally announces this guiding principle: "I say it, and it seems to me I have brought forth this work only to prove it: the spirit of moderation ought to be that of the legislator; the political good, like the moral good, is always found between two limits" (29.1, 602). This blend of philosophical sobriety and humility was offered four decades before the French Revolution and its ultimately radical stances on philosophy, human nature, politics, religion, and violence (see also *Spirit*, Preface, xlv).

The philosophically moderate Montesquieu and his disciple, the English jurist Blackstone – not the social-contractarian, analytic philosopher Locke nor any other radically rationalist minds – were the foremost philosophical influences upon the framers of the Declaration, the 1787 Constitution, and the Bill of Rights as a whole. The Lockean dimensions to our constitutionalism and to the thought of leading founders, most evident in the opening of the Declaration on individual rights and in ideas about separating church and state, should not eclipse the larger complexity of principles that characterize our founding. America simultaneously draws upon not only liberalism and modern republicanism but also classical philosophy, Christianity, and classic common law.[10] Such moderation among or balancing of diverse principles pervades American constitutionalism and extends beyond institutions to shape the complexity of our civic culture and thought, evident in our perpetual blending of pluralism and principle, individual rights and public purposes. *The Spirit of Laws* informs this American complexity more than any other book save the Bible; its only philosophical rival for this distinction, Blackstone's *Commentaries on the Laws of England*, draws heavily upon Montesquieu.[11] This is in part because Montesquieu's liberal constitutionalism analyzes and utilizes the model of liberty in the English constitution, praising it as the only government in the world dedicated to liberty as its main aim. Yet he also warns, at the close of his first portrait of England, against "extreme" elements in its liberty as well as extremes "even of reason" that characterize modern political thinking (11.4, 155; 11.6, 166).

We will hardly understand America if so few of us study this complex philosophy, given that America still is governed largely by the

---

[10] In *Democracy in Moderation*, 118 n. 20, I cite a range of scholarly sources on these points. I am indebted to several works by James Stoner for the basic insight.

[11] I argue this in *The Cloaking of Power: Montesquieu, Blackstone, and the Rise of Judicial Activism* (University of Chicago Press, 2003).

Constitution and amendments inspired by Montesquieu – encompassing not only the 1787 Constitution and Bill of Rights but also the Civil War amendments informed by Lincoln's effort to restore the original spirit of that constitutionalism. The demotion of his philosophy of moderation in turn cuts us off from his views on civic education, which offer crucial ideas about why this topic matters so fundamentally, and for assessing what kind of American civic literacy and forms of civic moderation are now needed.

1.2.2 A Moderately Modern Conception of Civic Education

The philosophy of moderation explains why, unlike Locke, Montesquieu analyzes civic education as a constituent element of a comprehensive political philosophy, and does so in the early books of *Spirit of Laws*. In the middle of Part 1 of the work's six parts is Book 4, "That the laws of education should be relative to the principles of the government." It is a perplexing book, with seemingly contradictory elements along with striking statements that have attracted scholarly discussion. We need, therefore, a broader perspective on why he addresses civic education so early in his comprehensive masterwork, and why this matters for America's constitutionalism and civic culture. In Books 2 and 3, Montesquieu had adapted Aristotle's concept of analyzing different regimes; he would investigate the structure or "nature" of four main types of government – democratic republic, aristocratic republic, monarchy, and despotism. He then analyzed the animating passion or "principle" that moves any given structure to function. It thus is telling that education is such an early, formative topic in his long analysis of the multifarious spirit of human affairs, ultimately requiring thirty-one books (in recent translation, over 700 pages). In the Preface and Book 1, he delineates the fundamental aims and premises of his political philosophy, including his conception of divine, natural, and human laws and the main constituent elements of the "spirit" of any government or set of laws. Books 2 and 3 then introduce his novel political science of three main types of government – republic (in two modes), monarchy, and despotism – and the further novel concepts of the *nature* (structure) and *principle* (animating passion) for each. The very next topic, significantly, is education: that there "should be" an alignment between the education and the principle in each type of government. An important place for education is hardly striking from the perspective of classical political philosophy; Plato's *Republic* places education at or near the center of philosophy and political philosophy, and Aristotle devotes two of the seven books of the *Politics* to education and the best regime. What is so striking in modernity is that Montesquieu agrees with this classical tenet even as a modern and liberal philosopher who thus is not primarily concerned, as were classical and medieval philosophers, with the search for the best political regime as the home for human virtue; understood as the excellence of an individual soul and of a community of souls.

Yet as a proto-social scientist, Montesquieu describes the kind of government – he calls it a democratic republic – that historically takes as its aim something like human excellence; thus, he defines its principle as "virtue" but gives that word a new meaning, as a kind of public-spirited, patriotic zeal. He also describes monarchy as having an elevated aim and character, deeming its principle "honor," which is neither the classical conception of virtue nor Montesquieu's new concept of a democratic citizen's "love of the laws and of the homeland" (4.3, 36; see also 2.3). This principle of honor, as the passion animating monarchy, is the dedication of the nobility and royalty to the self-regard required to embody a distinct code of conduct (Book 2, chapters 5–7). We can appreciate Montesquieu's distinctive approach if we recall that Locke has no time for this historical and theoretical messiness about virtue and honor, with its classical and medieval overtones. He does publish *Some Thoughts Concerning Education* after his *Two Treatises of Government*, but leaves readers to discern why he separates education from his main statement of political philosophy, and what this means for both education and his new and seemingly materialist philosophy. The *Second Treatise* defines the sole legitimate aim of government as security of radically individual rights to life, liberty, and property, coupling this with a theory that our natural asociality requires the mechanism of a social contract to construct an artificial thing called political society. Just as it takes no education in the state of nature to feel bodily insecurity and be pulled toward a mutual pact for reducing one's insecurity, so, Locke implies, there is no political, public-oriented education needed for citizens of the contracted society to feel whether the government is securing their material life, liberty, and property. One infers he saw no need for education to be a positive, integral element of political philosophy per se. Locke thus ignores the classical conception of civics as only indirectly relevant, at best, for the new individual-oriented aims of politics, the new philosophy propounding them, and sustaining both. *Thoughts Concerning Education* confirms this: education is a strictly private matter, not a public, civic one; best undertaken in the family, not in schools; and while he states an intention that this individualist, privatized education will serve the public good of vigilance toward government and defense of political society when needed, this result would be achieved not from instruction in a sense of duty or honor but out of strictly self-interested regard for protecting the social contract that secures one's own life, property, and at best family – but no wider sense of community.[12]

Montesquieu's reintegration of education as a positive, constitutive element of political philosophy, necessary to ensure the proper functioning of any government, thus reintegrates elements of classical and medieval philosophy to correct the materialism and skepticism of the radical modern philosophers of the prior century, Locke among them.[13] Montesquieu's account of education is an important step toward achieving a properly moderate liberal philosophy through a moderate constitutionalism. His positive role for education in republics (mostly in the democratic mode) and also in monarchy is evident when he states, "education in monarchies works to elevate the heart," and the education to virtue in democracies inspires citizens to strive for the "greatness and glory" of their republic – while a despot wants only "ignorance" in subjects (4.3, 34–35; 4.6, 37; see 2.9). This judgment in Book 4 reinforces a crucial point made near the end of Book 3, that while it is important to grasp the distinct natures and principles of the four types of government, there really are only two kinds. The basic distinction is "between moderate governments and despotic governments" (3.10, 29). Moderation, as rising above the politics of despotic fear, means rising above materialism, mere animality, and passions, such that reason can educate and elevate the passions toward a more humane politics. That said, the elevation can't aim too high, returning to the illiberal aims of classical political philosophy to find the one true account of virtue in the soul and the one true regime of strongly harmonized souls. Moderate elevation is needed.

---

[12] While not as critical of Locke as my account, the interpretation of Lorraine and Thomas Pangle generally concurs, in "The Lockean Revolution in Educational Theory," in *The Learning of Liberty*, 54–72, especially at 61, 65–66, 69–70; see also Rita Koganzon, "Locke's Authoritarian Education," in *Liberal States, Authoritarian Families: Childhood and Education in Early Modern Thought* (Oxford University Press, 2021), 93–128. An account more sympathetic to Locke is Nathan Tarcov, *Locke's Education for Liberty* (University of Chicago Press, 1984).

[13] Susan Collins, in *Aristotle and the Rediscovery of Citizenship* (2006), helpfully contrasts modern liberal theory with Aristotle's philosophy of a polity or regime, including citizen education toward the virtue that defines a regime; while she does not discuss Montesquieu, her critique of what modern liberal theory omits points to his distinction from Hobbes and Locke by restoring to a central place the issue of education toward the aims or ends of a given regime.

Thus, a theme running through Part 1 of *Spirit of Laws* is that classical republicanism (think Sparta and Rome) is despotic in demanding virtue as the individual's total commitment to the greatness and glory of the democratic republic.[14] This is why "in republican government the full power of education is needed" – because in the classical model of a republic, "political virtue is a renunciation of oneself, which is always a very painful thing" (4.5, 35; see also 5.2, 42–43). Montesquieu clearly has posed the question of what kind of civics is suited to sustain modern, moderate republics; to include those grounded in the principles of individual rights yet not repudiating a higher politics embracing some conception of civic virtue.

1.2.3 The Moderating Spirit of Christianity in Modern Civic Education

This concern with classical republican extremism explains why, from the opening of Book 4, Montesquieu elevates the status of what we now call constitutional monarchy within modern liberal philosophy. He states that "the laws of education," which "prepare us to be citizens," apply not only to republics but also to monarchies (4.1, 31; 3.6, 26). He also deems civic education in monarchies – a form of government he strongly praises in Book 6 for its judicial institutions protecting individual security – as relatively more moderate, thus just, than standard-model republics, which can tend toward the immoderate or despotic. As both a nobleman (a baron) and a judge in France's monarchy, his judgments on these issues hold some authority.

On first reading Montesquieu's analysis of honor would not seem to support any genuinely elevated qualities of citizenship akin to a reflective patriotism that balances self-regard with gratitude for the polity and a sense of civic duty. He had stated in Book 3 that "speaking philosophically" the principle of monarchy is "a false honor," because adherence to a code of honor doesn't directly seek to affirm the nobility or greatness of the kingdom, nor to serve one's community, but

---

[14] See Thomas L. Pangle, *Montesquieu's Philosophy of Liberalism* (University of Chicago Press, 1973); Paul Rahe, *Montesquieu and the Logic of Liberty* (Yale University Press, 2009); Diana Schaub, "The Regime and Montesquieu's Principles of Education," in *Montesquieu and the Spirit of Modernity*, ed. David W. Carrithers and Patrick Coleman (Voltaire Foundation, University of Oxford, 2002), 77–100; and David W. Carrithers, "Democratic and Aristocratic Republics: Ancient and Modern," in *Montesquieu's Science of Politics: Essays on The Spirit of Laws*, ed. David W. Carrithers, Michael Mosher, and Paul Rahe (Rowman and Littlefield, 2001), 109–58.

rather seeks "to demand preferences and distinctions." Thus a noble-man undertaking a great deed or adhering to the code in effect "works for the common good" even though his primary motivation is "believ-ing he works for his individual interest" (3.7, 27).[15] Montesquieu thus implies this medieval, feudal idea of honor really is quite modern in its focus on the individual's concerns. Indeed, Book 4 emphasizes the dis-tinction between the ancient and the modern modes of life and thought, devoting a chapter to "The difference in the effect of education among the ancients and ourselves" (4.4, 35). He contrasts the "extraordinary" character of the ancient democratic republic – their institutions and the deeds of their citizens – with "the dregs and corruptions of our mod-ern times," including monarchies (4.6, 37). The "effect" of the ancient education in virtue was deeds the likes of which "we no longer see" and which "astonish our small souls" (4.4, 35).

The puzzle, then, of these chapters is that Montesquieu simultaneously praises monarchy for educating citizens not subjects, and for elevating the heart, implying that monarchy essentially is modern or European not ancient or feudal; while also seeming to praise the grandeur of ancient republics in contrast to the pettiness of modern monarchies. Finding the full thread through this labyrinth requires recourse to several earlier and later passages in the work as well as other passages in Book 4. For our narrower concern with his main conclusions on civic education, we can focus on a particular instance of his praise of honor, and his use of a con-trast between ancient Greek views of republican civics and the modern views of William Penn, as ways he articulates a philosophy of modera-tion and a moderate civics for modern republics.

Montesquieu makes clear throughout the work that moderation requires affirming natural right, natural law, and the natural rights of individuals, as *Spirit of Laws* does in the Preface and fairly obviously in Books 1, 3, 6, 10, 12, 24, 26, and 29 – while also affirming, as he does in Book 1, that it is only reasonable that "the political and civil laws of each nation" would be different. "Laws should be so appropriate to the people for whom they are made that it is a very great chance if the laws of one nation can suit another" (Preface, 8). This is not relativism but the recognition that one can clearly discern despotism in its vari-ous forms as violating natural right, while necessarily admitting that a range of moderate governments can protect natural right by protecting

---

[15] Adam Smith, his thinking deeply shaped by *The Spirit of Laws*, arguably takes his idea of "the invisible hand" in free economies from this analysis of honor.

individuals against despotic acts (3.10, 29–30). These moderate governments are more likely to be modern, thus shaped by Christianity, than to be ancient and democratic-republican. In Book 4, he credits the monarchical code of honor with educating citizens to produce grand, elevated, virtuous actions; this includes frank or candid speech, not from "the love of truth" per se but because it is seen as "daring and free." His analysis of politeness in manners induces an observation echoing the definition in Book 1 that humans are naturally sociable, in contrast to Hobbes and Locke: "Men, born to live together, are also born to please each other" (4.2, 32; see 1.2, 7). Moreover, honor educates one to check the potential despotism of "the prince" if he should "prescribe an action that dishonors us." Thus a nobleman, Crillon, was ordered "to assassinate the Duke of Guise" but refused. Montesquieu then recounts an episode of religious intolerance extending to mass murder, when in 1685, after Saint Bartholomew's Day, King Charles IX revoked the toleration of some Protestants in the Edict of Nantes and "sent orders to all the governors to have the Huguenots massacred." The episode evokes one of the most remarkable passages in the work:

> The Viscount of Orte, who was in command at Bayonne, wrote to the king, "Sire, I have found among the inhabitants and the warriors only good citizens, brave soldiers, and not one executioner; thus, they and I together beg Your Majesty to use our arms and our lives for things that can be done." This great and generous courage regarded a cowardly action as an impossible thing (4.2, 33; see also 6.5, 79).

Americans in the 1760s and 1770s protesting the British government's increasingly imperious conduct toward the North American colonies cited this passage from Montesquieu to rally the self-governing spirit they had enjoyed for more than a century at the western edge of their constitutional monarchy's empire. Americans should resist as a matter of honor the King's despotic acts of taxation without representation and other violations of established Anglo-American legal traditions and principles. Montesquieu thus is a likely source of the Declaration's closing invocation of sacred honor.[16]

In Book 4, chapter 6, Montesquieu's deepens his characterization of modern Christian monarchies as moderate versus the fanaticism of ancient republics by contrasting "Greek institutions" with the peaceful moderation of William Penn's colony in British North America. Great

---

[16] See Paul Merrill Spurlin, *Montesquieu in America, 1760–1801* (Louisiana State University Press, 1940). I argue these points in my article "Montesquieu, the Declaration of Independence, and the Moderation of America's Founding Philosophy," forthcoming.

lawgivers such as Lycurgus of Sparta are the models Plato uses in his work *The Laws* to design a polity of pure virtue, but both the Spartan and pure philosophic laws are extreme in their "singular" civic education. Yes, the "extraordinary" results of that education contrast with, as noted, "the dregs and corruption of our modern times." But this is not the end of the story, for here he introduces Penn and also the seventeenth- and eighteenth-century Jesuit missionaries in Spain's colony of Paraguay, emphatically praising both: "That extraordinary [quality] which we saw in the Greek institutions, we have seen that amid the dregs and corruption of our modern times." Penn is a "legislator, a true gentleman" who

has formed a people in whom integrity seems as natural as bravery was among the Spartans. Mr. Penn is a true Lycurgus; and, though he has had peace for his object as Lycurgus had war, they are alike in the unique path on which they have set their people, in their ascendency over free men, in the prejudices they have vanquished, and in the passions they have subdued (4.6, 37).

This is unqualified praise of the Quaker founder of Pennsylvania for establishing through laws and civic education what Montesquieu presumably knew was a Protestant and commercial republic, further defined by religious toleration. This makes for more of a contrast to Lycurgus and Sparta than an imitation, for Pennsylvania rests not upon indoctrination in passion, *sans* knowledge, but upon education in a civic ethic of peace and self-government – and without the Spartan exploitation of slaves (called the Helots). The consent of the governed in Pennsylvania is freer because it is grounded in Protestant Christian ethics of mutual regard, and freely chosen by individuals rather than through tradition or ecclesial authority.

Montesquieu need not be deemed a believer himself in order to consider that he appreciates how Christianity can be a moderating, ameliorating influence in modern life. This may be a utilitarian approach, but seemingly in a higher, respectful sense, such as Tocqueville's strong endorsement of religion held as a philosopher while personally not believing the Christian faith.[17] Montesquieu portrays the effects of the severe civic education of ancient republicanism as rightly "astonishing" to modern, Christian, monarchical, moderate souls. In a work committed to moderation and avoiding extremes, this allows him to portray ancient republican single-mindedness in politics and civics as fanaticism and

---

[17] I make this argument in chapter 4 of *Democracy in Moderation*, "Religion and Liberty in America: The Spirit of Montesquieu and Tocqueville."

extremism, in contrast to a complex, balanced, pluralistic civic education that reduces political fanaticism and extremism. This theme, dramatized by praise of the Viscount of Orte and of Penn, in turn sets up one of the emphatic moments of *Spirit of Laws*, the longest chapter of the work to that point, analyzing and praising the blend of monarchy and republic in the English constitution (11.6). And in that book both the English and continental European (Gothic) constitutions, inflected with a monarchical code of honor, are praised as "moderate" forms of government (Book 11, chapters 5–8).

Thus, as a comment on civic education broadly, the praise for Penn foreshadows principles emphasized later in the work as Montesquieu develops a philosophy of moderation. This featuring of Penn as exemplary also would be commonsensical to Americans – all the more so if we note that in Montesquieu's second long analysis of England, focusing upon the changes in political culture and character affected by the complex monarchy-republic of their constitution, he particularly praises the success of the English colonies in North America given their adaptations of the complex constitutionalism of the mother country: "As this government would carry prosperity with it, one would see the formation of great peoples even in the forests to which it had sent inhabitants" (19.27, 329).[18] For Americans or advocates of complex constitutional liberal democracies, this striking praise of Penn as a modern Lycurgus is less perplexing, for it further casts ancient political virtue as despotic and previews the moderate alternatives Montesquieu identifies. This reading allows a briefer comment on his pairing of the Jesuits in Paraguay as the other modern analogue to Lycurgus. He greatly praises the Jesuits' gentle, humane approach to the indigenous peoples, thereby "repairing the pillages of the Spaniards" elsewhere in the New World, healing "one of the greatest wounds mankind has yet received" (4.6, 37; see 10.4, 142). Montesquieu lists the many improvements the Jesuits supplied to the living conditions of native peoples, and deems this law-giving effort "successful" in undertaking "great things," confirming that "governing men by making them happier will always be a fine thing" (37).

---

[18] Montesquieu, a Latinist, would know that "Pennsylvania" means "Penn's woods" or forests. Moreover, shortly after this he praises England's blend of religious toleration, moderate modern republicanism, and commerce – just what Penn achieved in his 1682 Pennsylvania Frame of Government: "This is the people in the world who have best known how to take advantage of each of these three great things at the same time: religion, commerce, and liberty" (20.7, 343).

Montesquieu's striking passages on the Protestant Penn and Catholic Jesuits remind us of the thread earlier in Book 4 that Christianity can temper both honor and political virtue. These premodern political qualities might be acceptably adapted to modern republics and monarchies – or governments that blend these two types, as England does – if the proper elements of Christian charity and humaneness also are present to temper the ends, ways, and means of politics. He signals that these portraits of supposed Christian successors to Lycurgus nearly transform the meaning of republican virtue, making moderate modern analogues. New ideas of civic education will be needed for the modern and potentially moderate peoples, with their larger scales of society and government in contrast to the ancient republics, especially in modern republics that blend some elements of monarchy – as England does. If in some senses this moderate, Christian modernity looks petty, as dregs and corruption against the glorious Spartan and Roman models of warlike republics turned empires, then Montesquieu ultimately is praising a moderate modernity with such faint damnation.[19]

1.2.4 Paths toward America's Moderate Civic Education

Americans of the founding era and today would need to grapple with the larger implication of Montesquieu's analysis of civic education, namely, that it leaves to thinkers and legislators in specific polities the task of discerning how his general approach and lessons might guide the formation of a civic education for their regime. Tocqueville, deeply shaped by Montesquieu's philosophy, describes an America more complex than the England sketched by *Spirit of Laws*; for he sees an initial American founding by New England Puritans (thus 1620 and the Mayflower Compact, not 1619), then a political-constitutional founding from 1776 onward (*Democracy in America*, I.1.2, then I.1.8). We are the kind of blended, complex constitutional order and political culture endorsed in the middle of the *Spirit of Laws* (especially Books 11, 12, and 19) as more moderate and humane. Awareness of that lineage, descending from a republic-monarchy blend, can guide American civic educators still today.

---

[19] This point is reinforced if his *Considerations on the Causes of the Greatness of the Romans and their Decline* is understood as a warning to any moderns fascinated by Rome's triumphs and dominance that their elements of greatness and virtue ultimately are outweighed by the inhumanity and butchery the Romans inflicted on others, and finally themselves as well, across centuries.

The general spirit of Montesquieu's philosophy of moderation has to be applied to a given polity, balancing discernment of universal natural principles of justice with judgment in particular circumstances on how to abide by them. We benefit from his restoration of civic education to a central place in his political philosophy and moderate constitutionalism. He seems to suggest that some blend of an education in honor and in civic virtue, each moderated by the influence of Christianity as well as the balanced spirit of his philosophy itself, would best undergird a democratic constitutional republic or a complex constitutional monarchy with strong republican elements. His implicit charge to philosophical readers and thoughtful statesmen is to take up their own work, in their nations and governments, to assess, build, or renew the appropriate constitutionalism and civics to achieve a moderate, humane life. America might be fortunate to inherit his broad outline for our complex constitution of liberty, which needed only adaptation; but we must forge our civic education ourselves.

As noted, after *Spirit of Laws* provides in Book 4 the call to a moderate civic education and broad guidelines, the remainder of the work illustrates moderating elements in politics so as to stimulate thinking about a more balanced political order and civic education. Broadly surveyed, these include judicial and legal reforms (Books 6 and 12), complex constitutional orders (Books 11 and 12), federalism (Book 9), legitimate military power for self-defense but not conquest (Book 10), severe critiques of slavery and polygamy across human history and cultures (Books 15–17), general praise for commerce (Books 20–22), and the proper role for religion, especially Christianity, in supporting a moderate political order (Books 24–25).[20] A moment of great interest to Americans is the analysis in Book 19 of the English political culture produced by the complex constitutional forms and "extreme" liberty featured in Book 11. This character sketch includes praise for the moderation and liberty the English enjoy, but also notes their extreme points, including individualism, materialism, and repression of a religious minority.

Montesquieu's two portraits of the English, in Books 11 and 19, could provide founders, legislators, philosophers, and educators of similarly complex, modern constitutional republics the grounds for designing a

---

[20] This view of a coherent theme in *Spirit of Laws*, of amelioration aiming at moderation, is affirmed in Bill Allen's new translation with extensive commentary; see *Montesquieu's The Spirit of the Laws: A Critical Edition*, ed. W. B. Allen, Translation and Commentary (Anthem Press, 2023); I reviewed this milestone of Montesquieu scholarship in "The Soul of Constitutional Government and Moderation: W.B. Allen's Edition of Montesquieu's *The Spirit of the Laws*," *The James Madison Review of Books*, no. 2 (Winter, 2024).

citizenship education reinforcing better elements and redressing dangers. Describing the English people with their individually minded ethos as "confederates more than fellow citizens" is not praise given Montesquieu's fundamental view, contrary to Locke, that humans are naturally sociable and meant "to live together" (see *Spirit* 19.27, 332). The closing comment in his portrait is also salient for America's current crises: warning that, in England's freewheeling modern republic, thinking can slide toward mere partisanship. Perhaps it takes a foreign visitor, as he was in England from 1729 to 1731, to discern the single-mindedness or philosophical extremism that can afflict thought in a liberal republic. The paradox of such liberty is that freedom for discourse, and for party conflict, tends to produce intellectual insularity or narrowness. Montesquieu mentions English historians, but since his own works (both *Considerations on the Romans* and *Spirit of Laws*) weave history and philosophy, his warning arguably addresses all intellectual schools or disciplines addressing human affairs: "In extremely absolute monarchies" or despotisms, "historians betray the truth because they do not have the liberty to tell it"; yet "in extremely free states, historians betray the truth because of their very liberty, for, as [liberty] always produces divisions, everyone becomes as much the slave of the prejudices of his faction as he would be of a despot" (19.27, 333).

These lessons on thinking for ourselves about constitutionalism and civic education, and wariness of descent into single-mindedness, are reinforced by an earlier moment in *Spirit of Laws* when closing the book on liberty in constitutions (including the English). Montesquieu tells readers to take up our intellectual and civic duty. As a philosopher he might "like to seek in all the moderate governments we know" the distribution of power and the liberty provided, but "one must not always so exhaust a subject that one leaves nothing for the reader to do. The question is not that of making him read, but of making him think" (11.20, 186). Leading American founders, as well as Tocqueville, took up Montesquieu's charge to think about how to utilize his general guidance for moderation and civic education in our new, somewhat unique circumstances.

The complex political science of Montesquieu and Tocqueville thus can be a guide for discerning America's needed civic education, and *Democracy in America* offers more particular guidance through its regular attention to education as a crucial topic for modern democracy and America. As discussed in Chapter 2, Tocqueville suggests we consider not only institutional forms and first principles of constitutional liberal democracy but also the new kind of "reflective patriotism" arising partly from the American approach to schooling, and fitting for our commercial and egalitarian polity. His comprehensive political science pushes us to consider how to balance and reconcile these complex elements. His assessments of and recommendations for civic education are so valuable because he had studied both Montesquieu and writings of the American founders, themselves influenced by Montesquieu. Moreover, he had directly observed our constitutionalism in light of its theory as well as its half-century of practice since its founding.

If Montesquieu and Tocqueville could visit twenty-first-century America, both philosophers would grasp why a kind of democratic license in America, among other factors, has weakened our understanding and appreciation of our founding constitutionalism – but they also would grasp why some of the complexity of our original political culture survives nonetheless. They would understand how a political culture that could yield the Declaration of Independence could still admire, after centuries and both triumphs and travails, the peculiarly honorable profession of the volunteer military above all other institutions and professions; even amid an era otherwise dominated as much or more by cynicism and apathy as by the angry political devotion of a few on the left and right poles. Their complex philosophies take seriously the aristocratic legacy of honor and how it might adapt and survive in changed circumstances. They would take some hope from the fact that the polarized, demoralized, and inadequately educated citizenry of our era still could honor the honorable, in accord with the spirit of the closing pledge made in 1776 – even if the Declaration itself is not so widely or deeply studied today as it should be.

1.3 THE AMERICAN FOUNDERS ON CIVIC KNOWLEDGE AND CIVIC VIRTUE FOR SELF-GOVERNMENT

It is remarkable that several of our leading founders wrote regularly about the importance of educating the citizenry of the new republic, and specifically regarding civic knowledge and virtues. Jefferson, Franklin, Adams, and Madison were institution builders and statesmen who also devoted considerable attention and energy to improving education. Benjamin Rush and Noah Webster are more directly known for writings and efforts to improve educational materials and institutions, particularly for civics. Rush proposed a federal university even before the 1787 Constitutional Convention. More remarkably still, the statesman whom these leaders, and all Americans, admired above all others as the leading founder – the Founding Father – grasped and greatly amplified this insistence upon the priority of civic education. Unlike these other founders, George Washington had not attended college; largely because his father died when he was ten. After completing basic schooling, he did have resources for self-education to utilize; from his father's library to neighbors in Virginia, including the prominent Fairfax family and fellow founder George Mason. Crucially for our history and world history, he did so, and continued with self-education his entire life. In later years he donated funds to educational institutions and served as a trustee of the College of William and Mary. From his first Annual Address to Congress as President (later termed State of the Union addresses) to his last, he urged Congress to establish a national university, for providing a citizen education to future leaders of the newly reforged, more perfect Union.[21] At his death, his library at Mount Vernon held over 900 books, including works of classical and modern philosophy and law, far beyond military and agricultural topics. The intellectual confidence he developed allowed him throughout decades in public service to consult a range of learned advisers, and rely upon one or another as he judged best. Richard Brookhiser's perceptive analysis concludes that Washington was "a leader who sought explanations and explainers all his life, and who mastered both what he was told and those who told him."[22]

Careful study of the 1796 document we call his Farewell Address, his parting statement from public life, shows that Washington revised every argument and draft, making it his own.[23] Among his nine points of counsel and warning, the sixth and seventh address the educational element of building the American civic character he deemed essential for sustaining the republic.

Of all the dispositions and habits which lead to political prosperity, religion and morality are indispensable supports. In vain would that man claim the tribute of patriotism, who should labor to subvert these great pillars of human happiness, these firmest props of the duties of men and citizens. The mere politician, equally with the pious man, ought to respect and to cherish them ...

It is substantially true that virtue or morality is a necessary spring of popular government. The rule, indeed, extends with more or less force to every species

---

[21] See Thomas, *The Founders and the Idea of a National University*, especially 2–5, 29–36, 64–72, 86–88.

[22] Brookhiser, *Founding Father: Rediscovering George Washington* (New York: Free Press, 1996), 139; see also his chapters on Washington's "Morals" and "Ideas," 121–56.

[23] See Matthew Spalding and Patrick Garrity, *A Sacred Union of Citizens: George Washington's Farewell Address and the American Character* (Lanham, MD: Rowman and Littlefield, 1996).

of free government. Who that is a sincere friend to it can look with indifference upon attempts to shake the foundation of the fabric?

Promote, then, as an object of primary importance, institutions for the general diffusion of knowledge. In proportion as the structure of a government gives force to public opinion, it is essential that public opinion should be enlightened.[24]

Washington signed into law in 1789 the re-enactment of the 1787 Northwest Ordinance of the Confederation Congress, stating the federal government's responsibility for education in the Northwest Territory. The new government under the Constitution endorsed the complex mode of civic education as the formation of civic character implied by Montesquieu: "religion, morality, and knowledge being necessary to good government and the happiness of mankind, schools and the means of education shall forever be encouraged." This vast area included the eventual states of Ohio, Indiana, Illinois, Michigan, Wisconsin, and part of Minnesota. As Lorraine and Thomas Pangle note, the fact that Madison managed, in the House, the repassing of the Ordinance while he also led the drafting of the amendments which became the Bill of Rights suggests that "no one thought at the time that state-sponsored education aimed at cultivating religious faith was contrary in spirit or letter to freedom of conscience or the First Amendment."[25]

The roots of the commitment by American statesman to education ran deep. Franklin wrote proposals for a new kind of academy in Philadelphia in 1749 and 1750, before any serious conflict between the British government in London and its North American colonies. He revised the proposals in 1789, shortly before his death. The traditional emphasis in pre-college schooling on classical Greek and Latin, and classical civilization, would be tempered by including more practical subjects for preparing the leading citizens of a modern and commercial republic (Pangle and Pangle, *Learning of Liberty*, 75, 78, 89–90). John Adams addressed the importance of laws for "liberal education of youth" in his influential pamphlet "Thoughts on Government" in early 1776, intended to help the new states with drafting their constitutions (as the Second Continental Congress had called the thirteen colonies to do in 1775, before the Declaration). He further addressed education in his 1787–88 *Defense of the Constitutions of Government of the United States.* An education in virtue was a crucial foundation for the new form of republic the Americans were establishing (*Learning of Liberty*, 2–4, 96). Adams

---

[24] In *The Political Writings of George Washington*, eds. Carson Holloway and Bradford P. Wilson (Cambridge University Press, 2023), Vol. II, 492–503, at 498–99.

[25] Pangle and Pangle, *The Learning of Liberty*, 198–99.

also was the main drafter of the 1780 Massachusetts constitution, which included responsibility for educating the citizenry:

CHAPTER V. Section 2. The Encouragement of Literature, etc.

Wisdom and knowledge, as well as virtue, diffused generally among the body of the people, being necessary for the preservation of their rights and liberties; and as these depend on spreading the opportunities and advantages of education in the various parts of the country and among the different orders of the people, it shall be the duty of legislatures and magistrates, in all future periods of this commonwealth, to cherish the interests of literature and the sciences, and all seminaries of them; especially the university at Cambridge, public schools, and grammar-schools in the towns.[26]

Several other founders, Washington among them, advocated for public schools funded by state governments, so that students of poor and middling means could gain the civic knowledge and civic virtues needed for republican self-government. Benjamin Rush, Thomas Jefferson, and Samuel Knox essentially share with Adams and Washington the view offered by Noah Webster in "On the Education of Youth in America" (1788) that in "our American republics, where government is in the hands of the people, knowledge should be universally diffused by means of public schools." In addition to "knowledge of spelling books and the New Testament," he argued that study of "ethics and the general principles of law, commerce, money, and government is necessary for the yeomanry of a republican state" (*Learning of Liberty*, 97; 91–98 generally).

Jefferson turns the American discourse of civic education toward a more democratic spirit with his 1779 Virginia proposal for a public school system emphasizing individual rights. His Bill for the More General Diffusion of Knowledge specified that "natural rights" of individuals must be focal; primary texts for instruction likely would include the Virginia Declaration of Rights, largely drafted by George Mason and passed by the Virginia Constitutional Convention in June 1776; and the Declaration of Independence, largely drafted by Jefferson. The Preamble to the bill states students must be educated "in the free exercise of their natural rights" to prevent the inherent tendency of all governments and anyone "entrusted with power" to decay "into tyranny"; indeed, a system of common education is "the most effectual means" of preserving liberty in order to "illuminate, as far as is practicable, the minds of the people at large." Further, because

---

[26] In *The Founders' Constitution*, eds. Phillip B. Kurland and Ralph Lerner (University of Chicago Press, 1986), Vol. 1, Chap. 1, Document 6. The reference to Harvard College continues the colonial tradition of being incorporated under the care and notice of the commonwealth.

"laws will be wisely formed, and honestly administered, in proportion as those who form and administer them are wise and honest," the state should develop a system for discovering those citizens and future leaders "whom nature hath endowed with genius and virtue." Free public education will allow common people equally with the wealthy to produce these future public servants, to "be rendered by liberal education worthy to receive, and able to guard the sacred deposit of rights and liberties of their fellow citizens" (*Learning of Liberty*, 98–99, 106–07). This contrasts with Locke's theory of strictly private education yielding contract participants vigilant about government securing rather than subverting their rights, and who serve political society only as it would serve their own interests. Jefferson emphasizes a free government undertaking education of all citizens, especially those capable of political leadership and service.

Lorraine and Thomas Pangle helpfully note that Jefferson arguably goes too far in emphasizing individual rights and democratic vigilance against government, with no mention of duty to serve one's republic or to obey the legitimately established laws. They turn to Washington, in his First Annual Message to Congress in January 1790, as harmonizing the new democratic view with the more traditional republican view of civics:

Nor am I less persuaded, that you will agree with me in opinion, that there is nothing, which can better deserve your patronage, than the promotion of Science and Literature. Knowledge is in every Country the surest basis of public happiness. In one, in which the measures of Government receive their impression so immediately from the sense of the Community as in ours, it is proportionably essential. To the security of a free Constitution it contributes in various ways: By convincing those, who are entrusted with the public administration, that every valuable end of Government is best answered by the enlightened confidence of the people: And by teaching the people themselves to know and to value their own rights; to discern and provide against invasions of them; to distinguish between oppression and the necessary exercise of lawful authority; between burdens proceeding from a disregard to their convenience and those resulting from the inevitable exigencies of Society; to discriminate the spirit of liberty from that of licentiousness, cherishing the first, avoiding the last, and uniting a speedy, but temperate vigilance against encroachments, with an inviolable respect to the laws.

Whether this desirable object will be best promoted by affording aids to Seminaries of Learning already established – by the institution of a national University – or by any other expedients, will be well worthy of a place in the deliberations of the Legislature.[27]

---

[27] See *Learning of Liberty*, 113–14; First Annual Message in *Political Writings of Washington*, eds. Holloway and Wilson, Vol. II, 122–24 at 123. On the tensions and paradoxes within American debates over education for citizenship – the democratic and republican tension, and the liberal education versus pragmatic tension – see Eva T. H.

This dialogue within the new democratic republic is strikingly pertinent in twenty-first-century America as we face the costs of a century of emphasizing democracy education rather than civic education for our constitutional democratic republic. This turn to democracy education has correlated with our descent to populism and perpetual campaigning by officeholders. The democracy-education approach has pushed even the half of the citizenry that still bothers to vote, as well as officeholders, to neglect the proper focus on governing – with its difficult arguments and conversations out of the public gaze, aiming toward compromises, practical measures, and needed accomplishments. As Yuval Levin recently argued in his primer on our Constitution, this has left America with little capacity in the citizenry to understand either rights or our forms of government, thus little sense of responsibility to elect officeholders likely to govern within these institutional forms. Washington's balance between rights and laws, seeking a properly democratic-republican liberty, strongly accords with Levin's diagnosis of an American politics and political culture that now disregards our constitutional forms; only to wonder why we face an explosion of the angry polarization and passions that the Constitution was designed to preempt and ameliorate.[28]

Jefferson modified his careful plan of 1779 in 1818 in his post-presidency years, when appointed by Virginia to lead a commission for framing the mission of a new University of Virginia as well as selecting the campus location. Jefferson's three-tiered system included public elementary schools for female as well as male students; more selective academies, which we would call secondary education, for talented students also likely to hold leadership positions in Virginia and the federal republic; then more selectively still, a state-funded and governed university education. The foundations would be laid in the academies for the demanding aims of civic education and liberal education in the university curriculum. These aims included:

To form the statesmen, legislators, and judges, on whom public prosperity and individual happiness are so much to depend;

To expound the principles and structure of government, the laws which regulate the intercourse of nations, those formed municipally for our own government, and a sound spirit of legislation, which, banishing all arbitrary and

---

Brann, *Paradoxes of Education in a Republic* (University of Chicago Press, 1979), 11–14, 31–33, 40–45, 52–58, 79–95.

[28] Yuval Levin, *American Covenant: How the Constitution Unified Our Nation – And Could Again* (Basic Books, 2024), 1–11, 257–60.

unnecessary restraint on individual action shall leave us free to do whatever does
not violate the equal rights of another;

... To develop the reasoning faculties of our youth, enlarge their minds, cultivate their morals, and instill into them the precepts of virtue and order;

... And generally to form them to habits of reflection, and correct action, ren-
dering them examples of virtue to others and of happiness within themselves.[29]

Jefferson and Madison (also a commissioner) carefully defined the
curriculum on government; specifying six texts: Locke's *Second Treatise*,
Algernon Sidney's *Discourses on Government* (advocating republics over
monarchies), the Declaration, *The Federalist Papers*, the 1799 Virginia
Resolutions condemning the Alien and Sedition Acts of the Adams presidency, Washington's Farewell Address. There is some balance here
regarding the controversies and partisan fissures since the early 1790s,
yet as the Pangles note, a clear lean toward Jeffersonian, Democratic-
Republican party views; further, there are no works of classical or medieval political thought, or even pre-Lockean modern thought (*Learning of
Liberty*, 166, 168–69, 173).

Washington's suggestion in his 1790 First Annual Message, and subsequent efforts on a national university, had not succeeded as his second
term came to a close. His Eighth Annual Message to Congress is more
direct. He notes he had already proposed to them "the expediency of
establishing a National University," and the merit of such an institution
"has so constantly increased with every new view I have taken of the
subject that I cannot omit the opportunity" to renew the case. Attesting
that the "enlightened" assembly surely supports higher education, and
is proud of America's many private colleges, nonetheless only a national
institution could attract a full range of "the ablest professors in the different departments of liberal knowledge." This was crucial for an American,
republican civic education for leaders of the Union, and for other aims:

the assimilation of the principles, opinions, and manners of our countrymen,
by the common education of a portion of our Youth from every quarter, well
deserves attention. The more homogeneous our citizens can be made in these
particulars, the greater will be our prospect of permanent union; and a primary
object of such a national institution should be, the education of our Youth in the
science of *Government*. In a Republic, what species of knowledge can be equally
important? and what duty more pressing on its Legislature, than to patronize a

---

[29] Rockfish Gap Report of the University of Virginia Commissioners, August 4, 1818, the
Papers of Thomas Jefferson, at *Founders Online*, National Archives, www.founders
.archives.gov/documents/Jefferson/03-13-02-0197-0006; Pangle and Pangle, *Learning
of Liberty*, 114–24.

plan for communicating it to those, who are to be the future guardians of the liberties of the country?[30]

So important were these aims to Washington that in his last will and testament in 1799, he devoted three long paragraphs to urging his fellow citizens to establish a national university. He worries that future civic leaders are not being educated in the common principles of the American republic and "the true and genuine liberties of mankind," whether because of going abroad for study, or that colleges in their own states are too susceptible to "State prejudices." He pledged shares in the Potomac River Company he had been awarded by the state of Virginia for service in the Revolutionary War, a considerable sum of money, "towards the endowment of a UNIVERSITY to be established [in] the District of Columbia, under the auspices of the General Government."[31]

As George Thomas notes, a national university was supported by the first six presidents, through John Quincy Adams. Benjamin Rush had urged the Confederation Congress to found a "federal university" in early 1787. While a federal military academy was established in New York in Jefferson's presidency, sufficient opposition in Congress prevented action on a university – partly on constitutional grounds. With no separate clause in the Constitution on education, the view was held among enough members that education was a state matter; and while the Constitution's authority for national security eventually warranted the US Military Academy at West Point, a national university involved diffuse rationales about sustaining the federal republic (*The Founders and a National University*, 4–14, 20–42). Washington did what he could, endowing in 1796 the Liberty Hall Academy in Virginia, then in financial straits; in gratitude, its leaders informed him in 1798 it was now Washington Academy. When Robert E. Lee became its president after the Civil War, he, too, was credited with saving it; we know this institution today as Washington and Lee University.[32]

George Thomas formulated in 2015, through his study of the long reverberations in American history of the idea of a national university,

[30] Eighth Annual Message, December 7, 1796, Papers of George Washington, *Founders Online*, National Archives, www.founders.archives.gov/documents/Washington/05-21-02-0142.
[31] Thomas, *The Founders and a National University*, 2–3.
[32] Washington Academy Trustees to Washington, April 1798, Founders Online, National Archives, at www.founders.archives.gov/documents/Washington/06-02-02-0162#GEWN-06-02-02-0162-fn-0001-ptr.

a renewed argument for restoring to our colleges and universities a primary place for civic education. University presidents such as Derek Bok
and Ronald Daniels have articulated this view more recently in their own
terms. As our civic health has continued to deteriorate, these arguments
have gained wider attention. Yet the predominant response to our current troubles tends to echo the democracy education approach of the
past century, not the education in our constitutional principles, and in
the duties as well as rights of citizenship in our democratic republic,
that Thomas finds so strongly argued in the works of leading American
founders – and also so needed today. His closing argument is to consider
the civic commitments and foundations presupposed by our particular
constitutional order, and to take up the "constitutional patriotism" of
this original American approach to civic education in an appropriately
updated and Socratic spirit. I see this as the spirit of moderate civic education that Montesquieu urges, which influences both American practice
and Tocqueville's analysis, ultimately yielding the reflective patriotism
which Tocqueville encourages and seeks to buttress in America against
forces already corroding it in the 1830s. If Lincoln could close his 1838
Young Men's Lyceum address by invoking Washington, here we can
remind ourselves of Washington's challenge to Congress in 1796: "In
a Republic, what species of knowledge can be equally important?" And
we can take inspiration from Washington's will, one last time calling
friends and fellow citizens to take the concrete steps necessary to provide
young citizens an education for "acquiring knowledge in the principles
of Politics & good Government." In his mind this includes the formation
of the democratic-republican character and reflective patriotism necessary for and worthy of our country, and for our natural right to pursue
happiness.

2

Can Reflective Patriotism Protect Civics
from Propaganda and Partisanship?

One cause of the decline in civic education in the past century, in any mode other than democracy education for civic engagement, is the skepticism in academia toward America and generally toward any study and teaching about patriotism, love of country. As Ronald Daniels and coauthors recount in *What Universities Owe Democracy*, the new scientific definition of academic disciplines in the late nineteenth century, including the new social sciences, induced skepticism about civics. The new research model of the university, including the new discipline of political science, sought ever-new knowledge meeting the test of universal rationality and methods. The particularism of citizenship education, and of American patriotism even more so, failed these tests of rationality and was deemed nonacademic.[1] The social scientific distinction between facts and values, most prominently established by the German sociologist Max Weber, further demoted the liberal arts spirit in studying politics, law, and economics. Further, while skepticism from scientific rationalism and positivist social science demoted any patriotic dimension to an American civic education from one side, a Kantian universal moral idealism critiqued it from the opposite pole. The philosopher Martha Nussbaum prominently articulated this view in recent decades, promoting a cosmopolitan loyalty toward all humanity as morally superior to patriotism which, she argues, inherently tends to chauvinism or xenophobia about those not of one's country; a provincialism said to induce militarism and other injustices. In a later work, she develops a middle-ground approach to patriotism,

---

[1] Ronald Daniels, with Grant Shreve and Phillip Spector, *What Universities Owe Democracy* (Johns Hopkins University Press, 2021), 112–13, 120.

balancing love of country with critical skepticism to avoid jingoism, and cites Washington, Lincoln, and Martin Luther King, Jr., as embodying it. School children need patriotism, but with love toward the common good of one's country corrected by universal moral principles valid for all humans and urging respect for all.[2] Nussbaum does not mention Tocqueville's praise of a reflective patriotism that Americans have forged; nor does she indicate whether adults should be patriotic even in her critical sense. Steven Smith's recent *Reclaiming Patriotism* thus is bold in its extensive consideration of an enlightened patriotism as loyalty to country, arguing it is necessary for all citizens in a constitutional democracy, and particularly appropriate in one such as America, founded on universal principles of right.[3] A few scholars in higher education support this conception of a rational patriotism, and in K-12 public schools it has a slightly broader presence – but the predominant view in university schools of education and teachers colleges, thus most K-12 public schools, ranges from skepticism to aggressive cynicism about America and patriotism.[4]

The dangerously weak, dysfunctional condition of American civic culture and civics today recommends skepticism toward this academic-educational skepticism. On intellectual grounds, we have ample evidence that elite skepticism has been tested by reality and failed, just as Aristotle and Montesquieu would predict. There is only so long a free people can deficit-spend the civic culture that sustains free discourse, questioning, and dissent toward predominant moral and constitutional principles; the bill eventually comes due. American academics and educators must strike a better balance between replenishing our distinctive civic culture and maintaining appropriate space for discourse and critique. Thus, for both intellectual and civic reasons, we need to recover the concept of a rational,

---

[2] Martha Nussbaum et al., *For Love of Country: Debating the Limits of Patriotism*, ed. Joshua Cohen (Beacon Press, 1996); "Teaching Patriotism: Love and Critical Freedom," in *Political Emotions: Why Love Matters for Justice* (Harvard University Press, 2013), 204–39, 249–56. The replies to Nussbaum's initial 1996 essay "Patriotism and Cosmopolitanism" by Ben Barber, Nathan Glazer, Gertrude Himmelfarb, Michael McConnell, Charles Taylor, and Michael Walzer articulate helpful justifications for a rational patriotism, especially toward America.

[3] Steven B. Smith, *Reclaiming Patriotism in an Age of Extremes* (Yale University Press, 2021). Smith discusses the critiques of patriotism by Nussbaum and by George Kateb at 38–45.

[4] See William Damon, "Restoring Purpose and Patriotism to American Education," in *How to Educate an American: The Conservative Vision for Tomorrow's Schools*, ed. Michael Petrilli and Chester Finn, Jr. (Templeton Press, 2020), 75–85, and Jeffrey Sikkenga and David Davenport, *A Republic If You Can Teach It: Fixing America's Civic Education Crisis* (Republic Book Publishers, 2024), 25–43.

discursive patriotism that Tocqueville articulated, and that even Nussbaum admits leading Americans have embodied. Tocqueville's complex, rich argument that Americans have a unique kind of "reflective patriotism," sustaining this new democratic republic, deserves focal consideration.

To further dispute the skeptical or cynical view that any patriotic element to civic education opens the prospect for, or tends toward, propaganda and partisanship from right or left, it will be helpful to sketch some great Americans as civic exemplars of a discursive patriotism, one compelling them to advocate reform. Their belief in the ideals of the Declaration of Independence and constitutional self-government spurred them to address deficiencies in our politics, so that America would live up to her founding principles. These civic exemplars worked to develop reforms that could ultimately gain enough of a constitutional majority and national consensus to enact substantial change: Frederick Douglass and Abraham Lincoln in opposing slavery, Elizabeth Cady Stanton and Susan B Anthony in demanding equal political rights for women, and Martin Luther King, Jr., in demanding political equality and civil rights regardless of color or race. Since reflective patriotism is a civic virtue, and these great characters embodied several such virtues, the broader concept of civic virtue itself also must be rediscovered and featured in the civics renewal needed in our schools, colleges, and culture.

2.1 TOCQUEVILLE'S PRAISE OF AMERICA'S REFLECTIVE PATRIOTISM

A paradox of elite American intellectual culture today is that while there is great concern over angry polarization and the decline of reasonable, civil disagreement in our political discourse, we also largely neglect a once-strong foundation in our culture for civic unity, which supported a robust middle space for constructive debate and possible forging of compromises. This foundation is the civic virtues, importantly among them a rational, reflective patriotism befitting a free, argumentative people in a democratic republic.

America's continuing decline in civic knowledge among citizens and especially youth, measured by school test scores and polls, also tracks with a decline in awareness and formation of civic virtues, to include a considered patriotism. Recent analysis by Gallup shows continued deterioration in the top tier of patriotism, below the level in 2000 before the September 11, 2001 terrorist attacks (after which patriotism spiked). Now only 41 percent of adults are "extremely proud" to be American, and 26 percent are "very proud" – making for 67 percent as strongly patriotic.[5] Still more troubling, in the 18–34 group, a majority is *not* strongly patriotic; only 21 percent are extremely proud, and 24 percent are very proud, to be American. As to causes, one is that higher education, and relevant disciplines to include political science, no longer encourage such civic spirit; presumably on the premise that teaching or promoting it is akin to jingoism, thus unacademic. The dominant view implies that patriotism is a private choice for students; and, further, the foundations for it are the task of K-12 schooling, not higher education. Gallup's findings support this thesis; in the 18–34 cohort, college graduates are the least likely to be "very proud" to be American, at just 36 percent. Those with only some college, or a high school degree or less, were significantly more patriotic at 43 percent and 44 percent.

This academic neglect of patriotism also explains the strong correlation for the last seventy-five years between the declining status of civics in K-12 schools and the near-disappearance of required civics in higher education. The national, bipartisan study of K-12 civics and history education released in 2021, *Educating for American Democracy (EAD)*, included five professors among the seven coauthors; our disciplines spanning political science, history, and educational psychology. We recommended that higher education reform include "rebuild[ing] our own curricular offerings," and that colleges and universities assess whether they "adequately require rigorous American history and civic education – to include knowledge, skills, and virtues – of all their graduates."[6] The *EAD* report also recommends both schools and colleges offer, along with civic and historical knowledge, learning in "civic virtues." We emphasize three: civil disagreement, civic friendship, and reflective patriotism.[7] Higher education leaders independently confirmed this view, including Derek Bok, former Harvard president, and Ronald Daniels, Johns Hopkins president – warning that colleges and universities are failing in a basic academic mission by neglecting civic education, to include civic virtues.[8] A crucial reason to recover a rational,

---

[5] Megan Brenan, "American Pride Remains Near Record Low," *Gallup*, July 2, 2024.
[6] "Educating for American Democracy: Excellence in History and Civics for All Learners," iCivics, March 2, 2021. Available at www.educatingforamericandemocracy.org/.
[7] I discuss this in "Civic Preparation of American Youth: Reflective Patriotism and Our Constitutional Democracy," *The ANNALS of the American Academy of Political and Social Science*, 705 (January 2023), 36–52.
[8] Bok Derek, *Higher Expectations: Can Colleges Teach Students What They Need to Know in the 21st Century?* (Princeton University Press, 2020); Daniels with Shreve and Spector, *What Universities Owe Democracy*; see also engagement with civic virtues from the view of democracy theory in Tim Soutphommasane, *The Virtuous Citizen:*

discursive patriotism is grounded in the basic educational reality of the need to provide motivation for learning by addressing the purpose and larger meaning of the learning activity. From former Harvard president Bok to Stanford educational psychologist William Damon, who in turn cites psychologist Victor Frankl, prominent voices have recently noted this failing in both academia and K-12 education.[9]

To define a considered, discursive patriotism, the *EAD* report turned to Alexis de Tocqueville's judgments from the 1830s on the new patriotism in the New World. *Democracy in America* argues that ours is a "reflective patriotism" – blending gratitude for our country and its principles with insistence upon argument and questioning, aimed at both fellow citizens and government.[10] A further reason to investigate Tocqueville on patriotism and civics is the striking parallels between his analysis in 1835 and 1840, across both volumes of *Democracy*, and Lincoln's in his 1838 Lyceum address "On the Perpetuation of Our Political Institutions."[11] Lincoln sees decline in civics, and in a constitutionally informed patriotism, as causing increasing lawlessness. He warns that lack of an informed patriotism points to national "suicide" – two decades before our Civil War. *Democracy in America*, with its more comprehensive aims, also addresses the challenges to sustaining a rational patriotism and healthy civic culture in a modern era of rising technological dominance, secularism, and individualism.

2.1.1 The Six Elements of America's Complex, Reflective Patriotism

Tocqueville defines our "reflective" or considered patriotism as a love of country distinct from Old-World sentiment about blood and soil. Americans are proud of America, and thin-skinned about criticisms by foreigners; but the pride is only partly rooted in sentiment and fellow-feeling.

Patriotism in a Multicultural Society (Cambridge University Press, 2012); and an American Bar Association call for civic virtues in Christopher Callaway, "Civic Duties, Civic Virtues, and the Barriers to Effective Citizenship," *Human Rights Magazine* 43 no.2 (ABA, 2018).

[9] Damon, "Restoring Purpose and Patriotism"; Bok, "Helping Students Find Purpose and Meaning in Life," in *Higher Expectations*, 80–94.

[10] Alexis de Tocqueville, *Democracy in America*, ed. and tr. Harvey Mansfield and Delba Winthrop (University of Chicago Press, 2000 [1835, 1840]), "On Public Spirit," Vol. I, Part 2, ch. 6; pp. 225–27. Subsequent references will parenthetically cite this edition, by volume-part-chapter and page numbers.

[11] "On the Perpetuation of Our Political Institutions." Springfield Young Men's Lyceum address, January 27, 1838; www.contextus.org/Abraham_Lincoln%2C_Lyceum_Address_(1838).1?lang=en.

The pragmatic American spirit moves from knowledge of founding ideals on individual natural rights to realizing one's self-interest can only be secured through exercise of civic duties and self-government. Citizens calculate that civic participation, and a healthy political order, benefit one's family and friends. While Volume One of *Democracy* focuses on rational patriotism, Volume Two deems our utilitarianism toward civic participation and duties as an "enlightened self-interest." In that fuller discussion of the new kind of citizen, Tocqueville argues that Americans claim to act only on rational, self-interested grounds – but in fact, they undertake "disinterested and unreflective" acts of altruistic conduct (II.2, ch. 8; 502). This full picture sees Americans blending rational argument and self-interest with love of country and commitment to duty. A crucial foundation for both love of country and civic altruism, thus a healthy patriotism and civic culture, is America's original "point of departure" – our first founding, in the Puritan blend of religion and commitment to liberty. Yet Tocqueville also discerns in the 1830s that the efficacy of this first founding is fading, and in Volume Two proposes remedies for supporting it.

Thus, across several discussions in both volumes of *Democracy*, Tocqueville can be read as identifying six elements of this American patriotism – blending Christian and/or classical elements with modern, Enlightenment ones.[12] The six elements, and their textual locus, are:

(1) America's *Christian point of departure*, which balances "the spirit of religion" (including the Christian ethic of love of neighbor) and "the spirit of liberty" (self-rule, citizenship); this foundational and historically unique achievement also yields the ongoing American disposition to blend and balance seemingly rival principles (Vol. 1, Part 1, ch. 2)

(2) a *rational public spirit* arising from experience of *efficacy in local self-government*; blending love of country with a demand or expectation that America – all governments and communities, local to state to federal – should benefit oneself and one's family (I.2.6, I.1.5)

(3) the *political institution of religion* from our first founding continues into our second founding as the American republic (1776 onwards), teaching mores of political equality, liberty, and self-restraint grounded in fixed principles of right, patriotic concern for the common good, shared beliefs, and hope for the future (I.2.9)

---

[12] I am indebted to James Stoner for helping me to discern these six elements in Tocqueville's account of a distinctive American patriotism.

(4) *American exceptionalism* manifest in the testy pride shown toward any criticism of America, and professions of belief that Americans form the only enlightened *and* religious *and* free people in history, succeeding where other peoples failed (I.2.10, also I.1.2)

(5) interest well-understood or *enlightened self-interest*, the American philosophy that they undertake duties or service not from altruism but from reasonable expectation one's family and friends will benefit thereby; yet Tocqueville sees deep American altruism nonetheless, thus the limits to this rationalist self-analysis, and this further persuades him of the need to reinforce the religious grounds of altruism (and American civic culture generally) (II.2.8)

(6) *schooling, literature, and civic culture* – from home schooling, to mostly church-run local common schools for all students, to elite schooling in classic works (Greek, Latin), to a culture that values poetry; these dimensions of American civic culture support the metaphysical/altruistic foundation of reflective patriotism (I.2.9; II.2 chs. 9, 15, 17)

Tracing Tocqueville's analysis of this important theme throughout *Democracy* confirms James Ceaser's view that his complex, Montesquieuan political science praises both the original seventeenth century founding of America in Christian belief and political liberty and its eighteenth century political founding, influenced by modern, Enlightenment ideas of law and political philosophy.[13] Given today's deepening crisis of American civic knowledge and patriotic attachment, Ceaser was prescient to suggest a need to recover attention to civic passions, customs, and mores per the more complex political science developed by Montesquieu and Tocqueville. These moderate modern philosophers argue that emphasis upon abstract doctrines of justice alone – such as our tendency to focus upon only the opening claims of the Declaration of Independence – will not provide strong roots for civic attachment. A Montesquieuan political science further argues that rational doctrines alone do not promote a more moderate, less extreme politics, because they do not promote a robust civics, a reflective patriotism, and a healthy civic culture.

Both Tocqueville and Lincoln insist that a rational patriotism undergirds reasonable, peaceful disagreement among American citizens about their strongly held views, rising above extreme denunciations of opposing

---

[13] James W. Ceaser, "Alexis de Tocqueville and the Two-Founding Thesis," *The Review of Politics* 73 no. 2 (Spring 2011), 219–43.

views and fellow citizens – a passion-drenched civic culture that descends to anger and threats of violence. In today's terms, Tocqueville and Lincoln (and Montesquieu and Washington as well) are alert to the problem of negative or affective polarization in a democratic republic. One expression of such polarization would be opposing factions offering not an American civics but narrower instruction promoting their favored views. This approach becomes, in effect, an angry echo of the Old World patriotism of sentiment without rational grounding, susceptible to becoming propaganda and partisanship under guise of civics. For these great teachers of America, in contrast, a reflective patriotism supports the civic virtues of civil disagreement and civic friendship across philosophical and political differences. In this vein, Smith's *Reclaiming Patriotism* draws upon Tocqueville and Lincoln, and the American founders, to recover an American "enlightened patriotism" of head and heart; balancing rational understanding of our principles with loyalty and affection for the free political order which allows all to participate in the arguments of self-government, as well as a pluralism requiring further civic virtues of civility and moderation.[14]

Tocqueville's subchapter, "On Public Spirit" is his focal account of patriotism; arising within a late chapter of Volume I on "Real Advantages" American society derives from democratic self-government (I.2.6, 220–35). The unique patriotism of America's democratic republic is a real advantage. Others include the American idea of rights; of respect for the rule of law; and our characteristic busyness and activity devoted to private and public pursuits. As to public spirit, he defines it as "love of native country." The Old World version is "instinctive," sentimental, with "respect for ancestors" and "memory of the past" "bind[ing] to the heart" one's blood and soil (225). It "is a sort of religion itself; it does not reason, it believes, it feels, it acts." This is "patriotism" as "sentiment." In the New World and America, however:

There is another more rational than that one; less generous, less ardent perhaps, but more fruitful and more lasting; this one is born of enlightenment; it develops with the aid of laws, it grows with the exercise of rights, and in the end it intermingles in a way with personal interest. A man understands the influence that the well-being of the country has on his own; he knows that the law permits him to

---

[14] See also Ewa Atanassow, "Patriotism in Democracy: What We Can Learn from Tocqueville," in *Tocquevillian Ideas: Contemporary European Perspectives*, eds. Rau and Tracz-Tryniecki (University Press of America, 2014), 39–58, and Trevor Shelley, "A Political Science of *Mores*: Tocqueville on Citizenship and Civic Leadership," in *Citizenship and Civic Leadership in America*, eds. McNamara and Shelley (Lexington Books/Rowman & Littlefield, 2022), 69–82.

contribute to producing this well-being, and he interests himself in the prosperity of his country at first as a thing that is useful to him, and afterwards as his own work (225).

Monarchy's "instinctive patriotism" is not "the reflective patriotism of the republic" (226).[15]

A crucial element of a rational public spirit, the second of the six elements of patriotism Tocqueville delineates, is its foundation in a broad citizenry with incentives for participation: "the most powerful means, and perhaps the only one that remains to us of interesting men in the fate of their native country is to make them participate in its government. In our day, the spirit of the city seems to me inseparable from the exercise of political rights" (226). Every American citizen is "interested in the affairs of his township, of his district, and of the state as a whole as in his own" because "each, in his sphere, takes an active part in the government of society." The average citizen grasps "the influence that general prosperity exerts on his happiness." He "therefore sees in the public fortune his own, and he works for the good of the state not only out of duty or out of pride, but I would almost dare say out of cupidity" (226). Further, when America is criticized, citizens "are interested in defending all that is criticized ... for not only is his country then attacked, he himself is" – such that "national pride" takes on qualities of mere "individual vanity" (226–27). This is the fourth element of a reflective patriotism, a sense of American exceptionalism. This "irritable patriotism" is "annoying" and petty compared to the lofty, tranquil sentiments of the old patriotism; but its great advantage is in sustaining political attachment between individuals and democratic republics (I.2.6, 227).

Tocqueville's focal analysis sees in America's considered patriotism traces of traditional emotions and civic virtues; "duty" and national "pride" remain. Yet a new spirit of calculation and interest is strong. The tensions in the account, and the comment in Volume II debunking the American insistence about being civic-minded only to serve interest, requires analysis of Tocqueville's commentary throughout Volume I on this new kind of patriotism. He repeatedly instructs about the new democratic republicanism, the patriotism it produces, and its necessity for

---

[15] Tocqueville's phrase is *patriotisme réfléchi*; see the *Historical-Critical Edition of Democracy in America* (Liberty Fund, 4 vols., 2010), ed. Nolla, tr. Schleifer; vol. 2, 384. Schleifer uses "thoughtful patriotism"; Goldhammer (Library of America, 2004) "considered patriotism."

perpetuating America. Indeed, the theme is so important that he raises it very early in the work.

Democracy first mentions love of country in the Introduction when imagining an ideal democratic-republican society in the post-revolutionary era, in which "the love one would bear" for one's president would be "a reasoned and tranquil sentiment" (Introduction, 9). Patriotism is a benchmark of a just, healthy civic order (also Introduction, 10–12). Patriotism then features in the important discussion of "The Spirit of the Township in New England," with Americans experiencing the efficacy of self-government (in I.1 ch. 5, "The Necessity of Studying ... the Particular States Before ... the Government of the Union," 63–5). In fact, however, the first element of a considered patriotism implicitly arises in the crucial early chapter on "The Point of Departure and Its Importance for the Future of the Anglo-Americans" (I.1, ch. 2). This first founding of the Americans explains most political and cultural realities: readers of *Democracy* will find here "the key to almost the whole work" (29). The chapter's striking summation is that "the character of the Anglo-American civilization" combines, uniquely in human affairs, "the *spirit of religion* and the *spirit of liberty*." The sequel then notes Americans combine a religious devotion to Christianity – which gives clear boundaries for thought and action – with a political culture that is tumultuous and tradition-discarding, demanding progress (43, emphasis in original). This foreshadows a reflective patriotism of arguing with governments, and fellow citizens, about the meaning of America. This balance of Christian belief and liberty leaves citizens in a "moral world" with everything "classified, coordinated, foreseen, decided in advance" yet a "political world" where all is "agitated, contested, uncertain" – but the two cultures somehow "lend each other mutual support" (43). This foundational note of the work, linking America's religious, mainly Puritan character with a discursive patriotism, explains Tocqueville's initial praise for this new patriotism yet later warnings about the support from religious belief needed to sustain it – thus, in turn, to perpetuate such a complex constitutional and civic culture.

Tocqueville then initially delineates the second dimension of patriotism – a rational interest in self-government – in analyzing the New England township and its spirit of self-government. Such civic agency fuses the rights and duties of citizenship, and generates love of country. So many people share in multiple, dispersed offices that they combine a right to liberty with a sense of duty to perform needed township functions. Quotidian tasks gain a larger civic meaning. He marvels at "[h]ow many men thus exploit the power of the township for their profit and take interest in it for themselves!" (I.1.5, 64). Citizens also reframe their interest in self-government as patriotic ritual and duty: "In the United States they rightly think that love of one's native country is a kind of worship to which men are attracted by its observances" (64). The political benefits of this "administrative decentralization," with average citizens taking on many small offices in townships and counties, include generation of a blend of interest in and love for the success of one's township, the state, and the United States all at once. A citizen "applies himself to each of the interests of the country as to his very own":

He is glorified in the glory of the nation; in the success that it obtains he believes he recognizes his own work, and he is uplifted by it; he rejoices in the general prosperity from which he profits. He has for his native country a sentiment analogous to the one that he feels for his family, and it is still by a sort of selfishness that he takes an interest in the state. (I.1.5, 89–90)[16]

2.1.2 Challenges to Sustaining Patriotism and Enlightened Self-Interest

Tocqueville mixes in some warnings with description and praise of Americans, as Montesquieu does in his sketches of the English. The rational, considered element of American patriotism is endangered by the democratic, populist excesses of Jacksonian democracy. His analysis of "the Reelection of the President" notes the degradation of patriotism inherent in the pandering to the electorate that candidates for reelection must undertake, inviting crude passions to overwhelm the tranquil, reason-friendly political sentiments he has praised. "The principle of reelection therefore renders the corrupting influence of elective governments more extensive and more dangerous. It tends to degrade the political morality of the people and to replace patriotism with cleverness" (*Democracy* I.1.8, 129). America's founders – Tocqueville often uses Montesquieu's term "legislators" for makers of constitutions or political orders – knew of this potentially fatal vice in a democratic republic. They invented, in Article II of the Constitution, the college of electors, chosen by the people of each state to make an indirect, federalism-based selection of a president. Yet, by also allowing re-election, "they destroyed their [own] work

---

[16] Shortly after this passage Tocqueville also defines such self-governing liberty as a "natural right" by way of excoriating the centralizing spirit which eventually defined the French Revolution; I.1.5 92 and Note X to 92 at 692.

in part" by letting a democratic element invade via an incumbent's desire for reelection. Officials could be expected to employ flattery of the people – popularity – to retain office (129–30).

That said, Tocqueville mostly offers high regard for the Constitution and its founders. A later section declares the Constitution "Superior to the Constitutions of the States" in political wisdom and merit, and praises the 1787 framers in Philadelphia for their great character. He reminds readers he praised Washington strongly, along with Madison and Hamilton, in opening the chapter: "I have already observed above that the legislators of the Union were almost all remarkable for their enlightenment, more remarkable still for their patriotism" (I.1.8, 143; see 107). The question, however, given the rise of Jacksonian populism is how to sustain reflective patriotism in the people.

Tocqueville commends the Constitution's design of sharing sovereignty between member republics and the federal republic for allowing robust local patriotism to be shared upward to the Union. American federalism strikes a healthy balance, leaving most political activity with state and local self-government. Citizens also appreciate the advantages of pooling some state sovereignty in a federal government that ably manages foreign affairs and commercial, economic coordination. He admires that "in the United States the taste for and usage of republican government are born in the townships and within [state] assemblies." An American state, which hardly gives political leaders an arena for "much wealth or much glory," nonetheless animates political attachment, using ceremony to induce a sense of the great achievements of state and local governance – even in the quotidian tasks of opening a canal, or laying a road:

it is this same republican spirit, these mores and habits of a free people, which, after having been born and developed in the various states, are afterwards applied without difficulty to the sum of the country. The public spirit of the Union itself is in a way only a summation of provincial patriotism. Each citizen of the United States so to speak carries over the interest that his little republic inspires in him into love of the common native country ... [including] the general interests of the country and the glory of the nation (I.1.8, 153).

American federalism promotes a complex, dual-level patriotism because federalism works. In a dangerous world, in which most other governments reign over scarcity for masses who are subjects not citizens, Americans enjoy local liberty and national power; the latter, in both military and commercial dimensions. Echoing Montesquieu on the advantages of a federal republic (*Spirit of Laws* Book IX), he dramatically concludes: "The Union is free and happy like a small nation, glorious and strong like a great one" (154).

Yet notes of warning persist. There is perhaps too strong a tendency toward patriotism of the local and familiar (I.1.8). Tocqueville ultimately closes Part Two of Volume One with amplified concerns about the sustainability of American federalism; wondering whether a complex constitution of dual loyalty can survive a crisis or moment of passion that might pull the peoples of one or more states to abandon the Union in favor of their more-familiar home. In closing Part I of the first volume, he maintains a hopeful stance, that the Anglo-Americans have the geographic, cultural, and historical conditions allowing them to sustain federalism's tensions. A complex patriotism is one such tension. In the War of 1812 several New England states refused the President's order to mobilize their militias in the federal service (I.1.8, 159–60). The seeds of such a problem lie in the 1787 Constitution itself, given decisions made by its "legislators," for while there is real power in the federal government "the love and prejudices of the people" remain mostly with the states while the Union and its sovereignty is mostly "an abstract being ... attached to only a few external objects." State and local governments can rely "on memories, on habits, on local prejudices, on the selfishness of province and family; in a word, on all the things that render the instinct for one's native country so powerful in the heart of man" (157–58).

2.1.3 Christianity Moderating and Elevating a Democratic Patriotism

Tocqueville then turns more hopeful again in the focal discussion of "public spirit" and America's distinctive "reflective patriotism," in Part Two of Volume One. While Part I emphasized American laws and institutions, Part Two follows Montesquieu by examining mores and political culture. The focal discussion and praise of our reflective patriotism occurs here, the second of six dimensions of America's patriotism. Shortly after introducing reflective patriotism he offers a crucial discussion of the continuing influence of religion in American political culture. This introduces the third element of our patriotism: that the political founding in 1776 does not displace America's first founding in the Protestant culture of New England (the first element of our patriotism), for it persists in new form. Religious belief and mores become the informal but crucial foundation of the independent democratic republic, the "first political institution" of the American republic, moderating several extreme tendencies in modern democracy. This argument arises in several sections on religion in a chapter "On the Principal Causes Tending to Maintain a Democratic Republic in the United States" (I.2.9). This itself is effectively the first of two culminating chapters of Volume One; summarizing and emphasizing main lessons from his analysis; and it builds toward the thesis announced in the chapter's penultimate section, "That the Laws Serve to Maintain a Democratic Republic in the United States More than Physical Causes, and Mores More than Laws" (I.2.9, 292–95). It makes sense that patriotism would arise in this Montesquieuan discussion of mores; as Tocqueville defines them, mores are "the whole moral and intellectual state of a people" encompassing not only "habits of the heart" but also their various "notions," "opinions," and "sum of ideas" comprising "the habits of the mind" (I.2.9, "Influence of Mores," 275). Tocqueville declares religion a major component of mores; and addresses this crucial reality in three subsequent sections, starting with "Religion Considered as a Political Institution; How It Serves Powerfully the Maintenance of a Democratic Republic Among the Americans" (275–77). Given the early statement on America's Puritan "Point of Departure" as "the key to almost the whole work" (I.1.2) it is not surprising he would identify the third element of American patriotism as its religious basis. This discussion in turn prepares for the final explicit discussion of patriotism in the volume, in the epic closing chapter considering the fate of America's three races and America generally; and there Tocqueville reinforces patriotism's fourth element, the American sense of exceptionalism. In Volume Two, his discussion of America's fundamental civic and political orientation toward enlightened self-interest will echo this complex character of religious mores – beliefs and habits, both head and heart – as moderating and elevating the rationalist, self-interested, materialist traits of the modern democratic soul. There he introduces patriotism's 5th and 6th elements, enlightened self-interest and schooling; which, hopefully, can sustain it against threats it faces.

Tocqueville suggests the whole analysis of "The Principal Causes" sustaining America's democratic republic – not just the three sections on religion – reinforces his early "Point of Departure" analysis: the blending of religion and liberty in American mores is the key to understanding this democratic republic. The chapter opens by recalling that very early analysis, and renames this first founding the "Providential" cause sustaining our republic. It is:

the first and the most efficacious of all the causes to which the current prosperity of the United States can be attributed .... their fathers had long since brought equality of conditions and of intelligence onto the soil they inhabited, from which the democratic republic would one day issue as from its natural source. This is not all; with a republican social state, they willed to their descendants the most appropriate habits, ideas, and mores to make a republic flourish. When I think about what this original fact produced, it seems to me that I see the whole destiny of America contained in the first Puritan who landed on its shores, like the whole human race in the first man (I.2, ch. 9, 266–67).

Tocqueville further emphasizes that the Americans are fortunate that "their fathers" gave them "the love of equality and of freedom"; and he declares as "extraordinary" both their "social state as well as their laws" stemming from this foundation (267).

After a brief section on the importance of laws as a cause of America's democratic-republican success – stating he will not recapitulate his analysis of laws throughout Part One – Tocqueville turns to mores, and three sections of this "Principle Causes" chapter addressing religion. "Religion Considered as a Political Institution" makes the claim informing all three: religion "Serves Powerfully the Maintenance of a Democratic Republic Among the Americans" (I.2.9, 275). Next, "Indirect Influence that Religious Beliefs Exert on Political Society in the United States" addresses our distinctive patriotism by emphasizing the moderating influence of Christianity upon the rational, reflective dimension. The bold claim is that precisely when religion is not directly speaking of or oriented toward politics, its influence "is more powerful still," and "best teaches Americans the art of being free" (278). Tocqueville describes 1830s America as "the place in the world where the Christian religion has most preserved genuine powers over souls; and nothing shows better how useful and natural to man it is in our day, since the country in which it exercises the greatest empire is at the same time the most enlightened and most free" (278).

This analysis prepares an implicit reference to reflective patriotism. Whether or not Americans truly believe the "Christian dogmas" they confess, everyone wants to be seen as Christian; religion thus "reigns without obstacles." Moreover, Tocqueville reminds that he already noted (in "Point of Departure") the consequence that for Americans "everything is certain and fixed in the moral world," while "the political world seems to be abandoned to the discussion and attempts of men" (278). This leads to a Montesquieuan statement on "the spirit of the Americans" and its moderation. In this healthy nexus of mores and politics:

the human spirit never perceives an unlimited field before itself: however bold it may be, from time to time it feels that it ought to halt before insurmountable barriers. Before innovating, it is forced to accept certain primary givens and to submit its boldest conceptions to certain forms that delay and halt it …. Up to now, no one has been encountered in the United States who dared to advance the maxim that everything is permitted in the interest of society. An impious maxim – one that seems to have been invented in a century of freedom to legitimate all the tyrants to come.

So therefore, at the same time the law permits the American people to do everything, religion prevents them from conceiving everything and forbids them to dare everything.

Religion, which, among Americans, never mixes directly in the government of society, should therefore be considered as the first of their political institutions; for if it does not give them the taste for freedom it singularly facilitates their use of it (279–80).

Tocqueville then highlights patriotism by describing a political culture where "Americans so completely confuse Christianity and freedom in their minds" that easterners fund and organize missionaries for western territories from a "fear that religion will be lost in the midst of the woods." They want these future states to share a commitment to "be as free" (280–81). Thus "in the United States religious zeal constantly warms itself at the hearth of patriotism. You think that these men act solely in consideration of the other life, but you are mistaken: eternity is only one of their cares." Easterners tell him that, to preserve "the republican institutions" they enjoy, they "have an interest in the new states being religious so that they permit us to remain free" (281).

Yet it is precisely at this high ebb of praise for America's religious spirit that Tocqueville raises his first alarm in *Democracy* about the decline of religious belief in America. The rationalist and materialist attack upon religion from the radical Enlightenment in Europe reinforces other obstacles to belief, such that "all is well in America except precisely the religious spirit that I admire" (281). The great many who sincerely believe in and publicly profess Christianity mostly overlook that American society in fact is "an arena where religion must constantly struggle against a thousand relentless enemies"; that it receives "wounds" from this materialist, antitheistic atmosphere (287). Yet after these three sections on religion he returns to a hopeful tone, declaring sound mores – to include religion – the fundamental cause of America's political success. The "importance of mores" is "a central point" for him; it is "the end [aim or final point] of all my ideas" (I.2.9, 295). This hopeful conclusion about his political science, and America, implies religion still is largely healthy here, and there may be time and capacity for buttressing belief. The concluding section of this telling chapter on "Principle Causes" paints, in contrast to the American scene, a dark portrait of European politics given the consequences there of "[r]eligion having lost its empire over souls" (I.2.9, 299).

This indeed is the approach Tocqueville takes toward mores and religion in the volume's final epic chapter, on the three races; and on into Volume Two, with its numerous discussions of religion across its four parts. Christian belief and mores are a pillar of the success of American political society (Vol. I, Part Two) and in civil society with its social mores (all four parts of Volume Two), with both the political and civil dimensions of society and mores being crucial pillars for America's laws and political institutions. Nonetheless, Volume Two amplifies his warning on the weakening of religious belief, thus the concomitant decline of its capacity to moderate and elevate political mores and activity. Before the work's close he will raise the striking claim that enlightened statesmen in the modern democratic republics should take appropriate actions to reinforce, reinvigorate, and prioritize religious belief among the people.

This advocacy of the statesman's proper concern to both utilize and support religious belief actually first arises in the epic closing chapter of Volume One on the prospects for America's "Three Races," which also discusses patriotism (I.2.10). Returning to notes of warning, Tocqueville addresses American patriotism in a subchapter on "What Are the Chances That the American Union Will Last? What Dangers Threaten It?" (348–79). As noted in Chapter 1, Tocqueville's choice of "considerations" in the title of this longest chapter in all of *Democracy in America*, and also in the title of its penultimate subchapter – "Some Considerations on the Causes of the Commercial Greatness of the United States" – reminds of Montesquieu's influence. Tocqueville assesses the character and national trajectory of the Americans as Montesquieu assessed the Romans in *Considerations on the Causes of the Greatness of the Romans and Their Decline* (1734). Are the Americans primed to self-destruct, unable to moderate the tendency to excesses in their national character – dominating all the valuable land of North America from ocean to ocean, as he predicts here, but also ruthlessly subjugating the native peoples as well as spreading race-based slavery – akin to the Roman self-destruction after conquering so many peoples across vast territories?[17]

Tocqueville raises reflective patriotism, and its need for moderation and elevation by religion, just after the long, morally disturbing sections on the "Indian Tribes" then the "Black Race" (I.2.10, 302–48). His

---

[17] Harvey C. Mansfield, in *Tocqueville: A Very Short Introduction* (Oxford University Press, 2010), weaves Tocqueville's concern with greatness and pride across several topics and prominent chapters in *Democracy*; Mansfield does not address this particular moment, but does address patriotism and enlightened self-interest; for example, see "Tocqueville's Pride," 102–14.

section on "the Chances that the American Union Will Last" and the "Dangers" threatening it (348–790) – as Lincoln phrases it three years later in 1838, on the perpetuation of America's constitutional order – raises reflective patriotism as an important factor. He holds the Federalist view that the Union and federal government are weak relative to the states; from a legal-constitutional view the Union faces real danger of dissolution. Americans, as dual citizens of their (at the time twenty-four) distinct state republics and of the federal republic, might feel more attachment to their state than the Union (352–53). He had raised these issues in closing the first Part of Volume One (I.1.8 on the federal Constitution). Here, he emphasizes the strong material interests the states and citizens thereof have in maintaining the Union; chiefly the stronger commercial activity and prosperity gained by cooperation via national trade policies benefitting all Americans through a collective stance; thus also strength in relations with foreign powers and peoples. This collective capacity also includes a strong navy protecting America's merchant marine and commerce, and generally providing security to member republics and the Union (355–58). Having found a "tight bond" arising from these material interests, he turns to shared American opinions and beliefs – echoing his focus on mores in the preceding "Principle Causes" chapter. Here, too, he finds strong grounds for holding together the Union despite diversity across such a vast federal republic. This second consideration about what might bind, or separate, the Union is the context for renewed discussion of America's "reflective patriotism." His reintroduction of the term, however, is more critical about this second element of our patriotism:

The inhabitants of the United States speak much of their love for their native country; I avow that I do not trust this reflective patriotism founded on interest, and which interest, by changing its object, can destroy.

Nor do I attach very great importance to the language of the Americans when they express the intention daily of preserving the federal system that their fathers adopted.

What maintains a great number of citizens under the same government is much less the reasoned will to live united than the instinctive and in a way involuntary accord resulting from similarity of sentiments and resemblance of opinions.

I shall never agree that men form a society by the sole fact that they recognize the same head and obey the same laws; there is a society only when men ... have the same opinions ... [and] the same facts give rise in them to the same impressions and the same thoughts (I.2, ch. 10, 358).

Tocqueville argues that, from this vantage, anyone studying the Americans "would discover without difficulty" that even though the citizenry are divided into "twenty-four distinct sovereignties" they nonetheless "constitute a unitary people." Evidence for this "real" American "society" begins with the fact of shared religious beliefs: "Although the Anglo-Americans have several religions, they all have the same manner of viewing religion" (358). He rests his case for this ground of societal unity with this one sentence. Any serious reader, he implies, would grasp that earlier discussions of religion's importance for the existence and persistence of American constitutional democracy are so emphatic that any attempt to summarize them at volume's close would weaken the point; conversely, the brevity of the invocation reinforces its weight.

Tocqueville's second category of evidence for America's federal republic as a real society, as one people, is shared views on "the general principles that ought to rule human societies," which undergird secondary disagreements on policies, even on forms of government. Here, patriotism's fourth and fifth elements – American exceptionalism, and enlightened self-interest – arise from its religious elements, the first and third. The beliefs he lists echo his "Point of Departure" in Part I and analysis of religion as a political institution in Part II; including the belief that "the origin of all legitimate powers is in the people," and shared views of "freedom and equality" (358). Moving beyond "political and religious ideas" to "philosophical and moral opinions," Americans all hold such fundamental principles as that "universal reason," understood as "the sense of all," can be consulted to judge what is permitted or forbidden, true or false; and that "one's self-interest well understood" or enlightened self-interest is a sure guide to what is just and honest (359). The summary point affirming there is one real American society includes their patriotism:

For fifty years it has been constantly repeated to the inhabitants of the United States that they form the only religious, enlightened, and free people. They see that up to now, democratic institutions have prospered among them, while they have failed in the rest of the world; they therefore have an immense opinion of themselves, and they are not far from believing that they form a species apart in the human race (359).

Yet Tocqueville then abruptly shifts from Americans' confidence and patriotic pride about their exceptionalism to less optimistic terrain. He describes the starkly different characters of North and South among Americans and their states, offering grim reflections on prospects for a civil war over slavery. A section on whether the Union will last, and the dangers threatening it, closes with foreboding: the sovereignty and continued existence of the Union is "in peril," and he cannot foresee the result (379). Are the Americans hubristic about their exceptionalism, and their patriotism? Do they fail to see that the complex, novel, federal republicanism they are attempting includes real dangers to perpetuating the Union even amid shared belief in and gratitude for republicanism itself? Yes, a patriotism necessary for sustaining the Union supervenes' upon the patriotism more strongly felt for one's state; but will the latter adequately nourish, sustain the former?

Lincoln warned of national-federal suicide shortly after these observations, in 1838; and a civil war did nearly destroy the Union twenty-five years after Volume One was published. These facts suggest that Tocqueville's warnings of 1835 should be heeded in our own time, when we know there is less patriotic attachment among Americans to republican self-government at any level, whether local, state, or federal. Further urgency to consider this complex conception of a rational yet religiously supported patriotism arises from today's reality that Americans have much less religious belief than in the 1830s, entailing less efficacy for religion as our first political institution – instructing us on basic principles of self-government while also moderating and elevating our patriotism. Our first founding provides indispensable support for binding us as Americans by both grounding and elevating the basic political principles crystalized in our second founding. Today we can consider that America has overcome the division in the 1830s on proslavery and antislavery views; indeed there are reasonable grounds for dissenting from the reigning opinion among our elite institutions and intellectuals that, sixty years after the great Civil Rights legislation of the 1960s, and the launch of private and government affirmative action programs as well as Great Society programs for egalitarian redistribution of wealth and public support, America still is structurally and systemically racist. The elite sympathy for a categorically critical stance toward, and effective contempt for, America's fundamental justice indicates that today our danger of dissolution partly arises from decay and disintegration. We should consider that a major cause of this civic disintegration is neglect of both religious belief and civic education in a reflective, morally spirited patriotism – which Tocqueville had ranked, together, as great advantages and strengths of America.

Indeed, as Tocqueville continues to consider the prospects for perpetuation of the American constitutional republic, he turns toward a more hopeful fact:

For the forty-five years the Union has existed, time has done justice to a host of provincial prejudices that at first militated against it. The patriotic sentiment attaching each American to his state has become less exclusive .... More and more all are brought together into a common type. Each year thousands of men who have left the North spread into all parts of the Union: they bring with them their beliefs, their opinions, their mores; and as their enlightenment is superior ... they are not slow to take hold of affairs and to modify society .... This continuous emigration from the North toward the South singularly favors the fusion of all provincial characters into a single national character. The civilization of the North seems destined, therefore, to become the common measure by which all the rest will be regulated one day (I.2.10, 369–70).

Yet just as in the closing chapter of Part I, Tocqueville oscillates between hopefulness and foreboding in his larger reflections here on America's character and its fate; worries about a patriotism for America and Union persist. By the 1830s federal power clearly "is decreasing" relative to the first decades after the Constitution was ratified and the federal government established (370). The "very prosperity" and collective security they produced, which the Federalists anticipated, itself "began to make people lose sight of the cause that had produced it; the danger having passed, Americans no longer found in themselves the energy and patriotism that had helped to ward it off." As soon as "a strong government no longer seemed necessary, they again began to think it was a hindrance" (371). This paradox that "the federal government, by creating order and peace, itself brought on its decline" leads to deeper problems. A graver one is the democratic populism and demagoguery exploiting the shift in popular opinion. As soon as complacency toward Union arose, "party men, who live on the passions of the people, began exploiting it to their profit" (371). Tocqueville explicitly critiques Jacksonian democratism, and implicitly the Jeffersonian program that led to it; and his foreboding deepens about the Union's prospects. Nonetheless, at the section's close, some hopefulness returns: "I nevertheless believe that we are still far from the time when the federal power ... will be extinguished." Because "[t]he Union is [established] in mores," once it is evident "that the weakness of the federal government compromises the existence of the Union, I do not doubt that a movement of reaction in favor of its force will be seen to rise" (378). Moreover, "a change of [domestic political] opinion, an internal crisis, a [foreign] war could suddenly give it back the vigor it needs" (378).

Tocqueville offers one further section on perpetuation before turning this epic chapter to a section more bullish, considering the "Causes of the Commercial Greatness of the Americans" (I.2.10, 384–96). Then his Conclusion to the chapter, and Volume One, makes a striking prediction: in the future just two powers will dominate the globe, the Russians standing for autocracy and despotism, the Americans for freedom (395–96). The path from ambivalence about America's prospects to this prescient and pro-American view runs through the penultimate section, on America's "Republican Institutions" and "Their Chances of Longevity." The answer is more hopeful for republicanism than Union. This discussion also offers more prescriptions, to instruct American statesmen and citizens on their responsibility to perpetuate their free institutions and mores. This prescriptiveness also defines Volume Two's approach to patriotism and civic culture; including an emphasis on the sixth element of reflective patriotism, schooling.

2.1.4 Tocquevillean Remedies and America's Nonpatriotic Civic Culture Today

Republicanism has better prospects than Union because a culture of Christian liberty is America's natural political character. Tocqueville again emphasizes patriotism's first and third elements, its Christian core or foundation. "Republicans in the United States prize mores, respect beliefs, recognize rights." They believe "a people ought to be moral, religious, and moderate to the degree it is free." Republic means, in America, "the tranquil reign of the majority" (I.2.10, 379). This is a just, viable political order because reigning above the majority "in the moral world" are "humanity, justice, and reason; in the political world, acquired rights. The majority recognizes these two barriers" (379–80). The difficulty – as "I have already said, and I repeat" – is "the current movement of American society ... to be more and more democratic" (383). In its first half-century America frequently "changed laws," but "the foundation of the Constitution is respected." This epic chapter sustains from this point on a largely positive view of America's prospects; including his prophecy on eclipsing all European peoples as the world's strongest embodiment of liberty. Yet the admixture of warnings about unhealthy tendencies carries into Volume Two; and all such maladies bear on sustaining American patriotism. His greatest concerns in Volume Two include features of twenty-first-century America that are readily evident: first, the rise of a new kind of materialism and individualism, yielding an anticivic alienation among American democrats; second, weakening of Christian belief under increasing egalitarianism and materialism; and third, the rise of a new, tutelary kind of administrative centralism or soft despotism that lulls Americans into giving up active liberty and self-government. Again, *Democracy in America* still is studied 190 years later given such prescience. The dominance now of an egalitarian and materialistic intellectual culture suggests we also consider the probity of his proposed remedies for deterring or redressing these illiberal, anticivic trends.

A primary remedy is sustaining Christian religious belief and – in a more pluralistic spirit in Volume Two – any metaphysical theistic tradition.[18] Part One of the volume addresses Christianity in America accommodating yet elevating democratic instincts; how Catholicism is surprisingly prospering in America; and why democracy's friends should combat its tendency toward pantheism as replacing Christianity (II.1, chs. 5, 6,7). Part Two suggests how Christianity can elevate self-interest well understood; how religion helpfully turns Americans to metaphysical enjoyments; and the importance of reminding democrats about the horizon of eternity (II.2, chs. 9, 15, 17). On education, Tocqueville strongly endorses the classics – "How the Study of Greek and Latin Literature Is Particularly Useful in Democratic Societies" – and recommends poetry for elevating the mind and soul toward ideals and the metaphysical. This is the sixth element of reflective patriotism; schooling in higher meanings and duties from classical, Biblical, and metaphysical sources. These counsels on metaphysical elements to civic culture sharply contrast with the volume's opening view that pragmatism and materialism dominate the "Philosophical Method" of Americans (II.1, ch. 15, ch. 17, ch. 1). Yet Part II returns to that pragmatic trait when praising Americans for the way they "Combat Individualism with Free Associations" and "Combat Individualism by the Doctrine of Self-Interest Well Understood" (II.2, ch. 4 and ch. 8). These are the elements of Tocqueville that Robert Putnam restored to wider attention in recent decades, in his analysis of the "bowling alone" decline in American associational life.

Tocqueville does not invoke patriotism in analyzing self-interest well understood. He does refer to "several places in the work" which show Americans "almost always know how to combine their own well-being with that of their fellow citizens." Mansfield and Winthrop cite Vol. I, Part II, ch. 6 – the focal discussion of reflective patriotism as the American version of "Public Spirit" (see II.2.4, 501 and note). In Volume Two, the American doctrine behind their reflective patriotism now is explained as their view that "man, in serving those like him, serves himself, and that his particular interest is to do good" (501). Further, Americans "are pleased

---

[18] I discuss these ideas further in "Religion and Liberty in America: The Moderate Spirit of Montesquieu and Tocqueville," in *Democracy in Moderation: Montesquieu, Tocqueville, and Sustainable Liberalism* (Cambridge University Press, 2016), 208–17, including recent scholarship.

to explain almost all the actions of their life" by resort to this doctrine; how "enlightened love of themselves constantly brings them to aid each other" and "willingly to sacrifice a part of their time and their wealth to the good of the state" (502). Now, however, Tocqueville objects:

I think in this it often happens they do not do themselves justice; for one sometimes sees citizens in the United States as elsewhere abandoning themselves to the disinterested and unreflective sparks that are natural to man; but the Americans scarcely avow that they yield to movements of this kind; they would rather do honor to their philosophy than to themselves. (II.2.4, 502)

Why would Americans serve or sacrifice for others regardless of gain, or at direct risk to self-interest? Elements of emotional old-world patriotism remain (I.2.6), but are not likely candidates. Christian belief in a commandment to love and serve others is more plausible. For Tocqueville, enlightened self-interest is better than the degraded life of individualism, materialism, and soft despotism to which Americans could succumb; but the people are better than their rationalist doctrine. He warns their reflective patriotism increasingly will need to rely upon its first and third elements – the American blend of religion and liberty, the first political institution of Christian mores – to survive amid growing materialism and individualism. This dilemma later leads him to urge that statesmen and other leaders must teach Christian doctrines, or metaphysical beliefs, to perpetuate America's civic and political order; even though stating so is "going to harm me in the eyes of politicians." Statesmen and governments must "act every day" as if they believed in "the dogma of the immortality of the soul" by "conforming scrupulously to religious morality in great affairs." This is the only way to ensure "they are teaching citizens to know it, love it, and respect it in small ones" (II.2.15, 521). Further, in an age where "irreligion and democracy meet in an unhappy convergence, philosophers and those who govern ought constantly to apply themselves to moving back the object of human actions" – by teaching citizens that "only by resisting ... little everyday passions" will they "come to satisfy the general passion for happiness that torments them" (II.2.17, 523). Thus his striking counsel:

Governments must apply themselves to giving back to men this taste for the future which is no longer inspired by religion and the social state, and without saying so, they must teach citizens practically every day that wealth, renown, and power are the prizes of work, that great successes are found at the end of long-lasting desires ....

I therefore do not doubt that in habituating citizens to think of the future in this world, one would bring them little by little and without their knowing it to religious beliefs.

Thus the means that permit men up to a certain point to do without religion is perhaps, after all, the only one remaining to us to lead the human race by a long detour back toward faith. (II.2.17, 524; compare I.2.5, 190–91 on education, religion, and mores)

America's civic decline in recent decades, with flagging civic knowledge and patriotism in younger cohorts, suggests Tocqueville's prescience about decline in the religiously inspired mores that sustained our patriotism. Yet these higher mores, and a complex patriotism, persisted through great crises in America for well over a century after these warnings, and had prominent advocates into the late twentieth century. Inspiring moments of statesmanship, and patriotic art, suggest that the higher ethos transcending enlightened self-interest still could be invoked. Lincoln's Gettysburg Address and Second Inaugural still are widely regarded, taught, studied. Consider also the third verse of Katharine Lee Bates' "America the Beautiful" (1893) capturing the self-sacrificing heroism of Union soldiers in the Civil War; which so resonated with the great pianist and singer Ray Charles, descendent of slaves, that he began his famous rendition there. First recorded in 1972, he emphasizes the intertwining of patriotic sacrifice and Christian mercy which once inspired many Americans, and might again; it is inspiring anew in his soulful, jazz-and-gospel tribute:

> O beautiful for heroes proved/In liberating strife,
> Who more than self their country loved/And mercy more than life!

In calling us to blend metaphysical and religious principles with the rational, materialist, and pragmatic elements of our character, Tocqueville calls Americans to revive a capacity deep in our character for blending and balancing, for moderation. Lincoln's Perpetuation Address to the Young Men's Lyceum blends advocacy of a cold, rational civics in the Constitution and laws with a closing profession of faith in George Washington and Christianity.[19] Smith's recent argument for an enlightened patriotism sees a high middle ground between a narrow nationalism

---

[19] The peroration: "Let those materials be moulded into *general intelligence, sound morality*, and in particular, *a reverence for the constitution and laws*: and, that we improved to the last; that we remained free to the last; that we revered his name to the last; that, during his long sleep, we permitted no hostile foot to pass over or desecrate his resting place; shall be that which to learn the last trump shall awaken our WASHINGTON. //Upon these let the proud fabric of freedom rest, as the rock of its basis; and as truly as has been said of the only greater institution, *'the gates of hell shall not prevail against it.'*"

of some on the American right and a cynical, sophisticated disdain for America of some on the left. In the spirit of Tocqueville, Lincoln, and America's founders at their best, we must recover a greatly needed patriotism grounded in a discursive, informed civics, in religious and moral elements of our tradition, as well as in walking the path of the civic virtues it invokes – including civil disagreement, and civic friendship among Americans of divergent views.[20]

Tocqueville pays philosophers the compliment of suggesting they are akin to "those who govern" (II.2.17, 253). Thus, his admonition closing *Democracy in America* rests more heavily upon today's academics, educators, intellectuals, and other elites: have we set our constitutional democracy on the path "to servitude or freedom, to enlightenment or barbarism, to prosperity or misery?" (II.4.8, 676). Leaders of all kinds in our day must improve the prospects for America to find consensus on a renewed civics encompassing a thoughtful love of country and other civic virtues, grounded in considerable civic knowledge. That consensus must be strong enough to support substantial changes to priorities in schools and higher education. Our elite culture, and main educational culture in K-16, emphasizes only the final two elements of reflective patriotism, and narrowly conceived at that: a rational enlightened self-interest, and schooling. We need to rediscover how to blend in the other four elements: metaphysical foundations supporting republican liberty and equality and a shared culture of hope; participation in self-government; and pride in America. This is the only way to meet the charge recently and rightly laid down by Johns Hopkins president Ronald Daniels, that we educators undertake what we owe our democratic republic.

2.2 AMERICAN CIVIC EXEMPLARS OF PATRIOTISM AND REFORM

One way to recover and incorporate these largely missing elements is to study civic exemplars of reflective patriotism. Such great American figures are not mythical. Indeed, as real people, even their flaws or misjudgments permit us to imagine our own fallible selves emulating their discursively patriotic commitment to the idea of America. Especially given the predominant spirit of skepticism or cynicism about America in K-12 public schools and higher education, in either more active or

---

[20] Smith, *Reclaiming Patriotism*, ch. 5 "Enlightened Patriotism" and ch. 6, "Reclaiming Patriotism."

passive modes, we should feature civic exemplars who found American politics unjust in their time, failing to live up to our founding ideals, and took practical steps for redress. Expression of faith and hope in America fit with concerns about failing, and arguments for reform. I argued in the Introduction that George Washington is the first such reflective-patriot reformer; but given his status as Founding Father, later exemplars who sought to revise what he had established provide a more approachable example of the balance and insights we need today.

While there are further American exemplars to consider, five outstanding ones across our past two centuries should be on anyone's short list. We should consider and teach about Frederick Douglass and Abraham Lincoln bringing the Constitution into greater alignment with the Declaration of Independence by redressing the persisting crime of slavery; Elizabeth Cady Stanton and Susan B. Anthony making analogous arguments about depriving women of full citizenship; and Martin Luther King Jr. insisting on full protection of equal natural rights and civil rights without racial discrimination. A civics featuring these reflective patriots, grateful for America and her founding principles yet adamantly insisting upon deep reform, can help to hold to the high middle ground that defines a discursive civics: avoiding either narrow nostalgia or corrosive cynicism, thus protecting itself against temptations of partisanship and propaganda. This approach also will inspire American citizens and aspiring citizens, young and old; not least because only one of these extraordinary statesmen and stateswomen was a president of the United States. We must remember that this is not the only office – nor does one even need to hold formal office – to pursue great service and achieve great effect in our political and civic life.

I discuss in the closing section of Chapter 3, on schools, the extraordinary lives of civic knowledge and civic virtues embodied by Douglass and Lincoln, Stanton and Anthony, and King. To inspire us to acquire the knowledge needed for self-government, and appreciate then develop the civic virtues of civil disagreement, civic friendship, and reflective patriotism, most of us need the example of these and other extraordinary patriot-reformers. Those students, young and old, who are able to supply inspiration and motivation themselves can simply enjoy the journey of learning about, then trying to emulate, such statesmen and stateswomen. To justify that later discussion we might entertain here how a reflective patriotism would need to be considered if we are to explain the extraordinary balance these figures embody, eschewing extremes of passivity or cynicism or revolution while persistently demanding reform.

How could the escaped slave, and self-taught, Douglass retain hope in America across fifty years of his freedom, through the ups and downs of Emancipation, the assassination of his friend Lincoln, then Reconstruction and Reconstruction's failure? How could the self-taught Lincoln develop such practical wisdom to restore confidence in the Declaration's ideals as truths that must guide policy; and forge a compromise to defend the traditional concept of the Union against slavery advocates who would wreck it; then steer that compromise to ultimate success despite dissatisfied Northern abolitionists (including, to some extent, Douglass) but also Northerners who thought opposition to the spread of slavery and its moral acceptability was not worth fighting a war? How could Lincoln then in his final argument to avoid war, call Americans to recover the better angels of our nature? Once war came, how did he turn Northern public opinion from seeing it as a war for Union toward his view it really was a war about the evil of slavery, since the only Union worth saving was rooted in the ideal of universal equal natural rights, thus unwilling to endlessly compromise-away that principle; so that he could call Americans to continue fighting for "a new birth of freedom" – then once the war was practically won, resist the temptation of vengeful domination but instead call all Americans to atonement, to acceptance of God's inscrutable justice, and to "charity for all" in healing and rebuilding the nation?

How could Stanton and Anthony have faith in the Declaration's claims of equal natural rights when the Laws of Nature and of Nature's God it invoked always had held women in a second-class status or worse, including in America, segregating them in political life and voting, religious life, civil society, and economic affairs? After the near-universal denunciations of the women's rights movement sparked by the Seneca Falls Declaration of 1848, largely drafted by Stanton (and supported by Douglass), how could Anthony sustain her belief in the Declaration and the Constitution, insisting the true interpretation of their principles implied equal political rights, and particularly suffrage for women, all the more so after passage of the post–Civil War 14th and 15th amendments? Was their faith and hope in America rewarded by our principle of federalism, when several Western states included women's suffrage in their new constitutions before Stanton and Anthony died early in the twentieth century, well before the national consensus accepted their half-century of public arguments by ratifying the 19th Amendment in 1920 to recognize equal suffrage for women? How could King in the mid twentieth century generate faith and hope in America after the joy of Emancipation and the post–Civil War Amendments was followed by the collapse of

Reconstruction in the South amid the rise of the Ku Klux Klan, then enactment of Jim Crow laws in the south subjugating blacks and denying them constitutional rights, and widespread racism in the rest of the country – raising the reasonable question whether any constitutional amendments or major legislation could reform American racism? How did he resist the cynicism seeing the Declaration as false – thus seeing America as really like most of the rest of the world across most of history, with politics simply being sheer power held by some over others? How did King marry his Christian faith to hope that the Declaration indeed was true, the Constitution and laws could be reformed, that brute power and violence could be lovingly and effectively met by civil disobedience and the self-discipline of peaceful action, even after he had been beaten, arrested, jailed, stabbed, threatened, and many others in the Civil Rights Movement had been killed? Such that he could praise the American founders and both the Declaration and Constitution in his most famous address in 1963 (chosen as the centenary of the Emancipation Proclamation and Gettysburg Address), about his dream that one day the American dream could fully be shared by all? Then, after several years of his escalating critiques of America given frustration that his major successes in advocating passage of the 1964 Civil Rights Act and 1965 Voting Rights Act weren't actually eradicating the economic and political suffering inflicted by persistent racism, how could he again praise the Founding Fathers, Declaration, and Constitution in his final public address, the night before he was assassinated?

One of my civic education efforts for the department of civic thought and leadership I was asked to build at Arizona State University was a Pocket US Constitution, for use with students in our courses but also to distribute at our public speakers series the Civic Discourse Project, as well as to school teachers and students, public officials, and anyone in Arizona and beyond who asked for copies. I had seen Robert George, founder of the James Madison Program in American Ideals and Institution at Princeton University, add Lincoln's 1863 Gettysburg Address to the typical pocket Constitution lineup of the Declaration plus the Constitution with all amendments. This was meant to prod Princeton students and a wider set of citizens to consider how Lincoln had fought for and achieved a new birth of freedom grounded in the founding principles, through reform of the Constitution and laws in the wake of the Civil War, and how similar challenges of understanding, abiding, adapting await all generations of Americans. This made a US pocket Constitution into a Socratic teaching tool, an embodiment of reflective patriotism. It occurred to me that a further helpful step would be to add King's 1963 "I Have A Dream Address," indicating into a further century that American ideals and law are a grounded yet continuing argument, about our founding principles and whether or how we are living up to them. King also brought a reminder of the culture of Christianity, religious belief, and mores that in part had produced the Declaration, and Constitution, and Lincoln's statesmanship – in fact had been in dynamic, productive tension with legal and philosophical principles of liberty since the Puritans in 1620 forged the Mayflower Compact as the first political covenant in America.

In this spirit of a thoughtful patriotism and a higher civics, what one or two other classic American texts would you add to an ideal US Pocket Constitution? (I should add that our school at ASU also developed Arizona's first-ever printed brief constitution – an Arizona Pocket Constitution – given the fact that Arizonans are citizens both of a state and the United States, thus deserve a serious civics in state law, civic knowledge, and civic culture as part of an American civics.) The challenge is to abide by the constraint of a small, printed booklet that fits in a pocket, to be carried nearly anywhere and anytime, in order to have the intended civic effect. We can't add long texts, or many texts, so that it becomes a backpack constitution. As with seemingly every American ideal, this one has to be a practicable, achievable aim.

3

What Should American Schools Teach?

The extremes of political anger and apathy dominating American politics today correlate with a nearly seventy-year period of decreasing priority and support for civics in schools and colleges, since shortly after the Sputnik crisis of the Cold War in 1957. Intellectual polarization in academia and in civil society is another likely cause of the declining status of civics; the fracturing over the meaning of America, what history should be taught, and which civic principles are most vital. A further fracture across the past century is the democracy education approach arising from John Dewey, highlighting civic engagement and participation mostly for transformation, versus the democratic-republican approach to constitutional education emphasizing American civic knowledge and civic virtues for citizenship in our democratic republic.

In 2019, this was the set of challenges facing the lead authors of a national study on civics and history education for schools, amid the extremes of angry polarization and civic apathy marking the close of the first Trump presidency and start of the Biden presidency. The *Educating for American Democracy* (*EAD*) report, released in 2021, was the product of two years of discussions across a national network we assembled, committed to producing a national-consensus view of the challenges and prospects for improving civic education.[1] We worked with more than 300 scholars, educators, practitioners, and students to develop guidance and a framework for excellence in history and civics. Funded by the

[1] *Educating for American Democracy: Excellence in History and Civics for All Learners.* iCivics; at www.educatingforamericandemocracy.org/. I will refer to the report by its acronym, *EAD*.

National Endowment for the Humanities and US Education Department, we used task forces, convenings, and constituency focus groups to analyze the main ideas and the ground reality of history and civics learning in schools, to discern how to better serve all learners. The *EAD* report and its proposed "Roadmap" was an effort by a diverse, cross-ideological group of scholars and educators to devise guidance for states, local educational leaders, and teachers to use in assessing how to ensure students can better appreciate, understand, and operate our constitutional democracy and civic life.

As noted in the Introduction, I was the constitutional conservative among the lead authors; I am grateful for the intellectual and civic bravery of professors Danielle Allen and Jane Kamensky of Harvard and Peter Levine of Tufts University, and the director of iCivics Louise Dubé, in ensuring this would be a national-consensus study. The seven-member lead group also included Kei Kawashima-Ginsberg of Tufts and Tammy Waller of Arizona's Department of Education. As Allen and I wrote to introduce the final *EAD* report to a national audience, we sought a path out of the stalemate that had blocked any improvement in, and reprioritizing of, civics since at least the 1990s. One example was the effort begun in 2009 by the National Governors Association to develop Common Core State Standards: The initial goal was "standards for English language arts; math and STEM; and social studies. Standards for the first two were achieved. But social studies was left on the cutting-room floor. The reason was the deep disagreement about how to teach US history – whether to emphasize triumphs and achievements or wrongs and crimes of both commission and omission."[2] Another low point in this civic-intellectual polarization, blocking any improvement in civics, erupted just as *EAD* was released: The dueling single-minded visions of The 1619 Project of *The New York Times* and the 1776 Commission of the first Trump administration. Among other problems, these combatants ignored a basic reality of recent decades: The declining funding and priority for civics, history, and social studies education in states and school districts across the country. Although most school funding occurs through state and local budgets, an indication of the deplorable condition of civics is a metric we cited in the *EAD* report, a 2016 federal study that found federal funding for schools of roughly $50 per student per year on STEM fields and approximately $0.50 per student per year on

---

[2] Danielle Allen and Paul Carrese, "Our Democracy Is Ailing. Civics Education Has to Be Part of the Cure." *The Washington Post*, March 2, 2021.

civics; a 1000:1 difference. The dueling denunciations of the 1619 and 1776 gladiators were only deepening this problem, by reinforcing the reluctance of states, districts, schools, and teachers to invest time and resources in a controversial area. It's safer to keep the priority for science and math, and for reading and language arts, while ignoring the terrible condition of civics teaching and learning.[3]

This daunting reality, of a national crisis of civic illness and ignorance with no practical path up and out, motivated the spirit of compromise in the *EAD* report. Some of us took as a model Washington's view of the proposed 1787 Constitution: It was "the result of a spirit of amity and of that mutual deference and concession which the peculiarity of our political situation rendered indispensable."[4] Our recommended approach to civics, in a grade-level-appropriate mode, was to strike a balance between essential content and the reality of debate and disagreement in America, as well as in learning about America. We debated disagreements productively across differences of viewpoint, background, geography, and disciplines, then forged consensus about what and how to teach for an excellent civic education. Those are the very principles and civic virtues we recommended for teachers and students in schools – because, as we put it, disagreement is a feature not a bug of our constitutional democracy. The civic virtue of civil disagreement fits well with America's reflective patriotism. Five years after the report's release it is being discussed, and its Roadmap guidance implemented and adapted, across the country in the complex, spontaneous mode of American federalism – state by state, district by district; and the *EAD* approach recently was featured by the National Association of State Boards of Education in a special journal issue on civic education.[5]

My own reading of the *EAD* report and its Roadmap for improved K-12 history and civics curricula finds it more grounded in America's original

---

[3] A recent policy brief by the Sandra Day O'Connor Institute, "When and Why Did America Stop Teaching Civics?," September 2024, documents the sharp decline since the 1960s in the priority for, and teacher preparation to properly offer, a serious citizenship education, including this metric: "Whereas until the 1960s American public high-school students were typically required to take three courses in civics – Civics, Problems of Democracy, and U.S. Government – today most get by with a single semester-long class."

[4] "Washington to the President of Congress, 17 September 1787," *Founders Online*, National Archives, www.founders.archives.gov/documents/Washington/04-05-02-0306. I have modernized spelling and capitalization.

[5] Danielle Allen, Paul Carrese, and Louise Dubé, "The Challenges of Crafting Excellence in Civics and History for All," *State Education Standard* 25 no. 4, September 2025.

approach to civics than it appears at first glance. The *EAD* approach features civic knowledge, civic virtues, and reflective patriotism – concepts stemming from our founders, Tocqueville, and the nineteenth-century effort to actually achieve a common American civics in common schools. After recounting that feat of establishing civics in publicly funded and supervised schools, pioneered by Horace Mann and reinforced at the century's end by the new American Institute of Civics, I turn to a summary of the seven themes *EAD* recommends for kindergarten through high school. These are Civic Participation; Our Changing Landscapes; We the People; A New Government and Constitution; Institutional and Social Transformation; A People in the World; and Contemporary Debates and Possibilities. Through these Themes we weave five Design Challenges for teachers and students to confront – tensions between important principles that every citizen, and every curriculum, must grapple with – such as the fourth Challenge: "Civic Honesty, Reflective Patriotism." Finally, to overcome the dominance in schools and national discussions of the contending single-minded visions, of cynicism toward America's history and principles countered by a narrow nostalgia, I suggest schools develop curricula featuring civic exemplars of America's enlightened patriotism; statesmen and stateswomen grateful for our country and its founding principles but on that very basis seeing failings that demand reform. As noted in earlier chapters, these are Frederick Douglass and Abraham Lincoln redressing slavery; Elizabeth Cady Stanton and Susan B. Anthony redressing the political and civic exclusion of women; and Martin Luther King, Jr., redressing the persisting political and civil exclusion of blacks. A focus on such models offers students and schools hope about America while reinforcing genuine civic knowledge and virtues, including a discursive patriotism.

3.1 TOCQUEVILLE, COMMON SCHOOLS, AND THE INVENTION OF AMERICAN CIVICS

Stanford professor Josiah Ober and his coauthor Brook Manville argue in *The Civic Bargain* that an important step in the renewal of American civic education is to build on "America's rich tradition of civic education."[6] A larger point is that it is not nostalgia to seek counsel, in a confusing and contentious era, from time-tested ideas, figures, and principles

---

[6] Brook Manville and Josiah Ober, *The Civic Bargain: How Democracy Survives* (Princeton University Press, 2023), 237–39.

of our political order. A striking example is President Dwight Eisenhower, seeking guidance on the parting message to give his country at the end of two terms, and a half-century in public service. In 1959, considering an address for January 1961, he faced the Cold War: Two opposing global superpowers wielding nuclear weapons on missiles, aircraft carriers, and space satellites at the dawn of the computer age. He asked his staff to begin planning a statement, with one point of guidance: Consult Washington's 1796 farewell address. How could this commanding general in World War II, now the most powerful executive in the world, find views from horse and buggy days to be relevant? For Eisenhower, basic American principles and approaches to statesmanship gave crucial guidance amid unprecedented, bewildering challenges; as well as a likely path toward national-consensus strategies for navigating uncertainty.[7]

This is the spirit in which I suggest twenty-first-century teachers, curriculum designers, professors, district and state leaders, and serious citizens consider the origins of public schools and American civics, to find guidance and fresh perspective as we dig out of our civics crisis, and national crisis. Having discussed in Chapter 1, the persistent attention to civics voiced by leading American founders, we should note how their intentions for common schooling in civics were eventually achieved, institutionally, in the mid nineteenth century. As also noted in earlier chapters, Alexis de Tocqueville is an evergreen source about American education and many other topics, because his outsider's perception has proven accurate and prescient across nearly two centuries. In closing the first volume of *Democracy in America*, published in 1835, one summary statement about why our novel form of politics is succeeding praises our attention to schooling: "the instruction of the people serves powerfully to maintain a democratic republic."[8] Continuing his focus on "enlightenment" evident in New England, he praises their common schooling: "each citizen receives the elementary notions of human knowledge; in addition, he learns what the doctrines and proofs of his religion are; he is made familiar with the history of his native country and the principle features of the constitution that governs it." He admits this high quality diminishes as one moves west and south (he had traveled widely across

---

[7] I discuss this in "The Grand Strategy of Washington and Eisenhower: Recovering the American Consensus," *Orbis*, Spring 2015, 269–86.

[8] Alexis de Tocqueville, *Democracy in America*, ed. and tr. Harvey Mansfield and Delba Winthrop (University of Chicago Press, 2000), Volume One, Part Two, chapter 9, p. 291. Subsequent references will be parenthetical, citing part of the work and page in this edition.

the United States); this level of "civilization and enlightenment" is not matched elsewhere; and yet, "one would seek in vain in the United States for a single district that is plunged into ignorance" (I.2.9, 289).

In fact, Tocqueville had raised the importance of schooling in his crucial early chapter on the Puritan political-civic culture, defined as the "Point of Departure and Its Importance for the Future of the Anglo-Americans." Here are the seeds of nearly all his subsequent observations about American mores and laws: The reader will find here "the key to almost the whole work" (I.1.2, 27–44, at 29). Tocqueville declares regarding the Connecticut Code of 1650: "[I]t is by the prescriptions relative to public education that, from the beginning [i.e. from principle], one sees revealed in the full light of day the original character of American civilization" (41). He notes "provisions that create schools in all the townships, and oblige the inhabitants, under penalty of heavy fines, to tax themselves to support them," and that "in the most populous districts, high schools are founded in the same manner" (41). When Tocqueville turns to studying the legacy of these origins, nearly two centuries later yielding a democratic, egalitarian social and political culture, he declares that nowhere in the world but America are "so few ignorant and fewer learned men" found; "[p]rimary instruction there is within the reach of each; higher instruction is within reach of almost no one" (I.1.3, 51). He then emphasizes the need to study state and local government to grasp America – before studying the federal Constitution and government – with continued focus on New England given its highly developed culture of local self-governance; and he regularly highlights its regulation of schooling.[9] Tocqueville warns about excesses of democracy as Volume One proceeds; in Part Two of the volume he proposes such excesses can be preempted by education: "In New England, where education and freedom are the children of morality and religion," the people "respect intellectual and moral superiorities," thus "one sees that democracy in New England makes better choices than everywhere else" (I.2.5, 191; see also 210).[10]

Tocqueville's final word on education fills out his portrait of enlightenment as crucial for America's success by emphasizing the need to prioritize the constitutional dimension of civic education. At the close of Volume Two, thus the entire work, he observes that such education will be essential for reinvigorating a spirit of citizenship in local

---

[9] In I.1, ch. 5, see these references at 60, 63, 69 n. 20, 87, and 87 n. 51.
[10] He later observes, in a note, "The greater part of education is entrusted to the clergy" (I.2.9, 283, n. 4).

self-governance. He fears signs of a democratic life dominated by economic and material concerns, narrowly focusing on oneself and perhaps family and friends at best. Over a century later observers of American life picked up this thread in the late twentieth century as Americans grew worried about individualism, materialism, anomie, and alienation from civic and political life – even before the digital revolution amplified these maladies. If we can admire Tocqueville's prescience for worrying that (to adapt Robert Putnam's insight) bowling alleys might survive as businesses but voluntary local bowling leagues disappear, then we should heed his urgent counsel to combat and preempt such individualism through education in citizenship, which in America means a civics of constitutional self-government. Tocqueville warns of rising civic apathy among Americans, happy to let centralizing authority in state and federal governments manage political life for them. To counteract this, all genuine statesmen, "those who lead peoples today," must respect "forms," those constitutional structures which "slow down" politics by providing space and time for everyday citizens to participate, think, and deliberate about political affairs. So important are these constitutional forms and institutions that leaders "must consider the least of them with respect." Indeed, in this democratic era "we must have an enlightened and reflective worship of them" – a kind of reflective patriotism (II.4.8, 669).

Horace Mann achieved more than any other nineteenth century leader to adapt the civic education ideals of leading American founders, which Tocqueville summarizes and endorses, into an institutional system of public schooling. As noted in Chapter 1, the Massachusetts Constitution of 1780, largely drafted by John Adams, declared education a state responsibility.[11] As Mann shifted careers and roles in the 1830s from lawyer to elected state representative to education reformer, concern was growing about how to assimilate the large population of Irish and German immigrants coming through the port of Boston, mostly Catholics. His 1839 address "The Necessity of Education in a Republican Government" affirms the founders' view that for a young democratic republic, a broad system of education was all the more indispensable: "without intelligence and virtue, as a chart and a compass, to direct us in our untried political voyage, we shall perish."[12] A citizen education in laws, forms of

---

[11] Paul E. Peterson, "Horace Mann and the Nation Builders," in *Saving Schools: From Horace Mann to Virtual Learning* (Harvard University Press, 2010), 21–36.

[12] "The Necessity of Education in a Republican Government" (1839), in *Lectures on Education* (Boston: Ide & Dutton, 1855 [1845]), 125, 119.

government, and rule of law is crucial given the reality that America's democratic tendency unleashes human energies and desires. Mann's conception thus emphasizes moral and character formation equally with knowledge of history and constitutional forms. America might have excellent republic institutions, but if utilized by a "corrupt" people, justice and social progress would not result (149). Amid the chaos of passions, desires, and partisan anger in a democracy, a broadly available civics must be "a resource for the security of moderation and self-denial, and for the supremacy of order and law" (158). Further, too many citizens grow up with "no knowledge of the works, and opinions, of those great men who framed our government, and adjusted its various parts to each other" (154). "Each of two things is equally necessary for our political prosperity"; America needs "just principles of government and administration, on one side, and a people able to understand and resolute to uphold them, on the other" (160–61).

Mann, like Tocqueville, insists that citizen formation occur beyond schools as well; families, parents, local communities, religious communities all must undertake their roles. Yet state legislatures must enact institutional reform. "In our country, and in our times, no man is worthy the honored name of a statesman, who does not include the highest practicable education of the people in all his plans of administration" ("Republican Government," 162). He was urging construction, in effect, of the institutional system Jefferson sketched in his 1779 Bill for the More General Diffusion of Knowledge. Mann became the foremost leader in Massachusetts and beyond of the "common school" movement for tuition-free public education for children of all backgrounds and races, funded and supervised by states. When the state Department of Education selected Mann as its first secretary in 1837, the common school movement shifted from advocacy to institution building.[13] The new agency was designed to formulate and disseminate the best educational content and practices statewide, for improving curriculum, methods, and facilities. A crucial element of the plan was teacher training academies, called Normal Schools. (Arizona State University began in 1885 as the Territorial Normal School in Tempe.) This concept, originating in France, directed teachers to develop in students not only intellectual

---

[13] See Mustafa Emirbayer, "The Shaping of a Virtuous Citizenry: Educational Reform in Massachusetts, 1830–1860," *Studies in American Political Development* 6 no. 2 (Fall 1992), 391–419; and Carl F. Kaestle, *Pillars of the Republic: Common Schools and American Society, 1780–1860* (Hill and Wang, 1983).

but also moral norms, including civic capacities. Further, as a Calvinist turned Unitarian, Mann incorporated into the Common School concept a nonsectarian element of Christian moral principles.

Mann's legacy is the state-directed, locally administered system of public schools that educates most American children to this day. Yet like all institutions connected to politics and government, amid perpetual debate about the most pressing public priorities in changing circumstances, the original civic mission of public schools has fallen and risen in priority across the past two centuries. Not long after Mann's triumph a reform movement arose to reemphasize the core mission of citizenship education in schools, and into colleges and universities. Indeed, that reform leader coined the word "civics" itself.[14] In 1885 Protestant minister and writer Henry Randall Waite (1845–1909), who had been pastor of the American Union Church in Rome, Italy, from 1872 to 1875, founded the American Institute of Civics. Waite wrote in 1897 that a concern with "the ascendency of a spirit of chicanery, greed, and corruption" in American politics led him to seek discussion with, and support from, a range of leading American figures. A consensus formed to undertake "efforts for the promotion everywhere of the basic virtues of true patriotism, intelligence, integrity, and fidelity in citizenship relations."[15] He lists support from a Chief Justice of the US Supreme Court; presidents of Yale, Columbia, and Williams and Amherst colleges; the prominent historian, and US ambassador to Britain, George Bancroft (a Democrat); and former President Ulysses S. Grant as well as former Vice President Hannibal Hamlin (Republicans) (Waite, "Institute," 109). The Institute is a "national, nonpartisan, nonsectarian" organization encouraging "the qualities in citizenship which Washington sought to promote by his latest labors and final bequests, and which he, in common with Jefferson, Hamilton, and Madison, believed to be necessary 'to the security of a free constitution,' and to the welfare of the government and people of the United States." (The quoted phrase, uncited, is

---

[14] My *Educating for American Democracy* colleague Peter Levine notes in his "Blog for Civic Renewal" this origin story: "[the word] 'civics' is strictly American, and its first attested use is in the *Boston Daily Advertiser* in 1885: 'Henry Randall Waite, Ph.D., president of the American Institute of Civics, was the next speaker ... The use of the word civics for political science was explained.'" See www.peterlevine.ws/?p=22130 (no date).

[15] Waite, "The American Institute of Civics," in *The Arena*, ed. John Clark Ridpath, Vol. XVIII (July to December 1897) (Boston: The Arena Company), 108–15 at 109.

from Washington's First Annual Message to Congress urging support for citizenship education.) The Institute's charter states these formal aims:

1. To promote on the part of youths and adults generally, without reference to the inculcation of special theories or partisan views, a patient and conscientious study of the most essential facts relating to affairs of government and citizenship, to the end that every citizen may be qualified to act the part of an intelligent and upright juror in all affairs submitted to the decision of the ballot.

2. To promote, in the same spirit, such special attention to the study of Civics in higher institutions of learning, and otherwise, as shall have a tendency to secure wise, impartial, and patriotic action on the part of those who shall occupy positions of trust and responsibility, as executive or legislative officers, and as leaders of public opinion.

Its publications, lectures, and materials for schools and teachers supported activities on "good citizenship" ranging from "home studies" to "lectures, discussions, studies ... in connection with schools, lyceums, civic associations, labor organizations, and institute clubs" (110–11).[16]

A recovery of this cross-partisan spirit, emphasizing American constitutional and historical knowledge but also civic virtues including a reflective patriotism, was evident in the 1950s after several decades of the growing influence of John Dewey's new democracy-education approach. As noted in the Introduction, a 1954 volume on civics from the National Education Association (NEA) blends in some democracy-education elements of critical thinking and problem-solving skills, but its title theme is "American citizenship," and it primarily emphasizes loyalty to American ideals, particularly to the Declaration, Constitution, Bill of Rights, and equality for all under the rule of law.[17] After a resurgence of the democracy approach in the past fifty years, educational theorist E. D. Hirsch, Jr., who describes himself as a political liberal, has recently advocated a return to the strengths of the original American conception of a democratic-republican civics. He celebrates the Common School movement for providing in "the early grades ... a common core curriculum that would foster patriotism, solidarity, and civic peace as well as enable effective commerce, law, and

---

[16] The Institute published *Journal of Politics* from 1892, becoming *American Magazine of Civics* through 1897, then *The Arena*. Its Latin motto was *Ducit Amor Patriæ* (love of country leads).

[17] National Education Association, *Educating for American Citizenship*, Thirty-Second Yearbook (Washington, DC, 1954).

politics in the public sphere."[18] Educational theorists in the twentieth century, however, "had become optimistic about America. They no longer
worried that the very stability and peace of the Republic hinged on diffusing shared knowledge and preparing virtuous, loyal citizens who would
subordinate private aims to the good of the whole" (*Making Americans*,
6, 31). Hirsch argues that a national consensus now should form around
the stark fact that "neither a democracy nor a modern economy can function properly without loyal and competent citizens able to communicate
with one another" (25).[19] His call in 2012 for a renewed effort on "making Americans" anticipates, in my view, the national-consensus project of
EAD. That said, he admits that his proposed "civic core" in schools – that
"it is a duty of American schools to educate competent *American* citizens" – requires "rediscover[ing] some basic agreements about the United
States and its ideals that are shared by both the left and the right" (*Making
Americans*, 65–69).

3.2 EDUCATING FOR AMERICAN DEMOCRACY:
CIVIC KNOWLEDGE AND CIVIC VIRTUES

Based upon this history and theory of American civic education, what
should K-12 schools teach in the twenty-first century? The report issued
by the *EAD* study, on "Excellence in History and Civics for All Learners,"
explains the Roadmap of curricular guidelines we produced as balancing
essential content with an inquiry approach, to support the "civic strength"
of our constitutional democracy. Because of "the deep challenges" facing
America, and decades of "fail[ing] to prepare young Americans for self-
government," the "survival of our constitutional democracy is at stake."
Thus, we opened the report by stating that a healthy America requires "a
reflective patriotism" in which We the People "unite love of country with
clear-eyed wisdom about our successes and failures in order to chart our

---

[18] "The Inspiring Idea of the Common School," in *The Making of Americans: Democracy
and Our Schools* (Yale University Press, 2009) 1–33 at 6. See also Hirsch, *How to
Educate a Citizen: The Power of Shared Knowledge to Unify a Nation* (Harper/Harper
Collins, 2020).

[19] A recent report by the Center for Revitalizing American Institutions at the Hoover
Institution, Stanford University, on major American civics textbooks from 1885 to the
late twentieth century documents "the gradual de-emphasis on civic knowledge" about
"the structures of government and laws of the land" as well as civic virtues to include
patriotism, toward "promoting individual autonomy and action in the community." Jed
Ngalande, "A Century-Plus of Civic Education: What the Textbooks Show," September
2024, 13, see also 2–5.

forward path." We closed on this note as well: "Passing on a love and understanding of American constitutional democracy to future generations is an urgent civic necessity. We are all responsible for cultivating in ourselves and the young the reflective patriotism needed to navigate the dangerous shoals we now face as we chart a course between cynicism and nostalgia" (*EAD* report, 2, 25).

The *EAD* was also guided by federalism; thus, the Roadmap is not a national curriculum, nor a set of instructional standards. It is a guide for state and local authorities, and teachers, to chart their own paths. It recommends approaches to learning across seven content Themes; balancing core civic knowledge and civic virtues with an inquiry mindset; all to achieve five critical aims: (1) Inspire students to understand and become involved in their constitutional democracy; (2) tell a full narrative of America's plural yet shared story; (3) explore the need for compromise to make our democratic republic work; (4) cultivate civic honesty and patriotism so we can both love and argue about our country; and (5) teach history and civics both through a timeline of events and the themes running through them. These aims describe the five Design Challenges we wove through the Themes for K-12 study; tensions inherent in our constitutional democracy that we must understand, indeed utilize, both as educators and citizens.[20] What follows is my own bird's-eye-view summary of the Themes and Challenges, hopefully enticing educators, elected and appointed officials, and serious citizens to explore both the *EAD* report and Roadmap.[21]

3.2.1 *Theme One* Civic Participation and *Design Challenge One* Motivating Agency, Sustaining the Republic

Civic participation is both a right and a duty in America's constitutional democracy. The Declaration invokes both the right and duty of a people to overthrow a government threatening its God-given natural rights. Americans now mostly neglect the Declaration's stirring close: The signers invoke "the protection of divine Providence" and "mutually pledge to

---

[20] The *EAD* website, hosted for several years by iCivics and now by the Adams Presidential Center at www.educatingforamericandemocracy.org/, contains an Interactive Roadmap with suggestions for its use, and an Educator Resources section including a Pedagogy Companion as well as a curated list of content and curricular materials.

[21] I summarize here essays co-authored in 2022 with my ASU and *EAD* colleague Adam Seagrave, commissioned by *RealClearPolitics* for its American Civics portal; there are links embedded in the longer, original essays, and RealClearPolitics also developed a curated set of resources and lesson plans for teachers using the *EAD* approach; see www.realclearpublicaffairs.com/public_affairs/american_civics/lesson_plans/.

each other our Lives, our Fortunes and our sacred Honor" to support justice. Our Founders had a tendency to harmonize differing principles; here,
seeing rights and duties as complementary. They also grasped that civic
participation requires a foundation in civic education, offering students
a balance of civic knowledge and civic virtues, including a sense of one's
duties as a self-governing citizen and the motivation to perform them.

Because civics has a practical aim – to prepare citizens to undertake a life
of self-government – "Civic Participation" is the first Theme in the *EAD*
guidelines. A constitutional democracy requires every new generation of
citizens to understand it, work within its parameters for self-government,
and develop the civic virtues needed to operate and perpetuate such a
polity.[22] Civic education should blend the study of American history
and of political and civic principles to provide the blend of knowledge
and virtues needed for informed civic participation. Washington's 1796
Farewell Address, for example, is a touchstone of civic participation:
After decades of service to the republic, he offers a civic education in
knowledge and virtues, keyed to our nation's fundamental principles and
how to sustain them. The address invokes "Religion and morality" as
"indispensable supports" for a free people and politics. These are the
"great Pillars of human happiness" – echoing the Declaration's high concept of rights – and simultaneously "the firmest props of the duties of
Men and citizens." Washington thus urged that education itself be "an
object of primary importance," for "in proportion as the structure of a
government gives force to public opinion, it is essential that public opinion should be enlightened."

The theme of "Civic Participation" invokes the Founders and also exemplary statesmen and stateswomen, including Abraham Lincoln, women's
suffrage advocates, and figures such as Martin Luther King, Jr., as noted in
Chapter 1 and discussed later. Study of such statesmen and stateswomen
helps to develop what Tocqueville called civic "habits of the heart," including the three civic virtues *EAD* emphasizes: civil disagreement and civic
friendship among citizens with divergent beliefs and views, and reflective
patriotism. America's deliberately complex form of government – a separation of powers within both federal and state governments and federalism
dividing the federal and state governments – requires knowledge of the

---

[22] See Daniel Mahoney, "Civic Virtues as Moral Facts: Recovering the Other Half of Our
Founding," *RealClearPublicAffairs* American Civics portal, at www.realclearpublic
affairs.com/articles/2021/01/27/civic_virtues_as_moral_facts_recovering_the_other_half_
of_our_founding_656930.html.

institutional hardware but also of the software (so to speak) needed for the hardware to function. Yet the latter is harder than any technology: We need civic virtues, the dispositions and capacities of citizens enabling constructive participation. Our system of separate institutions compels debate, then compromise, two crucial virtues of civic participation; so that law and policy rest upon reasonable arguments and some consensus, not on force, or sheer majority power, or winds of current opinion. Thus genuine citizenship is developed through a culture of robust civic participation, with Americans working for the good of their communities, states, and the nation. Under federalism, citizens are self-governing in local communities, from legal tasks to the many civic associations, religious and educational to cultural, that embody the pursuit of happiness. Voting is the minimal level. Healthy self-government requires broader engagement from citizens, while drawing upon vibrant cultural and civic institutions beyond politics.

This is why the Civic Participation Theme is followed by the first Design Challenge of Motivating Agency, Sustaining the Republic; for educators and students to grapple with this inherent tension in civic life. How can students appreciate the responsibility of self-government and the complexity of America's political forms – and the reach of our global power – without feeling paralyzed or inadequate? How can citizens disagree about the justice of a policy while remaining civic friends? Such questions help us to understand and sustain American civic participation in the twenty-first century.

3.2.2 *Theme Two* Our Changing Landscapes

In Chapter 5, on civic culture, I discuss the inspired choice of the pianist-singer Ray Charles to start his classic rendition of *America the Beautiful* with the third stanza of the Katharine Lee Bates poem. There is wisdom, nonetheless, in the poet's choice to open her tribute to her country, and prayer for its reform, by invoking the land: purple mountain majesties, fruited plains, sea to shining sea. An American civic education should inculcate appreciation of the extraordinary fertility and variety of the North American setting that the first peoples enjoyed, and still understand in a distinctive way. Yet it was the Anglo-Americans and other Europeans who dominated, in part through an intensive agricultural, later industrial, approach to using the land for political and economic aims. This entailed a drive to expand the territory they controlled, partly through legal treaties with tribal peoples and other Europeans, and partly through war or other force. Anglo-Americans also were driven by worry that European powers on the continent – the Spanish and French but also Russians and British in the far West – had political cultures almost as distinct from their own views of liberty, equality, and industrious prosperity as were those of the first peoples. Thus, American expansion against rivals in North America was partly a preemptive defense of liberty, to make space for the American experiment.

Though American civic education involves universal ideas – the Declaration speaks to all "mankind" – it also educates about this particular polity, the United States of America. The nation's political, economic, and civic development across four centuries is a complex interaction with North America and the several peoples calling it home. The eventually dominant model of the Anglo-Americans was proposed as offering equal prosperity for all, and this promise explains the enduring American capacity of attracting immigrants from around the world. Yet the Landscapes theme does not evade the current reality that every dimension of civics and history education in America's schools is polarized between rival and sometimes-incompatible views. Teachers and students should identify shared American principles of rights, duties, liberty, equality, property, and prosperity that can frame constructive debates about our physical and cultural landscape. Strongly differing views about the justice of American expansion and prosperity require us to re-emphasize the civic virtues of reflective patriotism, with freedom to question and dispute, along with civil disagreement and civic friendship.

The civics and history questions posed to educators and students comprehend the religious, ethnic, and civilizational diversity North America has attracted from the fifteenth century onward. Religious liberty, a fundamental motive for the first Anglo-American immigrants, still propels people here from around the globe. The realities of African slavery must also be studied in the political, economic, and geographic story of the United States, a polity beginning on the Atlantic seaboard and extending across a vast landmass to the Pacific. As noted in Theme Six, "A People in the World," by the twentieth century the American polity extended to Alaska, the Hawaiian Islands, and other islands in the Caribbean and Pacific. In the twentieth and twenty-first centuries new questions have arisen about the so-called closure of the frontier and what this meant for the American polity – and whether new kinds of frontier exploration can be pursued. The land itself, and sea and sky, have become focal issues of concern as both the health of our natural environment and the sustainability of the predominant American approach of resource extraction, and domestication of land and sea, seem fragile. Our predominant spirit of liberty, with its confidence that economic and technological dynamism will provide greater relative prosperity than any alternative form of government, now faces internal challenges from competing views about economics, nature, and political community.

Thus the second Design Challenge, paired with Themes Two and Three of the Roadmap, addresses "America's Plural Yet Shared Story." How can there be a common American story, given this complexity of interactions across land, peoples, ideals, and historical actions?

3.2.3 *Theme Three* We the People and *Design Challenge Two* America's Plural Yet Shared Story

As historian Wilfred McClay argues, the opening words of the Constitution's Preamble are "the heartbeat of the American republic and its free institutions."[23] The first-person plural "We" provides an invitation to explore fundamental political agency – the subject of civic participation; and "the People" highlights a fixed point of American political belonging that gives coherence and meaning across historical change. The first "We" in the development of American constitutional democracy is the Mayflower Compact of 1620. Our Pilgrim forebears provided a paradigmatic statement of self-government, expressing liberty as both a right and duty. Tocqueville in *Democracy in America* marks this as our first founding, launching a tradition of local self-government in New England towns that prepared American colonists for independence. The Declaration provided a kind of culminating statement, asserting that because "governments are instituted among men, deriving their just powers from the consent of the governed," it is both a right and a duty of "the governed" to exercise control over what they have made. James Madison, writing as Publius (taking a famous name in ancient Roman liberty), expresses this spirit in *The Federalist* no. 39: Only a republican government would be "reconcilable with … the fundamental principles of the Revolution" and with "that honorable determination which animates every votary of freedom" to insist upon "the capacity of mankind for self-government."[24] The Constitution ensures the consent of the people by requiring popular

---

[23] McClay, "How the Mayflower Compact Changed History Forever 400 Years Ago," *RealClearPublicAffairs* American Civics portal, at www.realclearpublicaffairs.com/articles/2020/11/19/how_the_mayflower_compact_changed_history_forever_400_years_ago_650205.html.

[24] Alexander Hamilton, James Madison, John Jay, *The Federalist* (1788–89), no. 39, available at www.teachingamericanhistory.org/document/federalist-39/.

ratification in Article VI, and by their direct or indirect participation in all its institutional forms. It all begins, amendments as well, from "We."

And "the People"? This American "We" is animated by equality as well as liberty. All human beings in this polity are the foundation of its government, with their rights and happiness being the government's purpose. The word "person" occurs at various points in the Constitution and amendments, including in the important civil rights provisions (in the 5th and 14th Amendments) that no "person" shall be deprived of "life liberty, or property, without due process of law." This constitutional right stems from the Declaration: Because "all men" possess inalienable rights to "life, liberty, and the pursuit of happiness," the federal and state governments are prohibited from arbitrarily depriving any person of these rights. The universal moral status and dignity of "the People" so defined has been a powerful rationale for inclusion of black Americans, women, and other racial, ethnic, and immigrant groups in American politics; as discussed later when encouraging study of great American civic exemplars.[25]

The questions guiding this *EAD* Theme point to aspects of this complex relationship between the universal spirit of "We the People" and the particular histories, experiences, and backgrounds of the people comprising America over time. The challenge of enacting our national motto, *E pluribus unum*, captures this complex relationship. The *unum* of American political identity comes from the universal content of "the People" and the common civic action of the "We" who "ordain," "establish," and maintain our constitutional democracy. Thus, Design Challenge Two on "America's Plural Yet Shared Story" accompanies Theme Three, encouraging discussion of how a more complete and plural story of the history and foundations of "We the People" can also be the common story and shared inheritance of all Americans.

3.2.4 *Theme Four* A New Government & Constitution and *Design Challenge Three* Simultaneously Celebrating & Critiquing Compromise

America is indeed new in world history: The first republic to declare its founding principles before existing as a polity, and to immediately develop written constitutions ordering its self-government. As noted,

---

[25] See the classic essay by Robert A. Goldwin, "Why Blacks, Women, and Jews Are Not Mentioned in the Constitution," American Enterprise Institute, May 1, 1987, at www .aei.org/articles/why-blacks-women-and-jews-are-not-mentioned-in-the-constitution/.

the "United States of America," our first name, drew upon big ideas of natural rights and justice; and a political tradition dating to the 1620 Mayflower Compact. Declaring independence was a revolutionary act by the "United Colonies" against the British monarchy. Some members of the Second Continental Congress already had departed to fight, to make such big ideas a concrete reality. The most famous, a Virginian turned American named Washington, arrived in Philadelphia wearing his uniform from colonial service in the French and Indian War. The people of this part-idea, part-battling polity called America then set about writing state constitutions, the Declaration, and then a proto-constitution, the Articles of Confederation. The weaknesses of the Articles led to the momentous forging of a new Constitution in 1787. This *EAD* Theme thus calls American educators and students to study and (in upper grades) debate this fascinating, complex story of American self-government – the big ideas, the governments, the constitutions, the calls for reform.

To begin with, they should study how the rule of law informs the Declaration as much as the Constitution. Most of the Declaration is the indictment of King and parliament for violating law, civic or natural. The Founders held that the British constitution and laws that American colonists thought equally protected them conformed to the "Laws of Nature and Nature's God" and self-evident truths invoked in the opening paragraphs. Thus, amid the long list of indictments comes the charge that the king "has combined with others to subject us to a jurisdiction foreign to our constitution, and unacknowledged by our laws." The American founders invoked our constitutionalism long before drafting the Constitution in 1787.

These are intriguing historical topics and also pressing issues in America's current debates over the proper power of government. These debates embody our characteristic, ongoing tensions between individual rights and claims about social progress or the common good. Citizens need to understand the competing views in 1787 about the right kind of government for protecting and enjoying the rights and laws invoked in the Declaration. The most important product of the ratification debate is *The Federalist*, a series of eighty-five essays written by Alexander Hamilton, James Madison, and John Jay. It expounds the principles of the complex, balanced political science and constitutionalism informing this first-ever form of government: a tripartite separation of powers mixed with federalism. Yet don't the Federalist victors sometimes incorporate concerns of the Anti-Federalist, the opponents of ratifying the Constitution? We can learn about debate and compromise by noting that the Constitution's confident framers nonetheless included an amendment procedure, which, though ultimately used sparingly, has produced momentous changes to the American polity that still are consistent with founding principles. These include a Bill of Rights, a persistent concern of the Anti-Federalists; and later, abolition of slavery, adjustments to federalism to protect liberty and equality, and extension of suffrage to all adults. What compromises were made at the Constitutional Convention, how were they justified, what unresolved business did they leave to later generations? What arguments and compromises unfolded in the state ratification debates through 1788? What crucial ideas and concerns from the losing side, the Anti-Federalists, echo in American politics today? In our republic's 250th year – the semiquincentennial commemorations of 2026 – a serious civic education should help citizens and aspiring citizens appreciate and grapple with this exceptional polity, and understand both admiration for and contention about America's story. A serious study of and debate about our principles and practices makes it hard to accept the recent popular view that 1619, when the first African slaves were brought to North America, launched a legacy of oppression that marks America as fundamentally flawed and hypocritical to this day.

Indeed, the questions and Design Challenges the *EAD* Roadmap pose to educators across the first four Themes and first two Challenges provide avenues for understanding and responding to the grave charges made by proponents of the 1619 school. If our Declarational and Constitutional order is so defined by racism, and suppression of the colored powerless by the white powerful is still dominant, why, after four centuries, are people of color from across the world still seeking to become Americans – while some American people of color somehow gain power and prominence by castigating America? On the other hand, if America is simply a glorious story of the unfolding of the principles of 1776 across a quarter-millennium, why was there a horrendous civil war, followed by a de facto racial caste system ended only by the heroic efforts of the Civil Rights Movement just a half-century ago? The broader challenge: How can we grasp the distinctive American blend of religious, philosophical, and political-historical arguments for a constitutionalism of liberty, evident at the start of the American founding in the Declaration and in its close with Washington's Farewell Address? What is the Constitution's particular synthesis of a few democratic-egalitarian forms into mostly republican-selective governing forms? We must grapple with these original arguments and forms, focused on securing rights and promoting reasonable governance, before entertaining the arguments for transforming

America made by the Progressives (such as Woodrow Wilson) and their heirs (including Franklin D. Roosevelt).[26] Hasn't the complex system of separation of powers, checks and balances, and federalism provided more freedom, equality, security, opportunity, and prosperity for a wider range of people than any other form of politics in history?

This balanced approach to civic and constitutional knowledge also pairs aptly with education in mores and civic virtues such as civil disagreement and civic friendship – our bond with and regard for fellow Americans even amid strong disagreement. An understanding of "We the People" (Theme Three) thus pairs with grasping our dynamic constitutionalism to point to the third Design Challenge, the American trait of "Simultaneously Celebrating & Critiquing Compromise." How can self-governing citizens both appreciate and be demanding about compromises – including those the framers made, and citizens make still today, regarding our very forms of government – amid persistent argument and advocacy?

3.2.5 *Theme Five* Institutional and Social Transformation – A Series of Refoundings and *Design Challenge Four* Civic Honesty, Reflective Patriotism

It is difficult to constitute a new government on the very principles that inspired the overthrow of the old. Yet in the American case, the transition from Revolution to Constitution occurred through not just power but also principle. Thus it was the same people who engaged in both events, and the same animating principles. The ideas Thomas Paine and the Second Continental Congress in 1776 used as political dynamite were refashioned into building blocks of government by James Madison and Alexander Hamilton in 1787. The interplay between these two very different children of American political principles – revolutionary change and stable institution building – over the course of American history inspires this Theme on "Institutional and Social Transformation."

Thomas Jefferson, a father of the Revolution, wrote to his friend James Madison, heralded as the Father of the Constitution, in September 1789, claiming a new "self-evident" truth to add to those in the Declaration: "that the earth belongs in usufruct to the living: that the dead have

---

[26] Two thoughtful and recent guides to these issues and debates are Dennis Hale and Marc Landy, *Keeping the Republic: A Defense of American Constitutionalism* (University Press of Kansas, 2024), and Yuval Levin, *American Covenant: How the Constitution Unified Our Nation – And Could Again* (Basic Books, 2024).

neither powers nor rights over it." Thus, "no society can make a perpetual constitution, or even a perpetual law." Every generation must decide anew the laws and constitution under which it will live. In *Federalist* no. 49, Madison as Publius argues against a similar Jeffersonian proposal, warning that "frequent appeals [to the people] would, in a great measure, deprive the government of that veneration which time bestows on everything, and without which perhaps the wisest and freest governments would not possess the requisite stability." For Madison we are no longer in revolution; we are establishing a constitutional order. Reform and change must be tied to continuity and a prudent concern for perpetuating institutions to adequately protect our rights. Revolutionary principles are evident in the Preamble ("We the People ... do ordain and establish this Constitution"), Article V (the amendment process), and Article VII (ratification process). Article VII echoes the Preamble's reliance on "the People" as the ultimate source of authority by stipulating that ratification of the Constitution would occur by "conventions," not state legislatures. Article V, in particular, channels the need for change over time through an amendment process ensuring continuity and stability. Another, less formal method of constitutional change occurs through judicial review, when the Supreme Court interprets the Constitution in ways that allow it to apply more directly to contemporary questions.

The first change through formal amendment occurred soon after ratification, with the Bill of Rights in 1791. They both reflected the Revolution's principles of individual rights and paved the way for major institutional transformation. In combination with the emerging doctrine of judicial review and the Supreme Court's role as defender of "the rights of individuals" against other branches of government, the Bill of Rights has deeply shaped American politics. Another moment occurred in the aftermath of the Civil War, when the 13th, 14th, and 15th Amendments finally extended constitutional protection to the natural, civil, and political rights of enslaved and free black Americans. In this case, as in later transformational moments in American history such as the Progressive Era or the Civil Rights Era in the twentieth century, historians and commentators debate whether the extent and nature of the change is so significant as to represent a "re-founding" or, less radically, an extension of the founding. The answer often depends on one's view of the founding, including how the principles of the Revolution lived on in the founding and beyond. In the discussion below of American exemplars of reflective patriotism and reform, we can consider various arguments that the full implementation of the founding principles, deeply admired by these statesmen and stateswomen, required substantial constitutional or legal change.

The development of our commercial republic over time can be considered this way as well. Revolutionary principles invoked multiple conceptions of property; linking colonial grievances over taxation with the natural rights in the Declaration. Yet leading Founders conceived of property in psychological terms as well. External property was an extension of internal property – moral self-ownership reflected in the material world. Such moral property underpinned both political and economic freedom; thus the development of the early American republic and the development of our commercial economy over time. What do these ideas mean for debates today about equality and economic prosperity, about taxation and governmental provision of economic security? Perplexing questions like these point to the fourth Design Challenge, "Civic Honesty and Reflective Patriotism," encouraging the study of America's failings without indulging cynicism, and appreciating our Founding while admitting its imperfections.

3.2.6 *Theme Six* A People in the World and *Design Challenge Five* Balancing the Concrete and the Abstract

America began precariously, but now, in our third century, we have become a consequential people in history. From winning a long-shot revolution against a world power, we strove under President George Washington's first foreign policy or strategy – summarized in his 1796 Farewell Address – to be both independent and distinctively ethical in international affairs. We tend to forget that the opening counsel on foreign policy offered in the Farewell was not about "entangling alliances," a phrase that never appears, but a call for America to be secure, great, and good all at once:

Observe good faith and justice towards all nations; cultivate peace and harmony with all. Religion and morality enjoin this conduct; and can it be, that good policy does not equally enjoin it? It will be worthy of a free, enlightened, and at no distant period, a great nation, to give to mankind the magnanimous and too novel example of a people always guided by an exalted justice and benevolence.

After the United States departed from this blend of prudence and principle, a detour culminating in the near-disaster of the War of 1812, it restored the Washington strategy, including the restoration of a national bank as a national security measure. We extended that strategy via the Monroe Doctrine of 1823 to become both independent and influential.

This Roadmap theme explores an overview of American foreign policy so that students can think about how our nation can secure its interests in world affairs while affirming our ideals about law and justice.

Throughout the nineteenth century, the United States insisted on greater territory in North America to protect and spread a politics of liberty, pursued through diplomacy, force, and land purchases; against both native peoples and European powers; coast to coast. From the late nineteenth century into the mid twentieth, we struggled to accommodate our great economic power and potential military might with a properly American role in world affairs. At times, we chose engagement as a great power, while at others – as indicated in the July 4, 1821 address by Secretary of State John Quincy Adams – we sought to avoid conflict and adventurism. America played a major role in defeating Nazi and Communist totalitarianism in the great struggles of the twentieth century. By 1991, we made ourselves history's first sole, global superpower. Did our victory in the Cold War, foretold by President Reagan, portend that the historical development of all humanity had reached an endpoint, an "end of history"? A generation ago it seemed that way to some, yet today we are again one among several great global powers; and the others are decidedly not liberal-democratic. We also are beset by internal divisions over the proper principles and strategy for this complex and thoroughly globalized era, described by Harvard professor Samuel Huntington immediately after the Cold War as a "clash of civilizations." We have lost our unity and much self-confidence. Yet the American relationship with other states arguably has always been a more complex story than many commentators have suggested. Have we been either too inward-looking and self-interested, or too self-righteous and ambitious, as two recent views of American foreign policy contend? These debates have been highly polarized since the end of the Cold War, with a brief pause for solidarity after the September 11, 2001, terrorist attacks. America's lack of consensus now finds prominent voices pressing for national interest as our first principle, to avoid the costs of playing global policeman; while others press America to lead the free world and a rules-based international order. Students need the foundations for understanding and discussing, then debating, these views.

American debate and policy have not simply been bifurcated into advocates of self-interest versus ideals, or of isolation from a war-torn world versus global interventionism. As historian Walter Russell Mead articulates, Washington and other Founders, along with a Founder's son, John Quincy Adams, held a more complex view of how American statesmen need to balance principle with prudent policy.[27] Yes, our history has featured advocates of an American semi-imperial power (Theodore Roosevelt), or of leading an internationalist vision of perpetual peace (Wilson), or of a focus on national security and self-interest (from Henry Cabot Lodge to President Trump). Yet this pluralism does not show that the Declaration and Constitution provide no guidance on international affairs. It suggests the basic complementarity of principle and prudence, versus an abstract choice between a cosmopolitan idealism and a nation-focused realism. The Declaration appeals to both high universal principle and the necessity of taking up arms for our particular liberty. In *Federalist* no. 11, Hamilton finds the Constitution enabling a naval power to match America's global commercial potential, providing both national defense and capacity to defend universal rights – thus to "vindicate the honor of the human race." Fans of the musical *Hamilton!* will know that Washington, while utilizing his protégé's learning and patriotic energy, was more sober. Thus, Washington's strategy recommends neither a doctrine of isolationism nor of rights-crusading internationalism but instead a strategy to pursue global commerce – and deter conflict – while joining "temporary alliances" as needed, thereby to "gain time" for America to become "a great nation."[28] Being principled, we "give to mankind the magnanimous and too novel example of a people always guided by an exalted justice and benevolence." America will be capable, but more balanced than other great powers. If we followed his strategy, Washington foresaw Americans could "choose peace or war, as our interest guided by justice shall counsel." Are there echoes of this balanced strategy, blending principle and prudence, in the policy of a "Cold War" against global communism? Is another echo of this republican prudence evident in Eisenhower's 1961 farewell, recommending "balance" throughout, thus defending both a massive new national security apparatus yet also warning about undue influence from both a "scientific-technological elite" and "military-industrial complex"?

What should America's foreign policy be now? If the US has been not always just, has there been a less-unjust great power in history? Why is the all-volunteer military our most respected institution? Theme Six is

---

[27] Mead, *Special Providence: American Foreign Policy and How It Changed the World* (Routledge, 2002).

[28] Michael Doran and I offer this view in "Republican Prudence," *The American Interest* vol. 9 no. 5 (April 20, 2014), at www.the-american-interest.com/2014/04/20/republican-prudence/.

matched with Design Challenge Five, "Balancing the Concrete and the Abstract." That helps students and educators to consider the distinctive American effort to secure the nation's concrete interests but also the ideals of the Declaration and Constitution.

3.2.7 *Theme Seven* A People with Contemporary Debates and Possibilities

The final *EAD* theme explores the contemporary terrain of civic participation and civic discourse, investigating how competing historical narratives shape current political arguments, how both values and information shape policy arguments, and how Americans continue to renew or remake We the People in pursuing fulfillment of the high principles of our constitutional democratic republic.

Because American politics currently is so polarized, it is tempting for educators and local authorities to accept the demoted status of civics, and avoid contemporary issues. The *EAD* approach encourages educators to address contemporary civic topics on the basis of the preceding Themes and Design Challenges, along with more particular guidance to navigate this challenging terrain. Breakdowns of civil discourse reflect an absence of common ground – of both civic knowledge and civic virtues. If we dig deeper, however, can we reach shared views that unite most Americans? Whether the topic is technology, youth mental health, war and foreign affairs, issues of identity and inclusion, taxes, immigration, freedom of religion, or guns, how can we listen for understanding and seek productive pathways for problem solving in our pluralistic polity? As Madison wrote in *Federalist* no. 10, echoing Montesquieu's portrait of English liberty, when people are given freedom to form opinions, they will form conflicting ones – and tend to become attached to them like prized possessions. Yet Madison advocated thoroughgoing pluralism. In *Federalist* no. 51, he argued that in a large, diverse society agreement will be unlikely to occur "on any other principles than those of justice and the general good." Once people see that their pet opinions or interests aren't resonating with others, they will recur to "principles ... of justice and the general good" forming common ground between all members of society. When Madison wrote, the common ground was the moral and political principles expressed in the Declaration and other writings of the founding era, from Thomas Paine and Samuel Adams to John Adams. As John Jay indicates in *Federalist* no. 2 – confirmed by Tocqueville in *Democracy in America* – a common Christian culture, expressed across many denominations, further undergirded a basic political agreement about principles; today we would say people shared ultimate "values." Yet this *e pluribus unum* was greatly strained by the reactions to the French Revolution in 1789; the first party system began during Washington's first administration – indeed, in his cabinet.

Could we restore today anything like the moments in American history when a basic, widespread agreement on values and principles has held? If we dig deep enough, can we get to shared opinions about fundamental realities that unite all Americans despite political disagreements? The seven Themes and five Design Challenges of *EAD* prepare educators and students for that challenge. The particular resource of the three civic virtues prepares schools to investigate and discuss serious arguments on both sides of major contemporary issues, so as to understand better the sources of disagreements; thus to prepare for informed citizenship. That said, the Roadmap calibrates this aim, as with all others, to grade bands; particular approaches for K-2, others for 9-12. The thematic and driving questions of Theme Seven encourage educators to pursue these investigations and discussions with students, across both new and longstanding issues. This Theme also addresses emphatically a thread running through the Roadmap of information literacy and the civic duty to be careful, indeed appropriately skeptical, about sources for political, social, historical, and civic information. Digital and social media, along with cable news networks, podcasts, and talk radio, foster "echo chambers" reinforcing one's existing opinions, excluding open-mindedness and civil disagreement. In-person dialogue across disagreement is a rare and precious good, and schools should be a place to encounter and practice this civic institution. A challenge is the reality documented by the national organization Heterodox Academy in the past decade, that retreat into bubbles of groupthink now characterizes even many university and college campuses, and professional academic societies.[29] The larger issues cogently raised by Jonathan Haidt (a cofounder of Heterodox Academy) in *The Anxious Generation* about the malformation of young souls and bodies that we have facilitated through smartphones are related to this crisis of civic discourse; school reformers at differing levels could link these concerns in mutually constructive ways.[30]

---

[29] Heterodox Academy, at www.heterodoxacademy.org/.
[30] Haidt, *The Anxious Generation: How the Great Rewiring of Childhood Is Causing an Epidemic of Mental Illness* (Penguin Press, 2024).

K-12 classrooms, along with higher education classrooms and campuses, can and should be epicenters for the renewal of civil dialogue and civic friendship about contemporary issues. The *EAD* Roadmap underscores this point throughout, and facilitates its accomplishment.

3.3 AMERICAN EXEMPLARS OF REFLECTIVE PATRIOTISM AND CIVIC HONESTY

In closing Chapter 2, I recommended schools study the extraordinary lives of civic knowledge and civic virtue embodied by Douglass and Lincoln, Stanton and Anthony, and King; to inspire students to acquire the knowledge needed for self-government, and understand then develop civil disagreement, civic friendship, and reflective patriotism. I posed there a series of questions about these civic exemplars, and here I offer my brief answers.

3.3.1 Abolitionism and the Constitutional Confidence of Douglass and Lincoln

Frederick Douglass's ultimate confidence in the justice and prudence of Abraham Lincoln's persistent, complex opposition to slavery as a moral evil and constitutional stain should be studied in itself, and as a guide to studying Lincoln. Amid the voluminous writings on the great statesman president are recent works that focus on his greatest public addresses, and analyze his deeds as seeking the most plausible, prudent paths to achieving the high aims of his great words; in turn mining earlier Lincoln studies.[31] Diana Schaub's *His Greatest Speeches* guides us through three addresses by the reformer patriot: his 1838 Young Men's Lyceum Address on perpetuating our institutions, calling America to abide by and live up to the principles of ordered liberty in the Constitution no matter the injustice or controversy tempting us otherwise; his 1863 Gettysburg Address calling America to live up to the principles of equal justice in the Declaration and give "a new birth of freedom" to our Constitution and Union by defeating and eradicating slavery; and his 1865 Second Inaugural calling America to abide by the justice of Biblical

---

[31] An excellent introduction to Lincoln's thought and statesmanship is Steven Kautz, "Abraham Lincoln: The Moderation of a Democratic Statesman," in Bryan-Paul Frost and Jeffrey Sikkenga, eds., *History of American Political Thought*, 2nd ed. (Lexington Books, 2019), 408–29.

religion and the Christian spirit of "malice toward none ... charity for all" in repairing the Union after defeating slavery, thereby to "achieve and cherish a just, and a lasting peace, among ourselves, and with all nations."[32] For Lincoln's friend the statesman Frederick Douglass (1817–1895), two of his great addresses capture his reflective patriotism about America but its sore testing, given our compromise with slavery to forge the Union in 1776 and strengthen it in 1787. David Blight's *Prophet of Freedom*, a character study of this famous and accomplished escaped slave, guides us as to why these Douglass addresses are great in their own right, and also why his 1876 tribute to Lincoln – with which Blight opens his biography – is so valuable a guide to the statesmanship of the Great Emancipator.[33]

Douglass's 1852 address, "What to the Slave is the Fourth of July," excoriates the United States for failing to live up to the principles in the Declaration, and the higher promise of the Constitution's principles of self-government. Asked to deliver an Independence Day oration, Douglass would only agree to speak on July 5th – for given the continuing and then-expanding crime of slavery, even if now himself a citizen, as a black man he did not fully have a country to celebrate with his white fellow citizens. Yet many references in recent decades include only the first half of the address, omitting the second half in which Douglass reiterates his faith in "the great principles" of the Declaration and breaks with fellow abolitionists who argue the Constitution is proslavery. Rather, "interpreted as it ought to be interpreted, the Constitution is a GLORIOUS LIBERTY DOCUMENT." If we "take the Constitution according to its plain reading ... it will be found to contain principles and purposes, entirely hostile to the existence of slavery."[34] Douglass's April 14, 1876, "Oration in Memory of Abraham Lincoln" at the unveiling of the Freedmen's Monument in Lincoln Park, Washington DC, is similarly complex; and again, many recent references to it select only the portions critical of Lincoln as "the white man's president" and for his hesitation

---

[32] Diana Schaub, *His Greatest Speeches: How Lincoln Moved the Nation* (St. Martin's Press, 2021).

[33] David W. Blight, *Frederick Douglass: Prophet of Freedom* (Simon & Schuster, 2018); see also the introduction to Douglass's civic thought in Richard S. Ruderman, "'Proclaim Liberty Throughout the Land:' Frederick Douglass, William Lloyd Garrison, and the Abolition of Slavery," in Frost and Sikkenga, eds., *History of American Political Thought*, 388–407.

[34] *Frederick Douglass: Selected Speeches and Writings*, ed. Philip S. Foner (Chicago: Lawrence Hill, 1999), 188–206, emphasis in original.

in adopting the Emancipation Proclamation and pursuing abolition.[35] In attendance were President Ulysses S. Grant, the Chief Justice and members of the Supreme Court, and members of Congress. Douglass offers us a statesman's lesson on the trials, difficult judgments, and successful persistence of Lincoln's statesmanship. On behalf of black Americans who entirely funded and commissioned the monument, he declares, "Our faith" in Lincoln "was often taxed and strained to the uttermost, but it never failed" – for "we were able to take a comprehensive view of Abraham Lincoln, and to make reasonable allowance for the circumstances of his position." Lincoln rightly judged that he must pay more attention to shaping white majority public opinion than to immediately redressing the suffering of blacks, in order to achieve the ultimate aim of defeating slavery.

Had he put the abolition of slavery before the salvation of the Union, he would have inevitably driven from him a powerful class of the American people and rendered resistance to rebellion impossible. Viewed from the genuine abolition ground, Mr. Lincoln seemed tardy, cold, dull, and indifferent; but measuring him by the sentiment of his country, a sentiment he was bound as a statesman to consult, he was swift, zealous, radical, and determined.

3.3.2 Elizabeth Cady Stanton, Susan B. Anthony, and American Justice for Women

Douglass was an early supporter of the women's rights movement, attending then publicizing in his *North Star* newspaper the first Women's Rights Convention, in Seneca Falls, New York, in 1848. The Declaration of Sentiments it produced is striking for its use of the Declaration of Independence to ground and propel the argument for equal political rights of suffrage and broader participation for women, as well as equal civil rights. Elizabeth Cady Stanton (1815–1902) was the leader of the Convention, and lead drafter of its Declaration.

When, in the course of human events, it becomes necessary for one portion of the family of man to assume among the people of the earth a position different from that which they have hitherto occupied, but one to which the laws of nature and of nature's God entitle them, a decent respect to the opinions of mankind requires that they should declare the causes that impel them to such

---

[35] Douglass, "Oration in Memory of Abraham Lincoln," in *Selected Speeches and Writings*, ed. Foner, 690–99; also available at www.teachingamericanhistory.org/document/oration-in-memory-of-abraham-lincoln/.

a course. We hold these truths to be self-evident: that all men and women are created equal …

The history of mankind is a history of repeated injuries and usurpations on the part of man toward woman, having in direct object the establishment of an absolute tyranny over her. To prove this, let facts be submitted to a candid world.[36]

A list of Resolutions followed the Declaration, listing the equal status, privileges, and rights women should enjoy in religious life, and other roles in society. There was controversy about including "their sacred right to the elective franchise," fearing this was too much to demand too early in the movement. Stanton and Douglass spoke strongly in favor, and it was approved.[37]

The Convention provoked many condemnations of its religious, moral, and political errors. Susan B. Anthony (1829–1906) met Stanton at an abolitionist meeting in 1851, and the two began a partnership lasting for six decades until their deaths.[38] In their final decades some Western states included women's suffrage in their constitutions. In the second decade after their deaths, the 19th Amendment to the US Constitution was ratified in 1920, establishing equal voting rights for women.[39] Anthony was arrested in 1872 for attempting to vote in Rochester, New York, and stood trial in 1873. In addresses delivered before the trial, and in her statement at it, she emphasized the constitutional and legal basis, from the Declaration and Constitution to the passage of the 14th and 15th amendments, implying women's equal right to vote.[40] Stanton and

---

[36] The Declaration of Sentiments, often termed the Seneca Falls Declaration, in *History of Woman Suffrage*, eds. Elizabeth Cady Stanton, Susan B. Anthony, and Matilda Joslyn Gage, vol. 1 (Salem, NH: Ayer, [1881] 1985), 70–71; also at www.teachingamerican history.org/document/declaration-of-sentiments/.

[37] Seneca Falls Resolutions, in *History of Woman Suffrage*, 2nd ed., eds. Elizabeth Cady Stanton, Susan B. Anthony, and Matilda Joslyn Gage (Rochester, NY: Charles Mann, 1889), 71–73; also at www.teachingamericanhistory.org/document/seneca-falls-resolutions/. An introduction to Stanton's civic and political thought is Melissa S. Williams, "Feminism as an American Project," in Frost and Sikkenga, eds., *History of American Political Thought*, 446–57.

[38] Anthony met the escaped slave and preacher Sojourner Truth in 1851 at the Ohio Women's Rights Convention, where Truth delivered her "Ain't I A Woman" address. National Park Service, www.nps.gov/wori/learn/historyculture/sojourner-truth.htm.

[39] On Anthony's civic and political thought, see Elizabeth Beaumont, "Claiming Justice: Suffragists, Gender Justice Constitutionalism, and Pursuit of National Transformation," in *The Civic Constitution: Civic Visions and Struggles in the Path toward Constitutional Democracy* (Oxford University Press, 2014).

[40] Anthony, "Is It a Crime for a U.S. Citizen to Vote?" *Rochester Democrat and Chronicle*, April 4, 1873, available at www.teachingamericanhistory.org/document/is-it-a-crime-for-a-u-s-citizen-to-vote/.

Anthony later sought to utilize the American Centennial celebrations of 1876 for the cause, drafting the Declaration of Rights for Women to advocate women's suffrage and other political and civil rights as the proper fulfillment of America's founding principles.

3.3.3 Martin Luther King, Jr., and Persistent Hope in American Justice

Given the Martin Luther King Day federal holiday established in 1983, recognized by all fifty states as of 2000 – as well as the King Memorial on the National Mall in Washington, DC, established in 2011 – King's deeds and words are better known today than those of Douglass, Stanton, and Anthony. Yet he is not often viewed as an exemplar of reflective patriotism.

After the failure of Reconstruction in the 1870s and the imposition of Jim Crow segregation laws across the southern United States, and racist practices predominant in the rest of the country, the National Association for the Advancement of Colored People (NAACP), the black church, and other organizations began to achieve significant reforms in the 1940s and 1950s. President Truman's 1948 order desegregating the US military, and the 1954 Supreme Court ruling *Brown v. Board of Education* ordering desegregation of all public schools, were two milestones. A Baptist minister from Georgia, the Rev. Dr. Martin Luther King, Jr. (1929–1968), rose to a national role in the 1950s and, along with other leaders and institutions, including the Southern Christian Leadership Conference, sparked the Civil Rights Movement. King's practice of nonviolent civil disobedience against unjust laws of racial segregation, inspired partly by Mahatma Gandhi's civil resistance movement for Indian independence earlier in the century, led to arrests, beatings, and killings.[41] A classic King writing to study is "Letter from Birmingham Jail," written in June 1963 to White Christian ministers who criticized his civil protests; invoking Western political philosophy as well as Christian theology to define just and unjust laws, and the grounds for resisting the latter.[42]

---

[41] See Peter C. Myers's excellent introduction to King's civic and political thought in "The Two Revolutions of Martin Luther King, Jr.," in Frost and Sikkenga, eds., *History of American Political Thought*, 699–720.

[42] June 12, 1963; substantial excepts are at The Bill of Rights Institute, www.billofrightsinstitute.org/primary-sources/letter-from-birmingham-jail. Roosevelt Montás notes the "great books" course King taught at Morehouse College in late 1961 which informed the Letter, in "Martin Luther King as Teacher: What the civil rights icon found in texts that are falling out of favour with American academics," *Financial Times* (London), February 26, 2022.

King's most famous address, which exemplifies his reflective patriotism, was delivered at the March on Washington for Jobs and Freedom in August 1963. Standing on the steps of the Lincoln Memorial on the National Mall, he opens by invoking the 1863 milestones of the Gettysburg Address and Emancipation Proclamation as everyone stands in "the symbolic shadow" of this "great American."[43] He notes the crippling bigotry and racial segregation that persists a century after the hopefulness of abolition. Yet he praises "the architects of our republic" who "wrote the magnificent words of the Constitution and the Declaration of Independence." Their promise must be fulfilled, and now. He then turns to an extraordinary pledge of faith and hope, that despite the great difficulties obstructing justice, "I still have a dream" – one "deeply rooted in the American dream." This includes that his children "will one day live in a nation where they will not be judged by the color of their skin, but by the content of their character." King closes with the hope that national civil rights legislation finally will "allow freedom to ring" in all of America; and if so:

We will be able to speed up the day when all of God's children, black men and white men, Jews and Gentiles, Protestants and Catholics, will be able to join hands and sing in the words of the old Negro spiritual: "Free at last. Free at last. Thank God Almighty, we are free at last."

What turned out to be the final five years of his short life were tumultuous, filled with great achievements, but also his persistent demands for further amelioration of the plight of black Americans. Amid continued violence against the Civil Rights Movement, his statesmanship was decisive in passing the 1964 Civil Rights Act and 1965 Voting Rights Act. He was awarded the Nobel Peace Prize in 1964. Yet he pushed on to address economic inequality and his adamant view of the injustice of America's war in Vietnam, which drafted a disproportionate number of black men for military service. His frustration led to escalating rhetoric on the illegitimacy of an American political order maintaining such economic, social, political, and military injustice. In what turned out to be his final public address, at the Mason Temple Church in Memphis, Tennessee in April 1968, he urged continued struggle and unity, speaking of challenges overcome and challenges ahead. He noted, "when students all over the South started sitting-in at lunch counters," he knew "they

---

[43] August 28, 1963; Available at The Avalon Project, Yale University, www.avalon.law .yale.edu/20th_century/mlk01.asp/.

were really standing up for the best in the American dream, and taking the whole nation back to those great wells of democracy which were dug deep by the Founding Fathers in the Declaration of Independence and the Constitution." In closing, he spoke of his own passing from the scene before ultimate victory in the civil rights struggle. He was at peace, because he had been given a vision of what that greater justice would be. "I've been to the mountaintop." God has "allowed me to go up to the mountain. And I've looked over. And I've seen the Promised Land. I may not get there with you. But I want you to know tonight, that we, as a people, will get to the promised land!"[44] He was assassinated the following day.

A reflective patriotism calls all Americans to consider the daily efforts, studies, and commitments required of self-government as a matter of our sacred honor; of what we owe to higher principles, to our own dignity and pursuit of happiness, and to the rights and happiness of others. To be inspired to understand this and make the efforts and sacrifices required, it is helpful to know that extraordinary people like Washington, Douglass, Lincoln, Stanton, Anthony, and King actually lived, exemplifying such civic knowledge and civic virtues.

---

[44] April 13, 1968, available at American Rhetoric, www.americanrhetoric.com/speeches/ mlkivebeentothemountaintop.htm.

4

What Should American Colleges and Universities Teach?

The *Educating for American Democracy* (*EAD*) report urges higher education to rebuild not just civics and history education in schools but the entire K-16 "ecosystem" of civics: "after years of disinvestment in civic education," America faces "an undersupply of teachers" having "adequate college-level training in history and political science." Five of the seven lead authors were professors, making *EAD* also an internal argument for reform: Academia had a duty to America to better support citizenship preparation. Colleges and universities must "rebuild our own curricular offerings," and assess whether we "adequately require rigorous American history and civic education – to include knowledge, skills, and virtues – of all their graduates."[1] Yet as argued in the Preface and Introduction, higher education also needs to undertake for its own sake, its core missions, renewal of the priority for civic education. It is true there is an external dimension here, which Tocqueville would discern as enlightened self-interest. Danielle Allen argued in 2025, amid the second Trump administration's severe pressure on elite universities to comply with nondiscrimination law and redress their ideological imbalance, that academia should rediscover and elevate to a top priority its once-defining mission to provide serious citizenship education. The reason to do so rested on a needed introspection about why the Trump administration's pressure campaign, including a freeze or withdrawal of federal funding, was politically plausible: The sharp decline in public regard for

---

[1] Allen, Carrese, Dubé, Kamensky, Levine, et al., *Educating for American Democracy: Excellence in History and Civics for All Learners*, iCivics, 2021, at 20, 21. Available at www.educatingforamericandemocracy.org/.

academia in the past decade, which academia brought on itself. As discussed in the Introduction, this is a dimension of America's civic crisis; with Gallup polls showing in 2024, after campus protests about the Israel-Gaza war, a 21 percent drop in the top tier of confidence in higher education since 2015. A supermajority of Independents, let alone Republicans, register only some or little-to-no trust that colleges and universities serve American society. Responses suggesting ambiguities in the results typically don't address more specific surveys showing that concern about ideological bias is a major reason for the decline. Allen thus argued higher education, of itself, should propose "a new social contract" with America – prioritizing the public good of providing a serious, intellectually-balanced civic education.[2]

Allen also explained why this would be good for academia's core missions of pursuit of truth, robust debate and inquiry, and faculty intellectual diversity on important political and social questions. I would pursue this last point further: An array of evidence confirms a strong ideological tilt in higher education, across the past half-century, toward what is arguably now a 10:1 predominance of liberal-progressives to conservatives across all faculties in all institutions. The skew probably is 15:1 or more across the humanities and social science disciplines, and still greater in elite liberal arts colleges.[3] The larger argument Allen is invoking, in the spirit of John Stuart Mill's *On Liberty* and the recent national higher education association Heterodox Academy, is the need for robust discourse to pursue the truth. She proposes, as one measure, that scholars from conservative policy institutes hold two-year visiting fellowships

---

[2] Danielle Allen, "America and Its Universities Need a New Social Contract," *The Atlantic*, April 13, 2025; Jessica Blake, "American Confidence in Higher Ed Hits Historic Low," *Inside Higher Ed*, July 11, 2023, at www.insidehighered.com/news/business/financial-health/2023/07/11/american-confidence-higher-ed-hits-historic-low. See also Allen, "Trump's Imperfect Compact Is a Perfect Opportunity," *Chronicle of Higher Education*, October 6, 2025.

[3] Jon A. Shields, "The Disappearing Conservative Professor," *National Affairs* (Fall 2018), at www.nationalaffairs.com/publications/detail/the-disappearing-conservative-professor; Samuel J. Abrams and Amna Khalid, "Are Colleges and Universities Too Liberal? What the Research Says About the Political Composition of Campuses and Campus Climate," *Heterodox Academy Blog*, October 21, 2020, at www.heterodoxacademy.org/blog/are-colleges-and-universities-too-liberal-what-the-research-says-about-the-political-composition-of-campuses-and-campus-climate/; Samuel J. Abrams, "Liberal Arts Colleges Are More Liberal Than Universities," *RealClearEducation*, October 10, 2022, at www.realcleareducation.com/articles/2022/10/10/liberal_arts_colleges_are_more_liberal_than_universities_110774.html; Phillip W. Magness and David Waugh, "The Hyperpoliticization of Higher Ed: Trends in Faculty Political Ideology, 1969–Present," *The Independent Review* 27 No. 3, (Winter 2022/23).

at universities to quickly inject intellectual diversity into academic discourse. Allen may have had in mind the new partnership Johns Hopkins University and the American Enterprise Institute announced in 2025, The Civic Thought Project, to undertake collaborative research, teaching, graduate student pipeline projects and other initiatives to increase the presence of "heterodox faculty" across the university. Hopkins described the partnership as aiming "to model intellectual pluralism, convey the importance of rooting teaching and research with implications for the nation's common life in a broad range of points of view, and encourage greater intellectual diversity in the university community."[4] President Ronald Daniels, in his 2021 book *What Universities Owe Democracy*, raised this issue of "a dearth of conservative faculty" and the need to restore "intellectual diversity" to sustain the robust "intellectual discourse" essential to the university's core mission of "the endless refinement of ideas."[5] As noted in the Preface and Introduction, Daniels also has been a pioneering leader on this need: That every university and college owes its graduates, and America, a serious civic education in civic knowledge and civic virtues.

How to pull together the concerns raised by Allen and Daniels regarding loss of public confidence in higher education, the strongly ideological tilt in humanities and social sciences faculty especially, and the need to restore serious civic education to universities and colleges? The structural reform I've undertaken in academia in the past decade viewed itself from the beginning, in 2016, as trying to meet these three aims simultaneously – by establishing new colleges, departments, or centers of civic thought and leadership in public universities. As it turned out, this was just one element of a renewal of civic education in academia, arising from a heterogeneous, philosophically diverse set of actors. It is indeed significant that a cross-ideological consensus has emerged on civics and the related issues of ideological imbalance and declining public confidence. Allen and Daniels are not the only center-left scholars (Allen is a political theorist and classicist, while Daniels is a law professor) raising these concerns; they were preceded by former Harvard president Derek Bok, who, in his 2020 book *Higher Expectations*, identified the near-disappearance of a serious civic education requirement as the top deficit or failing that

---

4 "Johns Hopkins works to bolster intellectual pluralism across the university," Johns Hopkins University News Hub, April 21, 2025; www.hub.jhu.edu/2025/04/21/johns-hopkins-american-enterprise-institute-partnership/.

5 Ronald J. Daniels with Grant Shreve and Phillip Spector, *What Universities Owe Democracy* (Johns Hopkins University Press, 2021), 226–28.

twenty-first-century American higher education must redress.[6] Even the left-leaning *Chronicle of Higher Education* featured self-identified centrist and liberal institutionalist Steve Teles of Johns Hopkins, focusing on the problematic absence of conservative faculty in academia, endorsing the Civic Thought and Leadership reform as perhaps the most promising way to redress this set of concerns at once.[7]

4.1 RENEWING THE ACADEMY'S CORE MISSION THROUGH CIVIC EDUCATION

In 2016, the Arizona legislature and governor established the first department of civic thought and leadership at a public university. I served as founding director of the School of Civic and Economic Thought and Leadership at Arizona State University through 2023.[8] After the department's first half-decade, I reflected on its origin and the three main missions we developed: A rigorous blending of classical liberal arts education and American civic education to prepare leaders for service in the public and private sectors and civil society; public outreach on civics, including a speakers program featuring civic discourse and civil disagreement on important academic and civic topics; and support by PhD faculty in political science, history, and economics for K-12 teachers, providing workshops and curriculum resources to improve civics and history education in schools.[9] This reform, of a funded mandate by state government to

---

[6] Derek Bok, *Higher Expectations: Can Colleges Teach Students What They Need to Know in the 21st Century?* (Princeton University Press, 2020). In the Introduction above I also cite the Stanford Civics Initiative and a new national association, the Alliance for Civics in the Academy.

[7] Teles, "Why Are There So Few Conservative Professors?" *Chronicle of Higher Education,* July 1, 2024. In 2024 and 2025, the *Chronicle* published other positive accounts of the civic thought and leadership reform, whereas all references since 2016 had been mixed or critical; including Ben and Jenna Storey of AEI, "Will Republicans Save the Humanities," *Chronicle,* June 20, 2024; and an interview with the Provost of University of Texas at Austin, Will Inboden – formerly dean of the Hamilton School of Classical and Civic Education at University of Florida – in Evan Goldstein and Len Gutkin, "'We as Universities Have Lost Our Way'" *Chronicle,* October 28, 2025.

[8] In the remainder of this chapter I draw on and revise analysis I presented in "Civic Thought and Leadership: A Higher Civics to Sustain American Constitutional Democracy," *Laws* 13, no. 2: 19 (2024). www.doi.org/10.3390/laws13020019.

[9] In "A New Birth of Freedom in Higher Education: Civic Institutes at Public Universities," American Enterprise Institute, January 24, 2023, at www.aei.org/research-products/report/a-new-birth-of-freedom-in-higher-education-civic-institutes-at-public-universities/. A wide array of information about the School of Civic and Economic Thought and Leadership is at www.scetl.asu.edu/.

prioritize a higher civics, had spread by 2025 to a total of at least seventeen public universities in twelve states. While still nascent, the reform is likely to continue growing, and it has gained sufficient presence to warrant deeper consideration in itself. Moreover, while the efforts to renew a higher civics at Stanford University and Johns Hopkins noted in the Introduction are significant and still growing, the public university renewal has been more ambitious to date because it is more structural. New tenure homes for faculty in colleges and departments, or in centers with substantial autonomy, boost the prospects for new courses, curricula, degrees, and programming focused upon civic thought and leadership as a higher American civics appropriate to college and university education.[10]

As argued by Justin Dyer, founding dean of the School of Civic Leadership at the University of Texas at Austin, there are particularly strong grounds to restore the civic mission of public universities governed and funded by states. Benjamin Storey and Jenna Storey, scholars at the American Enterprise Institute, agree and further suggest a new academic field of Civic Thought is taking shape, which could renew core academic missions in a range of institutions.[11] Restoration of the traditional civic mission of public universities – to provide a blend of liberal arts and American civic education for committed, informed citizens and future leaders – offers even to left-leaning administrators and trustees, amid the legitimacy crisis facing higher education, a path to meet their enlightened self-interest. As the Storeys argue, private universities and colleges have analogous reasons to consider this practical, already proven model of reform that aims to recover a core academic mission, restore intellectual diversity, and reestablish public trust both by meeting a civic need and rebalancing academia toward intellectual pluralism and heterodoxy.[12] These scholars argue that, for the past half-century and

---

[10] Heterodox Academy produced a brief overview of the national scale of civic education and "civil discourse" initiatives across public and private institutions; Shiri Spitz Siddiqi and Michael Regnier, "The New Landscape of 'Civics Centers' in Higher Education: An Analysis of Missions, Structures, and Legislative Origins Across U.S. Colleges and Universities" (December 2025).

[11] Justin Dyer, "Embracing Civics Can Help Restore Trust in Higher Education," *National Review Online*, January 6, 2024, at www.nationalreview.com/2024/01/embracing-civics-can-help-restore-trust-in-higher-education; Benjamin Storey and Jenna Silber Storey, "Civic Thought: A Proposal for University-Level Civic Education," American Enterprise Institute, December 11, 2023, at www.aei.org/research-products/report/civic-thought-a-proposal-for-university-level-civic-education/.

[12] Jenna Silber Storey and Benjamin Storey, "Sometimes the Right is Right," *Inside Higher Ed*, April 9, 2024; and "How to Broaden the Academic Tent," American Enterprise Institute, April 8, 2025, at www.aei.org/social-cultural-and-constitutional-studies/

more in American higher education, faculty and administrators as well as trustees have forgotten, or deliberately ignored, the fact that phrasing about civic education is widespread across the charters and mottoes of our public universities. The 1789 charter of America's first public university, in North Carolina (established at Chapel Hill), included education in "social duties" as a main aim.[13] The University of Virginia, founded with the guidance of Thomas Jefferson and James Madison, is better known for the civic mission of its original charter. This model spread across the American states, and across the decades of the nineteenth and twentieth centuries, as new universities were established. As the Storeys note, "The mottoes of many of our colleges and universities reflect this view, such as the University of North Carolina's Light and Liberty, Ohio State's Education for Citizenship, and the University of Texas's Education Is the Guardian Genius of Democracy" ("Civic Thought," 2). Ohio State was founded in 1870, and UT Austin in 1883, indicating that for a century after America's founding and the founding of North Carolina as the first public university under the Constitution, this blend of liberal arts and civics held sway.

Johns Hopkins, however, was founded in 1876 as America's first research university, partly with the aim to supplant this traditional mission of liberal arts and civic education in both public and private institutions. As Daniels bravely documents in *What Universities Owe Democracy*, this new model has succeeded in supplanting the older approach, but with unintended consequences. Daniels and his coauthors argue that the new model of research university imported from Germany did not intend to undercut the provision of civic education altogether, but to offer it in a new mode; through emphasis on knowledge in new natural sciences and social sciences disciplines, thus in new dimensions of modern scientific, technological, and economic affairs increasingly dominant in modern industrial societies. Unintended or not, this and other progressive, secularizing changes in American political culture across the past 150 years have chipped away at the traditional civic mission of public and private higher education. As Jon Shields and Joshua Dunn documented in their study of the declining presence of conservatives in higher education, political science and several other disciplines in the humanities

how-to-broaden-the-academic-tent/. In 2025 AEI established a Center for the Future of the American University, with the Storeys as codirectors; www.cfau.aei.org/.

[13] Act Establishing the University of North Carolina, 1789; at www.docsouth.unc.edu/unc/unc01-08/unc01-08.html.

and social sciences have aggressively or quietly repudiated this traditional blend of liberal arts and civic education in recent decades.[14]

The new view in these fields, about their own disciplines as well as about general education requirements, held that civics was not a real academic field, and was merely a subject for K-12 schools. James Stoner helpfully explains one deeper dimension of the shift, in the emphasis on the fact-value distinction in the new social sciences, to include political science. The ambition to define knowledge as strictly "scientific or universal, as social science in the age of globalization has tended to become," yields the view that civic education in a given regime is narrow and unacademic. Stoner recounts the dramatic change in the past fifty years in his discipline (and mine) as evident in American political science departments. There remain "some remnants of the old practice of teaching students from a decidedly American perspective what a citizen interested in politics might want to know. Yet behavioral political scientists have different concerns."

The contrast between a classic course in constitutional law and a contemporary course in judicial behavior, or between a classic course in American foreign policy and a course in contemporary international relations, is illustrative. Universities still offer the classic courses because students flock to them, but political-science journals tend to publish research in judicial behavior and international relations.

Or consider a course on the presidency. Our chief executive, as all citizens know, holds the highest and most critical political office in American government. Yet it is hard to find a working political scientist to teach a course on the subject. Why? Because when it comes to the presidency, the sample size is one. A good social scientist knows you cannot draw valid conclusions from a sample that small.[15]

Further, universities and colleges replaced civics, as civic knowledge and civic virtues for our constitutional democratic republic, with an emphasis on democracy and civic engagement. Some scholars, such as Peter Levine, argue for a balanced conception of civic engagement that includes civic knowledge of the American constitutional order and its political development; Levine even invokes civic virtues and patriotism along with the more typical educational terminology of skills, habits, and attitudes.[16]

---

[14] Jon A. Shields and Joshua M. Dunn Sr., *Passing on the Right: Conservative Professors in the Progressive University* (Oxford University Press, 2016).

[15] James R. Stoner, Jr., "Civic Thought and Political Science," *National Affairs* no. 62 (Winter 2025).

[16] Peter Levine, *The Future of Democracy: Developing the Next Generation of American Citizens* (Boston: Tufts University Press), 2007.

Most advocates of democracy education in academia, however, ignore or eschew these traditional elements in their emphasis on democratic engagement with a leaning toward progressive activism; including the recent efforts by a Civic Learning and Democracy Engagement Coalition (CLDE) founded in 2021.[17] This politicized, ideological mode of civic engagement in universities, colleges, and scholarship eventually came to dominate what little space remained for civics and history education in K-12 schools as well. The American Political Science Association (APSA) links "civic learning" and "civic engagement" in its website section on educator resources, with the clearly predominant theme being engagement and participation rather than constitutional and civic knowledge.[18] The most recent APSA reports nominally on civic education are *Teaching Civic Education Globally* (2021) and *Teaching Civic Engagement across the Disciplines* (2017).[19]

This imbalanced view displaces fundamental civic knowledge of America's constitutional order, principles, and development and also of the civic virtues one develops through discussion of the classic as well as contemporary voices that have addressed these crucial topics. If one scans the panel and paper titles of recent APSA Teaching and Learning Conferences, there is occasional mention of deeper and broader ideas about citizenship, civic education, and civic culture, but the predominant focus is democracy activism, engagement, change, mobilization, commitment, service learning, and tactics. If first-order questions are posed at all (and it is rare) about the meaning of citizenship and education for informed citizenship in America's liberal democratic constitutional republic, they are implicitly approached through a hyper democratic, present-centered lens.[20] Missing is the liberal arts approach of addressing foundational ideas and ideals, and the perpetual American debate about

---

[17] See Association of American Colleges & Universities, *A Crucible Moment: College Learning and Democracy's Future*, The Civic Learning and Democratic Engagement National Task Force, 2011; and the College Civic Learning project, The Civic Learning and Democracy Engagement Coalition (CLDE Coalition), at www.collegeciviclearning.org/home.

[18] See the "Civic Engagement Resource Collection" section of the APSA website at www.educate.apsanet.org/civic-engagement-resource-collection; and elsewhere on the site the APSA emphasizes civic learning and civic engagement with a democracy focus at www.apsanet.org/why-political-science-the-science-of-democracy/. The APSA did establish in 2024 a standing committee on Civic Education, but as of 2026, it had not yielded much of an increased emphasis upon civic knowledge in APSA programming and publications.

[19] See the APSA website at www.web.apsanet.org/teachingcivicengagement/.

[20] The programs for recent Teaching and Learning conferences of the APSA are at www.apsanet.org/events/teaching-learning-conference/.

them. A recent interdisciplinary study by a political scientist (David Campbell) and two education scholars (Paula McAvoy and Diana Hess) argues this liberal arts approach concomitantly develops civic virtues of civil disagreement and civic friendship across diverse viewpoints through the very study of, and discussion about, such essential topics.[21]

Higher education leaders should work to restore prioritized space for higher education's core academic missions of pursuing knowledge and truth, debating contested ideas in properly academic ways, and teaching the next generation of civic, economic, intellectual, and social leaders for American constitutional democracy. New national organizations like Heterodox Academy have argued in a nonideological, transpartisan spirit about the suppression of these traditional missions and ideas, and the exclusion of important debates and viewpoints.[22] The recent exposure of ideological orthodoxy at several Ivy League and other elite campuses given the protests against Israel, including in the Congressional testimony of the university presidents beginning in fall 2023, indicates that this strong leftward bias is seen by a broad public as violating a public trust. Both public and private institutions proclaim they educate leaders for America, and receive enormous federal funding and societal status in return, as well as tax-exempt status; yet many of them are readily perceived to be acting not as academic institutions under an established trust with a broad public but as political, partisan agents. The protests and explanations by leaders and faculty who rebut this characterization would have more credibility if accompanied by significant structural reforms, particularly regarding faculty, courses, requirements, and degrees.

4.2 A HIGHER CIVICS: CIVIC THOUGHT AND LEADERSHIP

Arizona leaders discerned these problems in 2016, and took steps to restore at a public university the kind of civic education that once was central to all American universities and colleges. The legislature and governor, as ultimate custodians of public education in the state, mandated the establishment at Arizona State University (ASU) of a separate department, by name: The School of Civic and Economic Thought and

---

[21] Paula McAvoy, David Campbell, and Diana Hess, "The Relationship Between a Liberal Arts Education and Democratic Outcomes," *Mellon Foundation Research Reports*, 2019, at www.mellon.org/news-blog/articles/relationship-between-liberal-arts-education-and-democratic-outcomes/.

[22] The Heterodox Academy website is www.heterodoxacademy.org/.

Leadership. A decade later, a national reform movement by legislatures and governors (in some cases boards of regents or trustees) to mandate and fund separate departments or colleges at public universities, and some centers or programs below the department level, includes at least Arizona, Florida, Georgia, Iowa, Mississippi, North Carolina, Ohio, Tennessee, Texas, Utah, and West Virginia. These departments, colleges, and centers aim to provide the blend of classical liberal education and American civic education that had long prepared civic-minded leaders for public life, the private sector, and civil society. The public authorities in these states argue that a higher civics should at least be an option in publicly governed and funded universities.

As founding director, along with the first cohort of faculty I hired, we developed three missions for the School of Civic and Economic Thought and Leadership (SCETL). We were guided by the Founding Mission Statement drafted by an advisory board of distinguished scholars from Harvard, Notre Dame, and Stanford, discussed below. As founding faculty, we stated our first mission as providing a rigorous interdisciplinary education – through our own faculty, courses, and degrees, undergraduate and graduate – blending classical liberal arts education and American civic education. Working with broad guidance from the advisory board, we designed an undergraduate major in civic thought and leadership with four main themes: political and moral thought; American civic and constitutional thought; economic thought; and leadership and statecraft; all to be studied in the Socratic spirit of discourse, scholarly disagreement, and intellectual diversity. A second mission is programming and public outreach to provide space at ASU and for the community to build intellectual diversity and civil disagreement; in student mentoring and leadership experiences, and in a public-speaker series and other speaker events. Our main speaker series is The Civic Discourse Project, which partners with Arizona PBS. A third mission is supporting renewal of K-12 civics and history education through subject-expert faculty working on teacher preparation, teacher professional development workshops, and curricular materials; mostly through one of two centers under the School, the Center for American Civics.[23] (My work in coleading the *EAD* study was supported by Center colleagues, and the Center continues to implement

---

[23] See www.scetl.asu.edu/, under the tabs "About" for mission and origins, "Degree Programs," and "Student Life," and "News and Events" for the Civic Discourse Project and other programming. The "Centers" and "CivEd" tabs provide information about the Center for American Civics and its K-12 work.

EAD materials and themes in its work.) The departments, colleges, and centers around the country that have adapted the SCETL model mostly undertake all three of these missions, albeit – given the American genius of federalism – in their own ways.

The ASU senior leaders guiding the formation of the school, and distinguished advisory board they formed (discussed below), prioritized the spirit of restoring Socratic debate and discourse about the school's themes rather than conceiving the department as a space for politically conservative ideas. Jonathan Haidt's *The Righteous Mind* captures this approach to citizenship preparation for free societies and also the proper, Socratic spirit of higher education itself. Not accidentally, Haidt was a cofounder of Heterodox Academy; and we invited him to speak in SCETL's Civic Discourse Project in its inaugural year.[24] My own scholarship in political philosophy had explored the intellectual and political virtue of moderation, understood as wariness about taking any idea to an extreme and the need to balance or reconcile multiple important principles, as a crucial but recently neglected element of Enlightenment thought, and of the founding of American constitutionalism. Thus there was mutual agreement among ASU leaders and the SCETL founding director about the complex, Socratic approach to liberal education and American civic education we should develop.[25]

The Storeys and Dyer have been joined by Stoner and also Peter Berkowitz, Hoover Institution fellow and commentator on higher education, in efforts to articulate the philosophy that should inform these colleges, departments, and centers of civic thought and leadership, including their curricula and research.[26] Their writings, my own, and those by a few other scholars constitute a nascent public discussion about the blend of intellectual and civic virtues that the study of civic thought and leadership should offer to students, and American higher education. These virtues include civil disagreement about important academic and civic ideas;

---

[24] Jonathan Haidt, *The Righteous Mind: Why Good People Are Divided by Politics and Religion* (Pantheon Books, 2012). SCETL also invited the intellectual and civic friends Robert P. George and Cornel West to speak in that 2017–18 inaugural year; the civil disagreement they long have practiced across philosophical and political differences is explained in their book *Truth Matters: A Dialogue on Fruitful Disagreement in an Age of Division* (Post Hill Press, 2025).

[25] *Democracy in Moderation: Montesquieu, Tocqueville, and Sustainable Liberalism* (Cambridge University Press, 2016).

[26] Peter Berkowitz, "Higher Education Reform, Civic Thought, and Liberal Education," *RealClearPolitics*, February 11, 2024, www.realclearpolitics.com/articles/2024/02/11/higher_education_reform_civic_thought_and_liberal_education_150478.html.

knowledge of and truth-seeking about the foundational principles and historical development of free government, particularly American constitutional democracy; practical experiences for students of service, leadership, and civic discourse; and motivation to lead and serve in American life, in whatever path a student might choose. In just a short few years the new entities established across the country indicate a prospect that the presence itself of these colleges, departments, and programs can shift the academic and civic culture on the campuses establishing them, and beyond. The SCETL idea spread to other states within just two years, and now a larger concept is developing of a new field of civic thought and leadership embodied in these different-but-related kinds of academic units across higher education. Further, the early success of SCETL at ASU prompted the Arizona Board of Regents to establish a new graduation requirement for students in all of Arizona's public universities: the study of American institutions, ideals, and self-government.[27]

A course that SCETL already required for all of our majors and minors, Great Debates in American Politics, easily met the guidelines for the new American civics requirement. This sophomore-level course is a pillar of the school's approach to blending liberal arts education and an American civics informed by reflective patriotism. It introduces students to classic ideas, documents, and figures in American political thought, and to the basic institutions of our constitutional democratic republic, almost entirely through primary-source texts. The main theme is fundamental ideas and debates about liberty, equality, constitutionalism, and democracy – from the Puritans, the American Revolution and the constitutional founding, through the Civil War, and into the twentieth century challenges by Progressives to the meaning and relevance of some founding principles. At the start of the course, students receive the SCETL US Pocket Constitution, discussed at the close of Chapter 2, which adds to the Declaration and Constitution Lincoln's 1863 Gettysburg Address and Martin Luther King, Jr.'s 1963 I Have a Dream Address. A theme of the course is to enter the ongoing debates about the meaning and implications of the two most influential political documents in our history: the Declaration and Constitution; Lincoln and King being among the foremost voices to encounter. A major aim is to provide future civic and political leaders, and informed, committed citizens, a deeper foundation

[27] Johanna Alonso, "Making Students 'Angry and Proud': Arizona's New 'American Institutions' Requirement," *Inside Higher Ed*, February 20, 2023, at www.insidehighered.com/news/2023/02/20/new-civics-requirement-tests-arizonas-public-universities.

for thinking about the principles, institutions, tensions, challenges, disagreements, and questions that have defined the American experiment and that continue today to shape American civic life – including what it means to be a citizen of this constitutional republic.

Several SCETL faculty teach the course each semester from a common syllabus, in large and small sections, with minimal variations made by each professor. The emphasis on discussion and writing seeks to further develop independent thinking and capacities for expression, discussion, even debate and civil disagreement. Required texts are *The Federalist* and Tocqueville's *Democracy in America*, along with a reading packet including crucial documents, speeches by statesmen and stateswomen, and US Supreme Court cases. All the reflective patriots discussed in Chapters 1, 2, and 3 are included; from the founding era and Civil War era through women's rights, Reconstruction and its failure, and the Civil Rights movement. Students also discuss American economic thought, and principles and major statements on American foreign policy. They get a touch of philosophy in Locke, Montesquieu, and Tocqueville, and the debate on ratification of the Constitution between Federalist and Anti-Federalist views captures a crucial spirit of America and of the course.

I introduce my students to striking statements about that debate which were offered to me as an undergraduate in the 1980s by Professor Murray Dry at Middlebury College, who had worked as a junior editor with his teacher Herbert Storing to compile the first published collection of the Anti-Federalist writings. In Storing's introductory essay, written in the 1970s at the time of the Bicentennial, he states that this debate continues to reverberate; so that one cannot understand America without understanding the dynamic tension it exemplifies between shared principles and perpetual debate about them. "If the foundation of the American polity was laid by the Federalists, the Anti-Federalist reservations echo through American history; and it is in the dialogue, not merely in the Federalist victory, that the country's principles are to be discovered."[28] That was striking enough to this undergraduate student; more amazing

---

[28] Herbert J. Storing, "Introduction," *What the Anti-Federalists Were For: The Political Thought of the Opponents of the Constitution*, With the Editorial Assistance of Murray Dry (University of Chicago Press, 1981); Volume 1 of *The Complete Anti-Federalist*; p. 72 (see also Introduction, 3-6). Derek Webb's *The Spirit of Amity: The Original Meaning of Civility and the Creation of the Constitution* is a recent study in Storing's spirit, on the deeper lessons of civic knowledge and civic virtues evident in the ratification debate (Cambridge University Press, forthcoming).

was Storing's statement that, in his own view, the Federalists had the better argument; ratification was the sounder choice; this from the senior editor of the first-ever published collection of the *opponents* to ratification! He notes we probably would not have had the Bill of Rights if not for the Anti-Federalists; nor have the extraordinary writing in defense of, and explaining, the Constitution and its principles by Hamilton, Madison, and Jay if not for the criticisms levelled by the Anti-Federalists. Storing's larger point as a scholar and a citizen, which has stayed with me for forty years, is that he could not know whether the Federalists had the sounder view about the Constitution and ratification unless he had seriously studied the Anti-Federalist writings; and that the best of them – Federal Farmer, Brutus, Cato – rival the thinking and arguments of Publius (Hamilton, Madison, and Jay). In retrospect, I also was shaped by Storing's implication that the American principles and system of self-government being debated, providing for equal liberty under law, were a good thing. Altogether, though I did not know it at the time – because I hadn't yet studied Tocqueville with Professor Dry and his colleague Paul Nelson – I was encountering in these learned scholars, Storing and Dry, a model of reflective patriotism.

This case study of a foundational course for SCETL, now meeting an ASU graduation requirement, underscores a larger point about the advantage these civic thought and leadership units bring at this moment in American higher education, one discussed by Dyer, the Storeys, and Berkowitz. Study of civic thought and leadership restores space for a distinct mode of liberal education in American higher education. The Storeys argue that "[u]nlike many forms of liberal education understood as great books education," civic thought and leadership "asks students to understand their humanity through the lens of their work as citizens." The study of their own political and social contexts points toward consideration of "how living up to citizenship's inherent commitments requires fundamental inquiry into perennial human questions." So designed, a higher civics is "a kind of liberal education, aligned with Marcus Tullius Cicero's elucidation of the *artes liberales* – arts that enable one to live as a free person, capable of engaging with others in self-government" (Storey and Storey, "Civic Thought," 6). For Dyer, civics is "a central part of a liberal education in its original sense: the education befitting a free person. It rests on open inquiry, reasoned debate, and freedom of thought and speech, all in the pursuit of truth." American civics is "anchored in the study of Western civilization and American constitutionalism, and it fosters a patriotism that is spirited, thoughtful, and open to critical self-reflection" (Dyer, "Embracing Civics"). For Berkowitz, the new departments, colleges, and centers of civic thought and leadership "must accord with the governing aim of liberal education, which is to cultivate citizens who understand the principles that undergird, and who can contribute to the maintenance of, free and democratic political institutions" (Berkowitz, "Higher Education Reform"). These scholars agree that a higher American civics draws on a range of academic disciplines, from political science, history, economics, and law to philosophy, literature, and classics, but is not dominated by any one, and this blending and balancing aims at a sum greater than the parts. Its fundamental orientation toward preparing American citizens to understand, operate, and lead in a constitutional and civic order itself grounded in a philosophy of natural rights provides a restoration within these disciplines of space for more traditional ideas. Like all of the humanities and social sciences, these have shifted strongly leftward in the past half-century and are predominantly skeptical of the constellation of ideas informing America's natural rights constitutionalism and democratic republic.

Here a distinction must be kept in mind between the political versus intellectual modalities of the terms conservative and traditional. Some critical faculty at the seventeen or more public universities where civic thought and leadership units are established have protested that these are political projects launched by Republican politicians; and other voices have joined this condemnation. The new entities are not just conservative but "right-wing," and constitute a political attack on academic freedom and the institutional integrity of higher education.[29] As to the politics, it is noteworthy that the Institute of American Civics, established at the University of Tennessee Knoxville in 2022, earned strong bipartisan support in the legislature. SCETL at Arizona State University in more recent years has earned renewed annual funding with votes from Democratic legislators and, for three years running, with support from a Democratic governor. However, the deeper misunderstanding lies in the view that an intervention by a state's ultimate governing authorities, whether the political branches or regents, to restore a traditional civic mission to public

---

[29] See Stephanie Saul, "Arizona Republicans Inject Schools of Conservative Thought into State Universities," *The New York Times*, February 26, 2018; Emma Pettit, "How a Center for Civic Education Became a Political Provocation," *The Chronicle of Higher Education*, February 22, 2023; Richard Amesbury and Catherine O'Donnell, "Dear Administrators: Enough with the Free Speech Rhetoric," *The Chronicle of Higher Education*, November 16, 2023.

universities is by definition a partisan political intrusion – rather than meeting an urgent civic need and redressing obvious educational deficits and imbalance. As noted, the independent affirmation in recent years of this traditional approach to a higher civics by prominent scholars, academic leaders, and public intellectuals from the center and center-left – including Bok, Daniels and Johns Hopkins, Steven Smith on patriotism, Richard Haass on a bill of obligations, Josiah Ober and the Stanford Civics Initiative, the *EAD* report, and the new Center on Civic Thought at Yale – demonstrates that these recent reforms are not *per se* ideological or partisan. In support of Dyer's argument that education in a kind of patriotism is appropriate to America as a political order founded on ideas and individual natural rights, the Storeys cite Tocqueville's endorsement of the "reflective patriotism" he observed in Americans – blending gratitude for their country and its principles with insistence upon argument and questioning, pointed toward both government and their fellow citizens (Storey and Storey, "Civic Thought").

Interestingly, Berkowitz warns as a conservative that civic thought and leadership should tread carefully regarding the intellectual versus narrowly political implication of any reference to the field as "conservative." In response to the Storeys arguing in an opinion essay that "conservatives" should view the rise of these departments, colleges, and centers in just the way "the left" had developed new disciplines and fields in recent decades to include women's studies and African–American studies, Berkowitz counsels that "conservatives should reject the left's politicization of teaching and learning." They should not conceive of civic thought and leadership as conservative "in the narrow partisan sense of furthering a right-wing political agenda." Rather:

Civic thought programs should be conservative in the larger sense – devoted to preserving the treasures of Western civilization and other civilizations and transmitting them to the next generation. Such preservation and transmission, it must be emphasized, can only be accomplished by those who have learned to weigh the evidence, seek out and grasp the truth in contending opinions, and craft persuasive arguments. Conservatives should emphasize that civic thought programs are the best means in the present circumstances for restoring a traditional liberal education, one which serves the public interest by forming young men and women capable of exercising their rights effectively and preserving and improving free and democratic institutions.[30]

---

[30] Here Berkowitz, in "Higher Education Reform," is responding to Storey and Storey, "Follow the Left's Example to Reform Higher Ed," *The Wall Street Journal*, January 26, 2024.

This concern does deserve emphasis; but the Storeys and Dyer articulate this same view: That civic thought and leadership is traditional or conservative in an appropriately academic sense and is not an ideological project to indoctrinate a political orthodoxy. Dyer states that while civic thought and leadership "is not a value-free social science, neither is it partisan. If anything, it is pre-partisan." The essential foundation for reasonable views on current policy issues is "knowledge of the character and basis of the political institutions we have inherited and must now steward as Americans" (Dyer, "Embracing Civics"). In their academic proposal for a field of civic thought, the Storeys argue against any orthodoxy about the civic and political questions that form one part of the inquiries: "The practical questions that animate Civic Thought can serve as common points of orientation for many branches of inquiry without subjecting the freedom of research and teaching to a hegemonic intellectual system or an ideological litmus test." Indeed, "scholars of Civic Thought" should "emphasize prudence and persuasion in their modes of presentation," as part of learning from great theorists and practitioners of a free civic life just how to forge common, consensus views amid the pluralism that characterizes a free political order. The study of such great figures can teach "how to persuade people of things those people do not wish to see, yield before the more comprehensive views others may present, and gather diverse human beings for the sake of action." Thus the new colleges, departments, and centers should feature "[s]eminar-style classes that embody the conversational pursuit of truth" and "occasions for rhetorical presentation in which students must strive to master the logical, ethical, and emotional aspects of persuasion" (Storey and Storey, "Civic Thought"). If, in their briefer opinion essay, the Storeys focused on the strategy and tactics of reforming higher education – while referring readers to their full academic argument for restoring liberal arts and American civic education via a new academic field – the larger proposal nonetheless was academic: Intellectual conservatives concerned by intellectual imbalance and the lack of a higher civics should "do what scholars have always done," namely "to create new disciplines" that redress important omissions (Storey and Storey, "Follow the Left's Example"). In the ASU case, it was the very existence of the mandated department on civic thought and leadership that prompted the Regents to consider the new graduation requirement; with the result that all public university students in Arizona have better prospects for encountering liberal arts education and American civic education than prior to the structural intervention by the legislature and governor.

4.3 LEADERSHIP EDUCATION AND THE AMERICAN BALANCE OF THEORY AND PRUDENCE

Two further points of disagreement in this nascent academic discussion deserve consideration. The first concerns the proposal by the Storeys that civic thought and leadership should be a new academic field or discipline; the second concerns the name of such a field, which the Storeys, Berkowitz, and Stoner define as Civic Thought; Dyer defines as Civics or American Civics; and I define as Civic Thought and Leadership (CTL). Regarding a new academic field, Berkowitz responds that these new units of civic thought and leadership should not seek to be a new field or discipline, because "conservatives should reject the left's compartmentalization of the curriculum" via creating "new disciplines" in the social sciences and humanities that are so narrow they almost are fated to become ideological camps teaching a political orthodoxy and activism. Instead, he argues, civic thought "must be grounded in liberal education" broadly conceived, so as to draw upon "the wisdom that is gleaned from, and the toleration and humility that are developed by, study of history, languages, literature, the principles of politics and economics, and the leading opinions about ethics and faith" – and then scholars and students should apply such broad, complex learning to contemporary issues.[31] In reply I will draw upon an insight by Stoner, about the disciplinary and institutional realities of American higher education today, which suggests that a new field of civic thought and leadership instantiated in separate departments and colleges is precisely a strong path at present for restoring a balanced liberal arts education on American campuses. The reality is that the humanities and social sciences disciplines Berkowitz mentions are now strongly tilted against the Socratic, and traditionally civic, learning that civic thought and leadership provide. It seems unlikely that political science and history, to take two leading cases, will restore of themselves a space for a more respectful, while still Socratic or argumentative, stance toward America; and when bothering to address American civics at all, to regularly employ the words American, or constitutional, or republic, rather than simply democracy in the progressive-reforming spirit of John Dewey. The prospect is bleak of anything like a reflective

---

[31] The spirit of this argument resonates with The Cornerstone Integrated Liberal Arts program launched at Purdue University in 2017, which recently has emphasized the civic education dimension of its liberal arts approach, including the launch in 2025 of the Cornerstone Institute for Civic Thought; see www.cla.purdue.edu/academic/cornerstone/index.html.

patriotism finding a home in these disciplines after decades of each pruning back or eliminating that spirit. We also cannot expect these and related fields to restore of themselves space for a friendlier, Tocquevillian stance toward the central place of religion and faith in American civic life, both historical and contemporary.

Stoner explores the conception advanced by the Storeys that civic thought is rooted in the perspective of the citizen and focused on developing the knowledge required to promote healthy public life in a free society, then turns to his own discipline of political science to assess whether it is likely to return to a receptive stance toward such thinking, research, and teaching. Related to the barrier of the social-scientific adherence to the fact-value distinction and the prominence of quantitative methods, he finds political science unlikely to descend from its recent adherence to a rationalist universalism so as to give any attention to, academically speaking, the particular perspective of a citizen in a given polity. Such a view is not now considered academic thinking by this social scientific discipline, but rather as some kind of political, value-laden activity (Stoner, "Civic Thought and Political Science"). Similarly, the new political science has been shifting away from a traditional approach to political philosophy, and reducing support even for the newer analytical and critical-theory (postmodernist) modes of political theory, given the dominance of a behavioralist, fact-driven concept of science. It is no accident that many of the directors, deans, and faculty in the new CTL units are political scientists inclined to traditional political philosophy. Stoner sketches the stark reality that the new rationalist political scientists from one view, and the philosophical political scientists from the other, are talking past each other; but the former clearly dominate the discipline. The launch of a new field thus is a plausible way to keep alive "normative" thinking in academia. For the political philosophers, this is a crucial dimension of real and human thinking:

The political philosophers ... show that describing human or political reality is impossible in amoral [scientific, value-free] terms. Aggression, threat, oppression, prosperity, peace, democracy – all of these are value-laden terms. Yet it is difficult to describe, much less explain, the political world without them; when new-fangled neutral alternatives are proposed, they are either vacuous (e.g., "interactions") or soon take on value valences themselves (e.g., "pluralism"). As these philosophers recognize, political reality invites not only our understanding, but also our judgment. Indeed, our initial judgments often spur our attempts at understanding.

Only a separate institutional space and academic field can plausibly maintain, or recreate, the space for judgment Stoner describes. Indeed, he praises civic thought for restoring a focus on prudence, or practical wisdom. Often without knowing it, Americans in this moment of civic decline and disintegration are regularly complaining about the lack of prudence in elected and appointed officials: The blend of moral principle and practical awareness about plausible ways to do the right thing. The modern research university has no time for such fuzzy ideas grounded in older sources and authorities. The strength of civic thought, Stoner argues, is to promote "an integrated approach to facts and values because it supposes that people act for reasons and are formed by choices – in short, that they are free, not determined – and so it promotes the virtue of prudence or practical wisdom." Political science in its "traditional, prebehaviorist understanding was itself thought to cultivate" prudence. It also once promoted "institutions where citizens deliberate together and choose by consensus or by vote."[32] Civic thought and leadership is the field now advocating, and making space for, such inquiries and teaching; not political science, history, or philosophy. To sustain and spread this renewal, it should adopt the structures of an academic field, to include distinct PhD degree programs either independent of or collaborating with humanities or social science departments. A recent constructive model is the new field of Science, Technology, and Society as an interdisciplinary, integrative, broad-minded remedy for a deficit recognized in academia and society; requiring new degrees and departments, in a new field, including at the PhD level.

These themes lead to the second point of disagreement, whether "leadership" should be included in the headline concept of this new field (for those persuaded this national reform is a field). In the past half-century under the increasing pervasiveness of the research university culture, the social science and humanities disciplines have narrowed the range of worthy topics and now overwhelmingly favor more recent, and more progressive, content and modes of inquiry. To take just political science and history: The study of political philosophy in a more classical and historical mode, and of American constitutionalism and American political development, has shrunk as political science became at once more

---

[32] Lorraine Smith Pangle argues for renewed focus on the virtue of practical wisdom, as part of higher education renewal, in "The Modern Academy and the Ancient Virtue of Phronesis," in *Liberal Education and Citizenship in a Free Society*, eds. Justin Dyer and Constantine Vassiliou (University of Missouri Press, 2023) 11–30. See also in that fine collection the essay by George Thomas addressing similar concerns but recommending the study of American political thought and constitutional law as a focus, "Liberal Education and American Democracy," 327–45.

mathematized or narrowly analytical at one extreme and more critical or postmodernist at the other. The study of political, diplomatic, and military history and of Western civilization has shrunk as history has become more progressive and postmodernist. The space for the study of America shifted toward the quantitative and empirical, and at the opposite pole, more postmodernist and critical with a focus on Western imperialism, colonialism, slavery, and the fights for civil rights and economic equality. Leadership education now largely is the province of business schools and the social-scientific approach in public policy schools and psychology; political science and history rarely research or teach about statesmanship and great political leaders (and great villains). A related benchmark of the intellectual shift and new orthodoxy, also connected to America's current civic disintegration, is evident in the status of studying the American founding, our ideals and constitutionalism, and the founders and subsequent political leaders in our history who rose above leadership to statesmanship. Voices from both center-right and center-left have noted that all such approaches have declined precipitously in these disciplines in recent decades.[33]

The shift in these disciplines is quite deliberate. The Storeys and Dyer in fact refer to the importance of these new departments of civic thought and leadership for preparing American leaders who can understand, appreciate, and perpetuate our constitutional order and civic culture. They propose a broad, interdisciplinary, nonideological study as the best foundation for leadership in a pluralist society and complex system of government and civil society. However, they may not fully appreciate how valuable it is to keep leadership in the headline concept of this new field precisely for maintaining breadth and balance in its research and teaching; particularly a healthy balance between theory and practice. That latter balance is missing from most of the humanities and social sciences today; several (including economics) are dominated by extremes of abstraction and dogmatic theory, but many are marked by extreme theory coupled with the opposite extreme of indoctrination in activism against Western civilization and the American political-economic order. The middle ground of a dynamic balance between theory and practice in the human sciences, each tempering and grounding the other, largely is

---

[33] See Shields and Dunn, *Passing on the Right*; Yascha Mounk, "Renewing Civic Faith," in *The People vs. Democracy: Why Our Freedom Is in Danger & How to Save It* (Harvard University Press, 2018), 237–52; Steven B. Smith, *Reclaiming Patriotism in an Age of Extremes* (Yale University Press, 2021), 188–203; also Will Inboden, "Restoring the Academic Social Contract," National Affairs Number 65, Fall 2025.

gone. One great deficit caused by this recent academic transformation is its entire neglect or disdain of a hallmark of the American political order as founded, namely the moderate disposition toward a mutual balancing of theory or ideals with practice or prudential arrangements; thus, a disposition toward the difficult work of forging compromises. As Yuval Levin helpfully argues, this in fact is the defining spirit and aim of our Constitution as founded. Given a century of declining attention to and regard for the principles guiding its structure, we should not wonder that we are angrily polarized while also failing to elect officials who seek to govern according to their actual constitutional offices.[34]

Civic Thought as proposed by the Storeys emphasizes preparing American citizens for the joint responsibility held by self-governing citizens, thus the intellectual and civic virtues of thoughtful deliberation, civil persuasion, and mutual accommodations. This approach is excellent, but arguably incomplete for understanding America's complex constitutionalism and democratic republic, let alone sustaining them. It overlooks the deliberate emphasis in our constitutionalism on distinct offices calling for leadership and even statesmanship (as opposed to administrative or bureaucratic positions), thus the call for the distinctive role of a leading citizen apart from the fellow-deliberating citizen. For example, they rightly invoke the lessons to be learned from great civic figures who excelled in persuasion about the challenges of self-government, and in advocacy for justice: "The conversations of Socrates and Catherine of Siena and the speeches of Cicero and Frederick Douglass should be analyzed and imitated as models of how to seek truth in common with others" (Storey and Storey, "Civic Thought," 8).[35] Yet most of these figures never held high executive office, as, say, a consul or president, governor, or general. Yes, Socrates was a soldier, Catherine a diplomat, Douglass a great civic leader and eventually a diplomat, and Cicero briefly was a consul and proconsul, while his predominant service was as a senator and magistrate.

The study of deliberative excellence by fellow citizens, legislators, or diplomats is crucial, but should be balanced by the full CTL study of

---

[34] Yuval Levin, *American Covenant: How the Constitution Unified Our Nation – And Could Again* (Basic Books, 2024); see the similar argument in Dennis Hale and Marc Landy, *Keeping the Republic: A Defense of American Constitutionalism* (University Press of Kansas, 2024).

[35] Bryan Garsten's *Saving Persuasion: A Defense of Rhetoric and Judgment* (Harvard University Press, 2009) renews the case for artful persuasion from classical political philosophy, discussing its modern critics and defenders, with an eye to restoring a healthier civic life and citizenship.

great executives and the founders of institutions, their deeds as well as writings and speeches. From Thucydides and Plutarch, through Aquinas on kingship, on to the speeches and deeds of Washington, Lincoln, and Franklin Roosevelt – and arguably also the great opinions of a Chief Justice Marshall, and Hamilton's essays in *The Federalist* on the single executive and the judiciary – such study of leadership, statesmanship, and statecraft is both enriching and a healthful complement to studying civic thought and the deliberative duties of citizenship. The senior US diplomat turned Yale professor of humanities Charles Hill, in recovering the tradition of grand strategy and statecraft, anticipated the case for CTL by arguing that theory and hoped-for ideal circumstances must be grounded in the realities, constraints, and demands of high office with its burdens of decision-making amid inadequate information and limited time.[36] Further, as America has descended into democratic self-worship, and the focus on democracy has yielded a deepening descent into populism and polarization of ever more extreme degrees, it is a tonic to recall the warnings against democratic excess – and the concomitant defense of republicanism, discrete constitutional offices, and complex constitutional forms in balance with consent of the governed – offered by great minds and statesmen, from Thucydides to Montesquieu and leading American founders. The dynamic balance between the study of civic thought and of leadership is in these important dimensions enriching and tempering. In the spirit of genuine liberal arts education, this CTL balance also more effectively prevents descent into ideological orthodoxy and indoctrination toward activism.

Given the call by the Storeys to prepare citizens for judging leaders and office holders, the proper study of leadership, statesmanship, and statecraft also is necessary for understanding the capacities needed to fulfill the duties of particular constitutional offices, including the most exposed and demanding of them. Further, such education in statesmanship shapes the more ambitious souls that might seek these offices toward devotion to serve the constitutional order, and the consent of the governed, above their own desires or designs. Washington and Lincoln used to be celebrated in American civics and civic ritual in part for the character each forged to turn their immense ambition for greatness toward serving our republic. Thus another sage source for this CTL nexus of liberal arts and leadership education, in addition to Hill's *Grand Strategies*, is Timothy Fuller's

---

[36] Charles Hill, *Grand Strategies: Literature, Statecraft, and World Order* (Yale University Press, 2010).

collection *Leading and Leadership* which ranges from Cicero and Plutarch on statesmanship to the greatness of Washington, Lincoln, and King.[37]

A final pertinent resource is the Founding Mission Statement of the first CTL unit, the School of Civic and Economic Thought and Leadership at ASU. It was drafted in 2016 by Harvard's Harvey C. Mansfield, one of the senior scholars from Harvard, Notre Dame, and Stanford that ASU leaders formed into an advisory board for launching the school. The Statement embraces the dynamic balance between the study of theory and of practice. Mansfield was a good match for articulating the coherence of the topics in the school's name because, as a political philosophy scholar, his books and translations have focused on philosophers who also were statesmen – Machiavelli, Burke, Montesquieu, and Tocqueville. His work also features appreciation for America's founders, our founding political science, and the view that America has a constitutional soul.[38] The Mission Statement opens with the need in American higher education to redress "an atmosphere of a certain conformity of opinion" and "an obvious lack of debate." It then posts a warning against a counter-ideological project: "the solution is not to bring in more politics and greater contention from outside, thus disturbing the peace necessary in a university for study and scholarly inquiry."[39] The school will embrace the dynamic balance between the liberal arts spirit of civic thought and attention to American civic duties and constitutionalism implicated by "Civic" and "Leadership" in its name. Its fundamental ambition is "to introduce a new level of debate over the large questions of life that always arise." These include the best forms of politics and government, of economics, and of individual life, as well as questions about the character of knowledge itself and of moral choice. After indicating that the questions are as important as the many proposed answers, SCETL is pledged to "approach them in two ways."

The first, which Mansfield addresses in a separate paragraph, could be called classical liberal education: "to look beyond the time and borders of our present society to the great thinkers who have contended for the high status of teachers of humanity." The kinds of "poets" and "philosophers" studied are indicated by citing "Homer, Dante and Shakespeare" then "Plato, Marx and Nietzsche." Given Mansfield's scholarship on

---

[37] Timothy Fuller, ed. *Leading and Leadership* (University of Notre Dame Press, 2010). Below I note the salience of studying Lincoln's statesmanship in particular, and recent studies in this vein.

[38] Harvey C. Mansfield, *America's Constitutional Soul* (Johns Hopkins University Press, 1991).

[39] SCETL Founding Mission Statement (2016), at www.scetl.asu.edu/mission-statement.

Democracy in America, one inspiration for recommending to a modern democratic republic the study of texts from premodern minds or moderns antithetical to liberal democracy may have been Tocqueville's chapter on "Why the Study of Greek and Latin Literature is Particularly Useful in Democratic Societies." The classical poets and philosophers seek ideals of the beautiful and noble not typically addressed by modern democratic minds, and exposure to such diversity is a salutary influence on American thinking, mores, and politics. Tocqueville's defense of space for classical study in at least a few colleges could be applied to the liberal arts foundation for American civics more generally; it has "special qualities that can serve marvelously to counterbalance our particular defects. They prop us up on the side where we lean."[40]

The SCETL Mission Statement then devotes twice as many words to the second approach, which could be called civics and leadership, starting with this paragraph:

The other way of studying the fundamental questions is to look within ourselves to the American leaders, both intellectual and political, who have inspired us. Here we turn from the human task of thinking for oneself to the civic vocation of contributing to our common life. As citizens our students face the responsibilities of the nation and the world that will be theirs when their time to lead arrives. We need to know what principles and institutions have made us Americans and whether they need to be reformed or reasserted.

The statement turns, in its penultimate and longest paragraph, to what could be called a higher civics, highlighting American political leadership. Study of America's founding, one defined by ideals and principles, leads to reference of the current emphasis on democracy – but framed, it seems, to question it: "Ours is the most thorough and enduring democratic society in history, and yet we debate its faults." The School's studies should ensure that criticisms are adequately grounded: "We need to see how the ideas of the Founding Fathers were both invoked and reformed through the succession of leaders after them: by Thomas Jefferson, Abraham Lincoln, Woodrow Wilson, Theodore and Franklin Roosevelt, Martin Luther King and Ronald Reagan – and let's not forget Mercy Warren, Abigail Adams, Edith Wharton and Betty Friedan." (This quietly invokes Abigail's March 1776 letter to John Adams, that in debating independence and a new polity, the Continental Congress should "Remember the Ladies.") The

---

[40] Alexis de Tocqueville, *Democracy in America,* ed. and tr. Harvey Mansfield and Delba Winthrop (University of Chicago Press, 2000), Volume Two, Part One, Chapter 14, 450–52.

guidance on civics and leadership concludes by further noting the distinctiveness and the higher, reflective patriotism of such study: "Nor can we fail to mention the two greatest books on America – *The Federalist* and Alexis de Tocqueville's *Democracy in America*." The brief final paragraph begins by noting the scope and ambition of the new endeavor: "In sum, our new school looks outward to humanity and inward to America." That striking summation should not displace, however, Mansfield's striking guidance for the study of America not as a democracy but as a constitutional republic with democratic features, and with great founders and leaders. Our republic's great founding of a substantially new political science, constitutionalism, and political culture drew the admiration of a philosopher-statesman like Tocqueville. All of this is a higher-level civics of civic thought and leadership.

This CTL approach is entirely heterodox amid the social sciences and humanities disciplines and fields today, which predominantly are indifferent or hostile to the American experiment. Stoner notes that political science departments today "typically still count American government as a subfield ... but as social scientists, the faculty feel a bit guilty about this. From a scientific perspective, they wonder why the study of American politics is not just one option among many in comparative politics," a distinct subfield in the discipline. A survey of leading PhD-degree-granting political science departments would reveal that several have no tenured faculty teaching and writing about the presidency and Congress as constitutional institutions, or about constitutional law (as distinct from behavioralist studies of judges); let alone the dearth of political philosophy scholars beyond very modern, democratic, narrowly analytical, or postmodernist theory. Civic thought and leadership restores the space in such an academic landscape for arguing that America's ideals, constitutionalism, founders, and great statesmen and stateswomen deserve serious inquiry and debate – including major reform movements and critiques – but from a premise of respectful regard. A signature element of SCETL's heterodoxy, Mansfield implies, is appreciation for founders, leaders, and statesmanship of both thought and action.

4.4 AMERICA CIVICS AND RENEWED PLURALISM IN CAMPUS DISCOURSE

Academic leaders and faculty have launched initiatives on civil discourse, free speech, and free inquiry in recent years as a response to concerns about ideological imbalance, as well as to negative media attention over speaker events cancelled or disrupted by student or faculty protests finding a speaker's views harmful (overwhelmingly, in the past decade and more, centrist and conservative speakers) – and generally to declining public confidence in academia. The Institute of Citizens & Scholars recently launched College Presidents for Civic Preparedness, now with over 100 college and university presidents, public and private, pledged to preparing students for "active civic engagement" by ensuring their campuses are open to diverse viewpoints, free inquiry, and free expression.[41] There are many other specific initiatives on particular campuses supporting free speech and robust discourse, and all of this is an improvement. Yet the Presidents for Preparedness effort captures the limits of this kind of response, given that the emphasis still is democracy education, engagement, participation, and civic skills; not foundational American civic knowledge about our constitutional democratic republic, and the civic virtues needed to operate and sustain it; certainly not in new coursework and indeed graduation requirements meeting this deficit. An exception is the University of Chicago Forum for Free Inquiry & Expression, since this institutionalizes a longstanding priority of the University, and the Forum's faculty leaders have edited a collection of important texts on this theme.[42]

SCETL at ASU emphasized free speech, intellectual diversity, and free inquiry from our first year, including by establishing The Civic Discourse Project as a public speakers program. We partnered with Arizona PBS to ensure that rebroadcasts of the lecture and dialogue events, along with a video archive, would reach a wider audience. The Project's aim was to host academic and public-intellectual speakers holding a range of views on academic, political, and civic topics; often with dialogue events to feature diversity of views in a single event as well as across the series.[43]

Yet any speaker series or engagement-initiative on civic discourse is not likely to last, or reform the academic culture of a campus let alone of higher education, by itself. These efforts do not address the core reality and mission of a college or university: courses, tenured faculty, degrees, and general education requirements; and along with faculty come research priorities. Again, these civic initiatives are an improvement. It is valuable to have dialogue events with speakers like Cornel West and Robert

---

[41] See Institute for Citizen & Scholars at www.citizensandscholars.org/ and Presidents for Civic Preparedness at www.collegepresidents.org/.

[42] The Forum's website is www.thechicagoforum.uchicago.edu/.

[43] The main page for the Civic Discourse Project is www.scetl.asu.edu/civic-discourse-project.

George modeling constructive, reasonable disagreement in the shared pursuit of truth. Students benefit from participating in Braver Angels and Bridge USA programs offering structured spaces for practicing civil disagreement – indeed, all the better with the American Council of Trustees and Alumni (ACTA) having pulled together these two programs with ACTA to form the College Debates and Discourse Alliance (SCETL has worked with all three). It is important that some colleges and universities now include free speech and civil discourse themes in first-year orientation programs.[44] What is further needed is required coursework providing the foundations in civic knowledge about the what, why, origins, and how of the First Amendment protections of religious liberty, freedom of speech and press, peaceable assembly, and petitioning government. Doing more democracy studies, and engagement, will not address our civic and civics crises because we've now spent down our constitutional-cultural capital to the point that more democracy thinking, more advocacy for engagement, won't remedy our crisis and may exacerbate it.

Students need to study, in required courses, recent works like Jonathan Rauch's *The Constitution of Knowledge: A Defense of Truth* which grounds the case for free speech, open inquiry, and civil discourse in our constitutional order and the Enlightenment.[45] They should study Lincoln's entire career as a model of discourse, debate, and civil disagreement in pursuit of truths about America but also statesmanlike judgments and compromises about how to do the least evil, and the most possible good, while sustaining the long game for defeating slavery. Recent works by political theorist Michael Zuckert, and historians Allen Guelzo and Doris Kearns Goodwin, offer lessons on the theory and practice, the civic thought and leadership, of the great rhetorician, statesman, and president.[46]

---

[44] For ACTA and College Debates, see www.goacta.org/initiatives/college-debates/; Purdue University pioneered in 2016 a featured place for free speech in its orientation program, and the Foundation for Individual Rights and Expression (FIRE) has developed materials for orientation programs – see www.thefire.org/news/free-speech-orientation-program-keeps-conversation-going-purdue and www.thefire.org/research-learn/free-speech-freshman-orientation.

[45] Brookings Institution Press, 2021.

[46] Goodwin, *Team of Rivals: The Political Genius of Abraham Lincoln* (Simon & Schuster, 2005); Zuckert, *A Nation So Conceived: Abraham Lincoln and the Paradox of Democratic Sovereignty* (University Press of Kansas, 2022); Guelzo, *Our Ancient Faith: Lincoln, Democracy, and the American Experiment* (Vintage Press, 2025). I discuss in Chapter 3 Lincoln's reflective patriotism and statesmanship, citing scholarship by Steven Kautz and Diana Schaub; see also Chapter 6 on Lincoln's higher call to America.

The SCETL Founding Mission Statement defends a new space in the American academy for study and debate that can improve both the theoretical inquiries about larger civic truths of self-government and the particular, civic study of our American way of life, politics, and leadership – by strongly integrating the two. Academia and our broader elite culture need to shift toward more respectful study of American ideals and constitutionalism, both as a matter of restoring a central focus on the university's truth-seeking mission and to confront what universities owe to the American constitutional democracy that provides them so much prestige, security, and prosperity. I have noted a few leaders like Derek Bok, Ronald Daniels, and Danielle Allen who, since 2020 – and largely independent of the nascent movement for civic thought and leadership – have argued for similar reforms to higher education amid our country's continuing civic disintegration. It is also worth noting the even earlier contribution by scholar and public intellectual Yascha Mounk. Unlike the scholars discussed previously, who specifically analyze the new CTL field and are intellectual conservatives, Mounk is not a conservative, and his insights on academia's failure in civic education predate any real national awareness of civic thought and leadership. That said, he may have benefited from Mansfield's heterodox presence during his doctoral studies in government at Harvard.

Mounk's 2018 *The People vs. Democracy* argues that one cause of America's descent into an anti-democratic populism that could elect a Donald Trump is the precipitous decline of civics, from schools through universities. He reports being struck by the absence, during his Harvard training, of any encouragement to use political science for teaching students to become thoughtful citizens, or addressing concerns of the broader citizenry (*People vs. Democracy*, 244–52). He laments the loss of any commitment in the academy to "raising citizens," to imparting civic knowledge and a sense of "civic duty." He describes a healthier American political life from the time of Washington's call for Congress to establish a national university for civic education of "the future guardians of the liberties of the country" until well into the Cold War era, and laments: "Civics was an integral part of the educational system, from nurseries all across the country to the faculty lounges of the nation's leading universities. As a result, most citizens had a better understanding of the practices and a deeper commitment to the principles of liberal democracy, making them far less likely to give credence to conspiracy theories based on lies or disinformation." From Horace Mann's rationale for public schools as preparing intelligent citizens for "a republican form of government" to the Supreme Court's affirmation in the 1986 case *Bethel v. Fraser* that public schools "must prepare pupils for citizenship in the Republic," Mounk charts a contrast to the recent social science and humanities disciplines, and schools of education, which emphasize America's failings. Higher education thus mostly ignores civics or "turn[s] civics into an anti-civic enterprise." He calls for restoration of "the mission the Founding Fathers gave to anybody who occupies the high office of citizen" to uphold our institutions and political culture, which today requires an effort "to rebuild a country in which writers aim to spread the values of liberal democracy; civics stands at the core of the curriculum; [and] teachers at all levels spare no effort to impart a deep understanding of the Constitution and its intellectual moorings to their students."[47]

America and our system of higher education face grave deficits, but such voices from center-left to center-right in the past decade offer some hope. Brooke Manville and Josiah Ober conclude *The Civic Bargain* with a call to renew American civic education, focused on civic knowledge, and civic virtues including patriotism. They articulate the reform Ober is undertaking as founder of the Stanford Civics Initiative, which renewed at Stanford a course on citizenship now required for most first-year students.[48] Hopefully similar voices and efforts will be swelled by the commemorations of America 250, marking in 2026 the semiquincentennial anniversary of the Declaration of Independence in 1776. Educational efforts via commemorations ought to continue for two decades, at least through marking the ratification of the Bill of Rights in 1791, thus 2041. Given the desperate deficit of understanding statesmanship and statecraft in academia and our civic culture generally, the full effort would require study and commemoration of Washington's 1796 Farewell Address for

---

[47] Mounk might be happy to know that the current chair of the Government Department at Harvard, Daniel Carpenter, offers a course, "What Is A Republic?" which fulfills a general studies category of "Ethics and Civics," and given its scope of studying classical, medieval, and modern thought and practice to include the American founding, meets the concerns quoted here; its recent quadrupling of enrollment was a newsworthy event at Harvard – Christy DeSmith, "Government professor looks at long history, evolution of form of governance in class that's drawing high interest in current moment," *The Harvard Gazette*, March 4, 2025.

[48] Manville and Ober, *The Civic Bargain: How Democracy Survives* (Princeton University Press, 2023), 227–46; I noted above in the Introduction the hopeful reforms embodied in the Stanford Civics Initiative (www.civics.stanford.edu) and the new national association, the Alliance for Civics in the Academy, also launched by Ober (www.hoover.org/research-teams/alliance-civics-academy).

its guidance about both domestic affairs and rediscovering a plausible American grand strategy – thus taking A250 to 2046. Educators at all levels now must ask whether we are part of the problem of America's civic coarsening and decline, and whether we should question recent academic norms predominantly skeptical of patriotism and of America, thus emphasizing democracy and civic engagement over American constitutional civic knowledge. Private as well as public universities and colleges should consider the practical model that now exists for renewing a higher civics more conducive to American civic strength and health. It also is significant that three "public Ivies," UNC Chapel Hill, UT Austin, and Ohio State University have joined this national reform movement to establish civic thought and leadership, and that Yale has just established the Center for Civic Thought.[49]

Indeed, the reform at Stanford, the new graduation requirement at Johns Hopkins for a course in the category of "Democracy and Civics," and the new Yale Center for Civic Thought show that elite private universities can get the message. Before the second Trump administration began its pressure campaign, several Ivy League professors in 2023 and 2024 called publicly for restoration of civic education, truth-seeking, and healthy heterodoxy. Thousands of Penn faculty and other academics supported the "Penn Forward" statement, which includes reviving traditional liberal arts and civic education in the context of calling for a return to the university's core truth-seeking mission; and Penn's Jonathan Zimmerman, a historian of American education, has voiced such concerns for years.[50] A "Faculty for Yale" statement called for similar reforms, and its website lists what it considers analogous faculty statements and efforts at Harvard, Columbia, Princeton, Dartmouth, and the University of Chicago, as well as Penn.[51] After the resignation of Harvard president Claudine Gay, in part as fallout from the anti-Israel protests on campus, Mansfield urged his Harvard colleagues and other academics to take steps toward recovering the core missions of a university.[52] Since

---

[49] Lisa Prevost, "Yale launches Center for Civic Thought to Promote Thoughtful Discourse," *Yale News*, May 27, 2025; the website is www.civicthought.yale.edu/.

[50] Penn Forward: A Vision for a New Future of the University of Pennsylvania, December 2023, at www.pennforward.com/; Jonathan Zimmerman, "College's Purpose Is to Create Citizens, Not to Be a Job Placement Service," *Chicago Tribune*, February 16, 2023; "The Real Problem at Harvard," *The Philadelphia Inquirer*, January 4, 2024; and "Elite Universities, We Have A Problem," *The Hill*, March 20, 2025.

[51] Faculty for Yale, December 2023, at www.facultyforyale.yale.edu/homepage

[52] Harvey C. Mansfield, "Who's Holding Up the Ivory Tower?," *Wall Street Journal*, January 11, 2024.

early 2023 he has not been so lonely in articulating such reforms, after the establishment of the Council on Academic Freedom at Harvard, of which he was a founding member; among other institutions, Princeton, Columbia, and MIT also have established such a council.[53]

The leaders of the Ivies, private and public, and of other elite universities, should consider establishing departments, colleges, or centers of civic thought and leadership, making institutional space for students, faculty, alums, trustees, donors, and community members to participate in the restoration of the excellent education and research – and the cultivation of intellectual and civic virtues – that both higher education and American civic culture so deeply need.

---

[53] The Harvard Council's website is www.sites.harvard.edu/cafh/.

5

How Should Civic Culture Sustain America's *E Pluribus Unum*?

Alexis de Tocqueville broadens civic education by praising a distinctive American mode of it: Citizens learning to be free by practicing the arts of freedom, beyond schools. *Democracy in America* names political and civil associations as a crucial "school" for learning to be self-governing citizens.[1] The larger lesson is that a democratic republic needs a civic culture which teaches reflective patriotism and committed citizenship. This is especially so in our era of angry polarization, civic apathy, and a fraying civic order – even if partly caused, and aggravated, by the demotion of civics in academia and then in K-12 schools. Tocqueville's separate observations on how we show a considered patriotism reinforce the endorsement of learning through culture, thus the mutual reinforcement of culture and formal schooling. As discussed in Chapter 2, he notes that formal instruction is just one of the several important elements in forming patriotic citizens. The American civic culture and mores, especially Christianity and its prizing of participation in self-government, inform the very approach to schooling itself. As discussed in Chapters 1 and 3 as well, *Democracy in America* commends our enlightened civic culture that on the one hand informed, and on the other completed and elevated, formal instruction, helping to produce

---

[1] "Town-meetings are to liberty what primary schools are to science," Alexis de Tocqueville, *Democracy in America*, ed. and tr. Harvey Mansfield and Delba Winthrop (University of Chicago Press, 2000), Vol. I, Part 1, Ch. 5, subsection on the American system of townships and municipal bodies, 57; see also Vol. II, Part 2, Ch. 7, on the connection of civil and political associations: "Political associations may therefore be considered as large free schools, where all the members of the community go to learn the general theory of association," 497.

self-governing citizens who pursue happiness above and beyond politics as well as through politics.[2]

At our 250th year as a polity – four hundred years after what Tocqueville considered our initial founding in the political culture of the Puritans – America's civic strength and health face deep challenges. I have noted in the Introduction and Chapter 1 the facts of our angry polarization and civic apathy, the declining confidence in all national institutions and professions, and the shrinking attachment of younger generations to the idea of America – that is, to being self-governing citizens of our democratic republic. Renewal of civic education in schools and college needs the nurturing of a healthy civic culture. In turn, our civic culture itself would benefit from deploying its considerable capacities and resources to renewing the importance of the civic virtues, and rallying to promote civic strength.

Perhaps one way to encourage such a civic renewal is to strike a balance between sober reckoning and a hopeful confidence that we can dig out of our problems. A quintessentially American expression of that blend and balance is the blues and its later expression in jazz; the folk music turned art form that confronts the reality of how bad things are, yet bolsters our spirits to resist despair. Jazz forges European, African, and Atlantic-American musical traditions, and multiple races. It blends liberty and improvisation with order, sorrow with joy, the quotidian with longing for beauty and the divine. It is an American *e pluribus unum*. We should consult it as a tonic, resource, and achievement of which we all should be proud – thereby overcoming our angry division, and also the alienation, anomie, and individualism exacerbated by digital technologies and habits. These social conditions pull some Americans toward demonizing America, or the opposing party or factions; while they pull others into detachment and civic apathy, leaving no self-conception of being self-governing citizens. In either extreme – activity that is not constructive, or individualism – too many Americans are pulled away from the core of a healthy, strong civic culture and polity. Could we learn from the achievement of jazz, its blend of sobriety and enjoyment, of striving and hope, to work our way out of this civic crisis?

Yet even so, to understand jazz requires appreciation for the spirit of religious pluralism and liberty that is one of its origins and elements.

---

[2] John Stuart Mill in *On Liberty* (1959) emphasizes especially in Ch. 2, "Of the Liberty of Thought and Discussion," that laws protecting freedom of speech will not be fully implemented and realized unless a culture and society prioritizes and defends such freedom. Lindsey Cormack explains how parents and families must contribute in *How to Raise a Citizen (And Why It's Up to You to Do It)* (Jossey Bass/Wiley, 2024).

Lincoln draws on America's deep tradition of religious belief, including pluralism among differing and contending theologies, when calling in the Gettysburg Address to make, under God, a new birth of freedom. He deepens that effort in the political sermon of the Second Inaugural, urging acceptance of universal American guilt for slavery and war as the ground for Biblical mercy and charity, with these in turn necessary for rebuilding justice in our nation and peace with all nations. Still further, we need to appreciate that these forged harmonies of jazz and religious liberty in turn reflect the basic political principles, culture, and institutions of American liberty and equality. Our constitutionalism grew up in partnership with an evolving tradition of religious liberty; and the two together permitted and even encouraged the forging of jazz from various cultural sources. It is a hopeful lesson to consider jazz as arising from a unique American politics that reflects and reinforces the American tradition of religious liberty, yet also gives space for an art form that has proven the potential of our universal, color-blind principles of liberty for all and pursuit of happiness for all.

Our formal studies in schools and colleges, and our activities in civil society and civic culture, need to recover Tocqueville's broader approach: That our success in establishing a new kind of republic owes as much to our moral principles and culture as to institutions and laws. To be sure, the right institutions and laws are crucial; but they are neither self-producing nor self-sustaining. He thus reiterates that the spiritual and civic culture which infuses, informs, and guides American political institutions is the most important element of the polity's health and success (see *Democracy in America*, I.2.9, subsection "That the Laws Serve to Maintain a Democratic Republic in the United States More than Physical Causes, and Mores More than Laws"). His comprehensive approach develops Montesquieu's emphasis on the spirit and mores behind any laws, and moving through them; and we now tend to overlook that Montesquieu was the single most influential European philosopher shaping American thought from 1760 to 1800, across our founding era.[3] Thus it is no surprise that Tocqueville's warnings about challenges or vulnerabilities facing our culture and institutions also emphasize this power of mores and culture. Would we resolve the great failing of our treatment of native peoples and slaves, transcending the age-old human failings of racism – by

---

[3] See James W. Ceaser, "Alexis de Tocqueville and the Two-Founding Thesis," *The Review of Politics* 73:2 (Spring 2011), 219–43. I discuss these issues in "Tocqueville's Deepening of Modern Moderation," Ch. 3 in *Democracy in Moderation: Montesquieu, Tocqueville, and Sustainable Liberalism* (Cambridge University Press, 2016).

tempering our power and dominance with justice, thus living up to both our Christian spirit and our declared principles of justice? Would we temper our egalitarian, democratic demand for equal prosperity – and our fascination with the power yielded by science and rationalism to achieve economic improvement – with higher principles of religious belief, or, succumb to materialism? Would we sustain a strong civic culture of self-government, of mutual service in civil society and voluntary associations, as well as service in political roles and offices beyond merely voting – or succumb to the self-isolating pull of prizing individual interest and concerns, the hollowed-out life Tocqueville dubs individualism?[4]

To confront and reverse today's civic decline we could use a dose of sober hope. We should rediscover some American successes in forging an *e pluribus unum* despite deep social or political divisions. These are not myths. We have done this before, and could renew this spirit. I turn first to consider jazz and its lessons, then close the chapter by briefly invoking our successes in forging a complex constitutional order of pluralism, and also a pluralistic religious liberty. This is to move, admittedly, in reverse-historical order; jazz is a product of an American constitutional culture and a religious culture which provided space to blend liberty and equality – and more broadly to blend bedrock natural rights with pluralism, and materialist striving with higher pursuits of happiness. Our current predicament suggests we should begin with the more accessible, hopeful story of jazz since this might be more helpful in pulling out of our downward spiral of cultural-political conflict and civic apathy. Retired Supreme Court Justice Sandra Day O'Connor and the jazz musician and educator Wynton Marsalis, in their 2009 recorded discussions about jazz and American democracy, provide an opening to connect these topics.

5.1 *E PLURIBUS UNUM* AND CIVIC HOPE: JAZZ, CONSTITUTIONALISM, AND RELIGIOUS LIBERTY

The great political scientist Samuel P. Huntington commented on the sober America brand of hope when exploring the tensions between our clear, inspiring ideals and the complexity of our political institutions: "Critics say that America is a lie because its reality falls so far short of its

---

[4] These are among the questions posed in the longest chapter in *Democracy*, I.2.10 on the three races in America; see also II.2.1 on democratic peoples showing a greater love for equality than freedom, and II.4 Ch. 6–8 on the new mode of soft despotism democracy may bring.

ideals. They are wrong. America is not a lie; it is a disappointment. But
it can be a disappointment only because it is also a hope."[5] Of the civic
exemplars discussed in Chapters 1 and 3, perhaps Frederick Douglass in
his July 5, 1852, address best captures this spirit of distress contending
with hope; although the final five years of Martin Luther King's life, after
his 1963 "I Have a Dream" address, included strong expressions of disappointment in America without ever losing confidence in our founding
principles. Langston Hughes, a poet of the Harlem Renaissance when
New York was becoming a center of jazz as an art form in the 1920s,
captures this complex harmony in his 1926 poem *I, Too* – offering that
"I, too sing America" even though as "the darker brother" they now
"send me to eat in the kitchen/When company comes." Yet America provides the conditions for overcoming bigotry and achieving equality:

> But I laugh,
> And eat well,
> And grow strong.
>
> Tomorrow,
> I'll be at the table
> When company comes.
> Nobody'll dare
> Say to me,
> "Eat in the kitchen,"
> Then.
>
> Besides,
> They'll see how beautiful I am
> And be ashamed –
>
> I, too, am America.[6]

A decade later amid the hardships of the Great Depression, Hughes
mixed in more discontent in the poem *Let America Be America Again*;
yet hope remained. As Louis P. Masur notes, Hughes and Martin Luther
King, Jr., were friends. There is resonance between King's account of the
American dream in his 1963 oration and the invocations by Hughes in
1936 of the American dream as a demand, and disappointment, for so
many excluded from opportunity. Hughes urgently calls to the powerful

---

[5] Huntington, "American Ideals versus American Institutions," *Political Science Quarterly*,
97:1 (Spring, 1982), 1–37; drawing on Huntington, *American Politics: The Promise of
Disharmony* (Harvard University Press, 1981).

[6] "I, Too" (1926) in *The Collected Poems of Langston Hughes* (Knopf and Vintage Books,
1994).

and successful, including across racial barriers: We "[m]ust bring back our mighty dream again."[7] To pull up and out of today's angry polarization as well as civic apathy, it would be helpful to learn about our history of forging an *e pluribus unum* that more closely approximates the principle in the Pledge of Allegiance invoked by King in 1963 – of "liberty and justice for all." My own hunch, shared with my coauthors of the national study *Educating for American Democracy* discussed in Chapter 3, is that a fair-minded, discursive accounting of America's full history induces a sober hope about America, as part of a reflective patriotism.

Jazz, and our constitutionalism, and our achievement of religious liberty all are hard-won harmonies. Each has plenty of blue notes along the way, and these still are sounding; yet the harmonizing, the coordinated energy, the movement toward justice embodied in each can teach us about letting America be America again. We can see the reflectively hopeful, patriotic view of our polity in Louis Armstrong and Edward "Duke" Ellington as they forge jazz during the twentieth century; then its affirmation by Justice O'Connor and jazzman Marsalis in the twenty-first. We can see Lincoln in the nineteenth century discern the need to supplement his rational faith in the Declaration and Constitution with a Biblical faith that is pluralist, supporting liberty and equality; then King's invocation and affirmation of this sober hope in the twentieth century.

5.1.1 American Story and Song, Especially Jazz

Perhaps the most famous rendition of the patriotic hymn *America the Beautiful* was recorded in 1972 by pianist and singer Ray Charles, using the blend of gospel music, blues, rhythm & blues, and jazz he had forged – often termed soul music. One hallmark of his version is its opening with the third verse in the Katharine Lee Bates poem of 1911, giving thanks for the Union soldiers who died in the Civil War. Bates echoes the eulogy in Lincoln's Gettysburg Address for "the brave men ... who struggled here" and who already "have consecrated" the battlefield "far above our poor power to add or detract." Brother Ray (as he entitled his 1978 autobiography) powerfully emphasizes such a eulogy by placing this verse ahead of the widely remembered first verse beginning "O beautiful for spacious skies/for amber waves of grain." He pulls together the spirit

---

[7] Louis P. Masur, "Tuning Up: Let America Be America Again," *The American Scholar* (Phi Beta Kappa), September 8, 2020; "Let America Be America Again" (1936) in *The Collected Poems of Langston Hughes*.

of religion and spirit of jazz to celebrate America, first through gratitude for those who secured the freedom we enjoy. Lincoln and Bates harmonized Biblical religion and a political philosophy of liberty and equality to define and celebrate America. A century later Charles, a black American from Georgia and descendent of slaves, insisted we first give thanks to the mostly white soldiers moved by "mercy" to fight and die to free black people from slavery.

> O beautiful for heroes proved
> In liberating strife,
> Who more than self their country loved
> And mercy more than life!
> America! America!
> May God thy gold refine,
> Till all success be nobleness,
> And every gain divine![8]

Ray opens in military-patriotic mode with a single snare drum, soon joined by trumpets and brass in muted fanfare, before unleashing his gospel-blues-jazz organ playing and singing – the latter featuring syncopated voicings, swoops, and improvisations. He next offers only the first verse, with its gratitude for our landscape and prayer that God will "shed His grace" on America to "crown thy good with brotherhood/From sea to shining sea!" He omits the second verse on conquering the continent and the fourth on a patriot's dream of America's future. This editing emphasizes the opening eulogy on sacrifice – and its call to govern material gain with moral aims and Christian principle – by pairing it with the version most of us know from "when I was in school" (as Ray improvises between his first and second verses). The spirit of jazz moves Ray to add other vocal improvisations (along with the instrumental ones): Declaring his own love for America, that "my God he done shed his Grace on thee," and how we ought to be thankful to God for doing so – with Ray modeling this last point in exultant shouts. The blend of gratitude, humility, exuberance, and piety was so powerful and popular that it led to Charles performing this version for the final three decades of his life

---

[8] See Benjamin Railton, *Of Thee I Sing: The Contested History of American Patriotism* (Rowman & Littlefield, 2021), xv; Dwandalyn Reece, "Brother Ray's Message to the People," The Smithsonian Institution, February 2016, at www.music.si.edu/story/brother-ray%E2%80%99s-message-people; and Jack Doyle, "Ray Charles Sings America," *The Pop History Dig* website, at www.pophistorydig.com/topics/ray-charles-sings-america/ (November 2011, last updated July 2020). The official audio recording from the Charles estate is at www.youtube.com/watch?v=2FXN1Z6Qoo4.

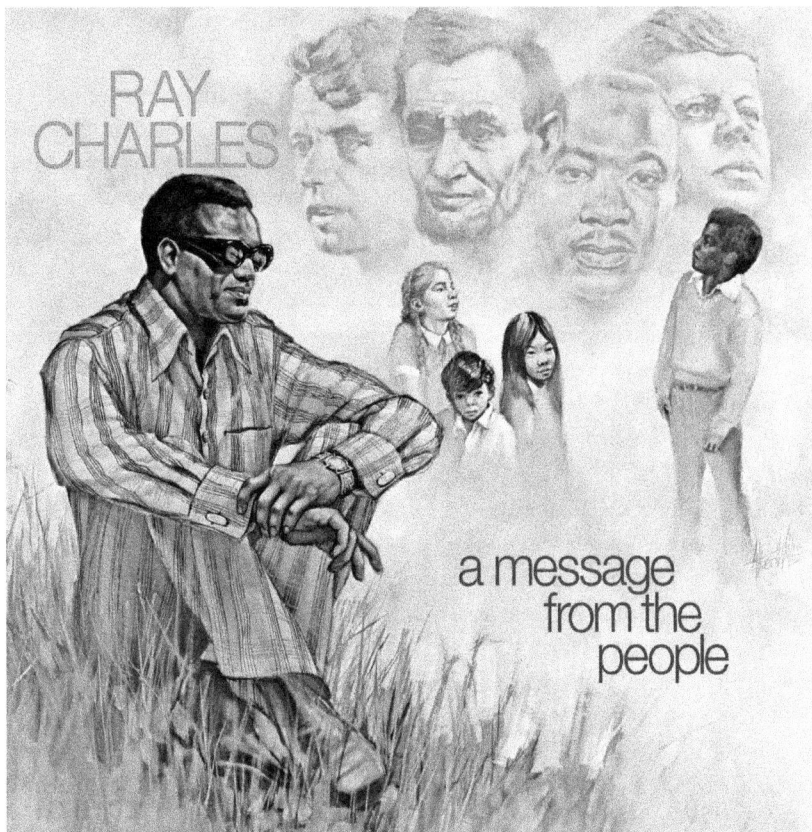

FIGURE 5.1 The cover to the 1972 Ray Charles album *A Message from the People*

(he died in 2004) – including at the White House, a 1984 presidential nominating convention, and the World Series.

The album on which Ray released *America* was entitled "A Message from the People." It contains notes of discontent, including the 1968 song for four martyrs of social change, *Abraham, Martin, and John*. The cover art (see Figure 5.1) features the four assassinated leaders in a Mount Rushmore configuration – Lincoln, John F. Kennedy, King, and Robert Kennedy – along with four boys and girls of different races, and Ray in a pensive pose.[9]

---

[9] The producer of the 1972 album was the jazz musician, arranger, and composer Quincy Jones – who a decade later produced some of pop performer Michael Jackson's biggest hits. Jones began his career in the 1950s with vibraphonist Lionel Hampton, who had played with the swing bandleader Benny Goodman; Jones also was a composer and arranger in the 1960s for the jazz-influenced singer Frank Sinatra, including Sinatra's work with Count Basie and his big band

In his autobiography Ray described the album as both criticizing America and expressing love, partly for "the spirit of America" that had allowed him to work hard and succeed despite his humble origins, his blindness, and racism. "I was saying, 'Listen, you need to clean up some of this s---, America, but I still love you.'" He notes a "black magazine wrote that I was selling out" with his patriotic *America*, to which he replies: "Ever since I started traveling round the world and seeing other places, I've been convinced that what we got – as rotten as part of it might be – is hipper than anything else I've noticed out there."[10]

Three scholars of political philosophy, literature, and American political thought recently have argued in the spirit of Brother Ray by providing an anthology of stories, addresses, and songs for cultivating a reflective patriotism. Amy and Leon Kass, with Diana Schaub, developed *What So Proudly We Hail* to inspire formation of "American identity, American character, and American citizenship" through close reading of, and seminar or reading group discussions about, a range of texts and symbols. A "reflective" patriotism requires education of "hearts as well as minds, exploiting the soul-shaping powers of story, speech, and song."[11] The stories range from Herman Melville, Mark Twain, and Willa Cather to Ralph Ellison, Saul Bellow, and John Updike; with speeches of great presidents from Washington and Lincoln through Theodore Roosevelt, and from great civic leaders including Frederick Douglass, W. E. B. Du Bois, and Martin Luther King, Jr. The selections, with brief introductions and Socratic questions on each, are grouped into sections including "The American Creed," "A Robust Citizenry: The Virtues of Civic Life," and "Making One Out of Many." "Songs for Free Men and Women" includes *The Star-Spangled Banner, My Country 'Tis of Thee, America the Beautiful*, and *Battle Hymn of the Republic* on to *God Bless America* and *This Land Is Your Land*.

The larger aim of *What So Proudly We Hail* is "to make Americans more appreciatively aware of who they are as citizens," thus to "produce better patriots and better citizens: men and women knowingly and thoughtfully attached to our country and devoted to its ideals, and eager

---

[10] Ray Charles and David Ritz, *Brother Ray: Ray Charles' Own Story* (New York: Da Capo Press, 2003 [1978]), 311–12.

[11] Amy A. Kass, Leon R. Kass, and Diana Schaub, eds., *What So Proudly We Hail: The American Soul in Story, Speech, and Song* (ISI Books, 2011), Introduction, x–xi. A volume with a similar spirit, collecting "classic speeches, poems, arguments, and songs" illuminating the American tradition, is Diane Ravitch, *The American Reader: Words That Moved A Nation* (Harper Collins/Perennial [1990] 2000).

to live an active life" (*Proudly We Hail*, xi). This requires striking the right balance between a universalism (whether that of the Declaration's most abstract principles or the recent emphasis among elites on cosmopolitanism) and an ethno-racial tribalism; "can there be a thoughtful national pride?" (xii). The forging of citizens, inspired to serve and lead beyond enjoying rights, requires Americans learning to "identify with their country, admire its institutions and ways, and devote themselves to robust civic participation" (xiv). This in turn entails "know[ing] who we are as Americans and why the blessings we share are worth defending and perpetuating," and developing "the affections for our country that can move us to act in public-spirited ways" (xv). They praise our uniquely important civil society, and endorse the need for robust voluntary associations from the religious to the secular and quotidian, yet warn that "if we lack public spirit, civic attachment, and the character needed for active and effective civic participation" then civil society will suffer (xvi). The larger challenge, then, is that "[a]ctive and attached citizens of good character are not born; they are made. Their making depends partly on explicit instruction, partly on habituation in character-shaping activities – in homes, schools, houses of worship, community organizations, youth groups, voluntary associations, branches of military service, and the like" (xviii). The hope is that "such reflective reading and discussion can foster a deeper sense of American identity," to include "honest" treatment of America as "not simply a success story" – for "[t]houghtful and engaged citizenship cannot be had by simple indoctrination into the American creed" (xx).

I invoke the jazz-inspired model of Ray Charles before the philosophical approach of *What So Proudly We Hail* because I think America's deep, systemic dilemma requires more accessible invitations in civic culture to rediscover the serious work of reflective patriotism. Some angry, culture-despairing culture warriors might be tempered by reflection on the bluesey yet joyful achievement of American unity in jazz, while the civically apathetic might be inspired to learn more about their country, one capable of such hopeful feats. This surely is the spirit of the brief dialogues between retired Justice Sandra Day O'Connor and jazzman Wynton Marsalis for Martin Luther King Day in 2009. The larger educational project of Jazz at Lincoln Center in New York City, where Marsalis long has been musical director, is "Let Freedom Swing." O'Connor, the first woman to serve on the U.S. Supreme Court, from 1981 to 2006, poses questions to trumpeter Marsalis in three videos: on our democratic constitutionalism and jazz; jazz and American racial unity; and jazz as our quintessential art form.[12] Each video opens with music by a Marsalis quintet (piano, acoustic bass, drum set, tenor saxophone, trumpet), and the music percolates throughout, sometimes coming to the fore.

When Justice O'Connor asks about similarities between jazz and democracy, Marsalis suggests that the Constitutional Convention in 1787, and the various equilibria of rights, institutional forms, and improvisations forged for our polity, is like a jazz quintet. The founders were "a collection of virtuosos" grappling with problems of political order, arriving at "a delicate way of balancing the rights of individuals, the rights of states, what is the central government's role. In [jazz] music we do that all the time." The jurist and the jazzman discuss which instruments are analogous to executive energy, judicial steadiness, and legislative capaciousness (the drum set, string bass, and piano, respectively). O'Connor emphasizes that "the point" of the entire arrangement is "to listen to each other"; which requires the discipline to balance improvisation with the rules embodied in the system's parameters, checks, and balances. Marsalis affirms that the discipline of hearing, and responding appropriately, is crucial for success. Perhaps because she had served as an Arizona legislator – indeed the first female president of a state senate in American history – O'Connor concludes by suggesting that legislators have the greatest challenge with listening, thus could benefit most from the model of jazz. We see the legislator and jurist find harmony with the trumpeter and educator on the reality that America's system of freedom and equality requires demanding virtues of all citizens, not only office holders, to achieve a functioning, enriching ensemble. These designed-yet-improvised conversations between two diverse leaders also convey symbolic lessons about America and civic friendship which are greater than the sum of their elements.

On American unity, O'Connor finds it fitting to recall on Martin Luther King Day that jazz "has helped us to bridge the gap between the races in our country," for while "many early jazz musicians were African American, we've had great jazz musicians" from other races,

---

[12] "Wynton and Sandra Day O'Connor discuss jazz music and government," February 9, 2009, at www.wyntonmarsalis.org/news/entry/wynton-marsalis-sandra-day-oconnor-discussion-jazz. Jazz at Lincoln Center and Teachers College at Columbia University collaborated to produce *Let Freedom Swing: Conversations on Jazz and Democracy; A Resource for Teachers Featuring Wynton Marsalis and Sandra Day O'Connor* (DVD, 2010), adding to the three conversations other interviews with professional and student musicians, and historians, on the themes of We the People, *E Pluribus Unum*, and A More Perfect Union; with suggested lesson plans.

such that jazz embodies "a mixture." Marsalis adds that King was pragmatic as much as idealistic, "a man of action," so embraced jazz "as an agent for change" given the power of "culture" to shape politics. He knew jazz was played "by all types of people, from everywhere." Duke Ellington, Marsalis notes, was from a middle-class Washington, DC family; Armstrong from awful poverty and racism in New Orleans; white musicians like Bix Beiderbecke, Benny Goodman, and Dave Brubeck from still other backgrounds in the Midwest and California; yet jazz let them play together and love the music made by their partners. O'Connor reads a Marsalis quote: "When a group of people working together feel something, when they trust that all are concerned for the common good, when they're determined to be in sync no matter what happens, that is swing." He replies: "Swing is a matter of equilibrium. The Constitution is a supreme example of swinging. How can we figure out how to meet each other's objectives and be together and for it to feel good? Now, when we look at swing, it brings together opposites ... When [the instruments] get along and they work it out, you have a great time. When they don't [pauses, winces], you got a long night." The conversation prods us to consider that amid failure there may be disagreements on the bandstand, as there surely are in politics, as to who is the greater obstacle to equilibrium; yet if it's got that swing, we should emulate the citizens who negotiate to produce a lively harmony. Of course a jazz group starts from greater agreement on a common good – the forging of an ensemble to play a particular kind of music – than a legislature or government divided by parties and branches; yet the need for civic commitment, to working across divergences, holds for both endeavors.[13]

In the third video O'Connor notes their different backgrounds – from a small ranching community in rural Arizona, versus New Orleans – yet each enjoys jazz, and they converse easily. Marsalis offers that improvisation on a jazz standard, or a new musical arrangement, is analogous to amendments to the Constitution: It's still the same legal order – "the ideals are valid, they are timeless" – yet they can be adapted to new scenarios. O'Connor concludes that jazz is the quintessential American art form, and "it belongs to us as a people"; Marsalis notes it has been embraced by people around the world, and she agrees; he adds "they

[13] The founding director of the Center for Jazz Studies at Columbia University, Robert G. O'Meally, uses Ralph Ellison's observation that jazz is "antagonistic cooperation" to guide his analysis of twentieth-century African-American art, in *Antagonistic Cooperation: Jazz, Collage, Fiction, and the Shaping of African American Culture* (Columbia University Press, 2022).

love it" because all peoples "like the best of what America has to offer the world."[14]

A comprehensive and inspiring study of this pillar of American culture is the ten-part documentary *Jazz* produced by Ken Burns, first broadcast on public television in 2001. The main writer for *Jazz*, Geoffrey C. Ward, joined Burns to produce a companion text on "America's music" which deepens the video analysis, featuring commentary by Wynton Marsalis and by historians and writers including Stanley Crouch, Gerald Early, Gary Giddins, and Albert Murray. Burns, in the preface "Our Art," quotes the great pianist, composer, and band leader Duke Ellington on jazz embodying freedom, having evolved from "certain ideals of freedom and independence" that define America. The series and book offer "the explosive hypothesis that those who have the peculiar experience of being unfree in a free land might actually be at the center of our history," teaching us about "our great promise and our great failing," serving as "our oft-neglected conscience, a message of hope and transcendence, of affirmation in the face of adversity, unequaled in the unfolding drama we call American history" (*Jazz*, vii and ix).[15] Yet jazz also is "much more," a story of "a million nights when, against all odds, men and women of all colors and astonishing gifts came together and made great art, in each instance recalling centuries of human suffering, cruelty, negotiation, search, and finally joy." Thus jazz embodies the American need, and capacity, for "reconciliation" – that "our national character and soul" contains "a certain amount of risk and challenge, of tension and attention, a certain presence that suggests how we might become as a people" (*Jazz*, ix).

Ward and Burns also follow Marsalis, and other performers and scholars interviewed, in honoring the path blazed by the genius of trumpeter and singer Louis "Satchmo" Armstrong across the twentieth century. Armstrong's blending of "sophisticated rhythms, elegant lines" with "power" and personal presence is to American music what Einstein is to physics, the Wright Brothers to travel. He invented swing by liberating

[14] In an extended interview in 2001, "Freedom of Expression with a Groove," Marsalis more expansively discusses these analogies of democratic constitutionalism and jazz; in Geoffrey C. Ward and Ken Burns, *Jazz: A History of America's Music* (Alfred A. Knopf, 2021 [2001]), 116–21. He also comments on the genius and contributions of Louis Armstrong and Duke Ellington.

[15] Burns and Ward make these claims having already produced multi-episode documentaries on the Civil War and on America's pastime, baseball; they see *Jazz* as completing their "American trilogy." In November 2025 they released their six-part documentary *The American Revolution* on PBS, to mark the American semiquincentennial; and the companion book *The American Revolution: An Intimate History* (Knopf Doubleday).

the solo performer amid the ensemble – first on trumpet, then in his singing. Many musicians and scholars invoke his great "heart" and "humanity" and spirituality, seeing him as a "gift of God or an angel." Marsalis finds Armstrong "chosen by God to bring the feeling and message and the identity of jazz to everybody," in America and beyond, and that his "overwhelming message is love" even in the face of life's hardships, which he knew well (*Jazz*, x; see also 340–41).[16]

Ward and Burns cite powerful testimony on jazz's fundamental lessons about America offered by a prominent law professor at Columbia and Yale, Charles L. Black; upon seeing Armstrong perform in 1931 in Austin, Texas where Black was a university freshman.

He was the first genius I had ever seen ... it is impossible to overstate the significance of a 16-year-old southern boy's seeing genius, for the first time, in a black. We literally never saw a black, then, in any but a servant's capacity.... But genius – fine control over total power, all height and depth, forever and ever? It had simply never entered my mind ... that I would see this for the first time in a black man. You don't get over that ... the lies reel, and contradict one another, and simper in silliness and fade into shadow. But the seen truth remains (*Jazz*, 2).

Black's most famous legal case occurred two decades later when he volunteered for the integrated legal team arguing *Brown vs. Board of Education of Topeka, Kansas*, with future Supreme Court Justice Thurgood Marshall as a partner. The US Supreme Court ruled in 1954 that racial segregation in public schooling violated the 14th Amendment to the Constitution.

Armstrong may also have shaped the 1957 crisis President Eisenhower faced when the Governor of Arkansas used National Guard troops to block integration of Little Rock high school, as ordered by a federal court pursuant to *Brown*. Armstrong had been criticized by younger black jazz musicians as an Uncle Tom who didn't protest discrimination or call for civil rights reforms. Billie Holiday had recorded in 1939 a protest song about white mobs lynching black people in the south, *Strange Fruit*; with its brutal lyrics about "Scent of magnolias, sweet and fresh/

---

[16] Jazz at Lincoln Center asked the Louis Armstrong House Museum to compile "The 20 Essential Louis Armstrong Recordings"; see www.syncopatedtimes.com/the-20-essential-louis-armstrong-recordings/; notice also the five bonus numbers. To capture Armstrong's genius across the eras of his career, I suggest from the chronological list the 1929 *Ain't Misbehavin'* (no. 5), the 1954 *St. Louis Blues* (no. 15), and the 1967 *What A Wonderful World* (no. 20); though a more traditional version of the last is instructive, such as the 1968 live recording at BBC Studios in London with a small integrated sextet, at www.youtube.com/watch?v=CaCSuzR4DwM.

Then the sudden smell of burning flesh." It was a surprising hit, reaching number sixteen on the record charts. Yet Armstrong had avoided politics for decades. Ward and Burns argue he "was proud of his race, but unblinking about the reality of race relations in America." He demanded fair treatment for himself and musicians travelling with him, and privately expressed political views, but avoided public statements (*Jazz*, 182–88; see also 352–54; 269–70). He gained further prominence in 1956 when the State Department asked him to join its program of goodwill tours during the Cold War, with integrated jazz groups performing in Africa, Asia, and the Middle East. Armstrong led a successful tour to West Africa; was now called "Ambassador Satch"; and was being mentioned as the clear choice to lead the first jazz tour to the Soviet Union. But when he learned of the Little Rock standoff on September 18, Armstrong entered politics with fury. Eisenhower had "no guts." He added he would not go to Russia for the State Department. He doubled down the next day: The federal government needed to "straighten that mess down South." No more "ignoring the Constitution." He was criticized by blacks and whites, but didn't back down. A week later Eisenhower sent in a famous, elite Army combat unit, the 101st Airborne, to ensure the court order was heeded. Louis sent the President a telegram: "If you decide to walk into the schools with the little colored kids, take me along Daddy. God Bless you" (*Jazz*, 392–97).[17]

Jazz was born in New Orleans, a strikingly cosmopolitan city for centuries and still so at the dawn of the twentieth. French, Anglo-American, African, Native American, Caribbean, and Latin American civilizations blended; as did slavery and freedom, hierarchies of race and wealth, Protestant and Catholic faiths. Historian David Hackett Fischer examines New Orleans as a locus of "the deep moral paradox in America, between the continuing horror of race slavery and persistence of racial injustice on the one hand, and the hope of expanding ideals of human rights, social justice, the rule of law, and dreams of liberty and freedom." New Orleans and jazz epitomize Fischer's thesis that love of liberty would shine especially brightly among enslaved peoples and their descendants. Whether manumitted, escaped, or still in bondage, across centuries they developed "forms of resistance" that significantly enriched American

---

[17] See also Nat Hentoff, "How Jazz Helped Hasten the Civil Rights Movement," *At the Jazz Band Ball: Sixty Years on the Jazz Scene* (University of California Press, 2010) 113–17. Hentoff was a prolific journalist, civil liberties advocate, and jazz aficionado whose commentaries appeared in publications ranging from the left-leaning *Village Voice* to the right-leaning *Wall Street Journal*. A later Holiday recording of *Strange Fruit* from her 1956 album *Lady Sings the Blues* is at www.youtube.com/watch?v=Web007rzSOI.

culture and civic life. The most successful efforts were "to build complex cultures and associations among themselves by collective efforts from which the master classes were largely excluded." These in turn "helped to shape a broad array of Afro-European cultures which in turn shaped North American cultures."[18] Jazz is among the most important of these.

Fischer draws from Gwendolyn Midlo Hall and other historians who built databases of African and slave culture in North America, particularly noting how Louisiana could become a source of jazz given the French colonial attitude of civilizational pluralism and blending, which persevered through racism and class structure to embody "an enduring idea of a common humanity" (*African Founders*, 465, 475–76, 478, 583). Louisiana and the Gulf Coast, especially New Orleans, epitomize this "dynamic process" of black people blending African and European-American religious, musical, and cultural traditions to build "systems of comity, association, interaction, identity, and belonging" amid oppression. The particular contribution in music was to introduce intricate rhythms, unequal notes, accented upbeats, and complex interplay of performers – including from the black church with its worship practice of call and response (*African Founders*, 470–78). Fischer sees the centuries-long tradition of musical "comity and creativity" in New Orleans evident in the recent mentoring of Troy Andrews, a child prodigy on the trombone, by Wynton Marsalis and other prominent jazz musicians; now known by his stage name, Trombone Shorty. The culture of comity developed in Congo Square from the eighteenth century onwards, with gatherings combining diversity and solidarity, slaves and free people of color, whether African, American, or West Indian. Eventually this culture produced jazz as a blending of sorrow (slave work songs, blues, spirituals) with joy (ragtime) – a musical genre of perseverance, expressing hope that the ultimate truth of the humanity of all God's children would show through (*African Founders*, 581–82, 585, 740–46).[19]

---

[18] David Hackett Fischer, *African Founders: How Enslaved People Expanded American Ideals* (Simon & Schuster, 2022), 749, 23. Marsalis similarly notes the paradoxes of the African-American contribution of jazz in "Freedom of Expression with a Groove," cited above; as does writer and jazz critic Albert Murray in "The Embodiment of the American Experience," in *Jazz*, 342–43 – as "a music played by Americans to get rid of the blues." Ellington explained why he used so much dissonance in compositions, such as "Mood Indigo" (1931): "Dissonance is our way of life in America. We are something apart, yet an integral part" (*Jazz*, 198).

[19] Fischer finds the musical *Hamilton!* as in this tradition, with writer/composer Lin Manuel Miranda using hip hop and rap, descendants of jazz, to speak in a fresh voice to new generations about their history, affirming a sense of belonging in American culture (*African Founders*, 737).

Ward and Burns, following Marsalis and other New Orleanians, explain jazz as a gumbo – the traditional stew of the Gulf Coast – "stirred and seasoned by hundreds of hands." Along with ragtime, ingredients include the black American tradition of folk spirituals, the sacred music of the Baptist church, and "that music's profane twin, the blues" (*Jazz*, 25, 15). Somewhere around 1900 the distinct genre of jazz could be heard, a gumbo greater than the sum of its parts: "the distinctive blend of blues and church music, ragtime and military marches, and all the other elements of the New Orleans mix" (*Jazz*, 21, 22). New Orleans musicians spread the music to Chicago and New York among other cities. James Reese Europe led a pioneering concert of African-American music at Carnegie Hall in 1912, with his 105-piece Clef Club Symphony performing "ragtime, spirituals, plantation songs, choral works, show tunes" – to a rave review from the New York *Evening-Journal*. Reese Europe and his musicians "have given us the only music of our own that is American – national, original, and real" (*Jazz*, 57–9).[20]

By 1920, Ward and Burns argue, jazz was sparking racial enlightenment among a few young white listeners; they "began actually to hear their own feeling mirrored in the playing of the African-Americans, and to look for ways they might participate." Both law and custom forbade the races to compete against each other or perform together; but "these young men were willing to brave a brand new world created by black musicians and in which black musicians remained the most admired figures. *Nothing quite like it had ever happened before in America*" (*Jazz*, 79, emphasis added). Trumpeter Bix Beiderbecke, guitarist Eddie Condon, and cornetist Jimmy McPartland were among the first to admire and learn from black musicians in the early twenties. By 1925, they were joined by a Chicago-born Jewish clarinetist, Benny Goodman, later dubbed the King of Swing (*Jazz*, 80–84, 88, 91, 131–32). Indeed, Goodman would be the first to integrate his ensemble, incorporating pianist Teddy Wilson and vibraphonist Lionel Hampton by 1936 (*Jazz*, 234–40). In 1923, Jelly Roll Morton, a New Orleans Creole pianist who

---

[20] Musicologist Gunther Schuller, in *Early Jazz: Its Roots and Musical Development* (Oxford University Press, 1968), repeatedly describes as "democratic" the civilizational blending that is jazz; swing is a "democratization" of rhythm and inflection (both "weak" and "strong" beats are important, and any note can be phrased or accentuated for effect), achieved by using African polyphonic and polyrhythmic elements to shift the monarchical, hierarchical forms of Europe; and with Armstrong, further inserting the American individual spirit of improvisation; see 3–19, 27, 32–38, 43, 47, 50–51, 54–59, 62, also addressing form, harmony, melody, and timbre.

declared himself the inventor of jazz, became the first black to record with white musicians when he joined the New Orleans Rhythm Kings on six numbers (*Jazz*, 94). Armstrong made his first interracial recording in 1929 with a group including trombonist Jack Teagarden (*Jazz*, 165). The spirit of equality and *e pluribus unum* also is evident in Frankie Trumbauer, by the mid-1920s the first saxophonist with a sweet, "beautiful" sound – who was half Cherokee (*Jazz*, 140–41). Trumbauer's new sound influenced the great tenor saxophonist Lester Young; who in turn shaped the singing of the great Billie Holiday. Those two, in turn, influenced the instrument-like vocal style of an Italian-American from New Jersey, Frank Sinatra (*Jazz*, 193–94, 257).[21]

All genres of popular music that developed later in the twentieth century, from rock and roll onward, arguably descend from Armstrong and this complex jazz lineage. Henry Louis Gates, Jr. and Cornel West feature jazz artists in their turn-of-the-millennium account of how black Americans in the twentieth century rose to positions of cultural leadership and significantly defined American life. These two prominent academics offer portraits of formative figures such as Scott Joplin, Jelly Roll Morton, Louis Armstrong, Duke Ellington, and Billie Holliday, on to such later jazz masters as John Coltrane, Miles Davis, and Wynton Marsalis.[22]

After Ellington's extended jazz suite *Black, Brown, and Beige* debuted at Carnegie Hall in 1943, he responded to critics who analyzed it in European classical terms by asserting he was composing in "the American idiom" – comprising blues and spirituals to Caribbean dances and improvised solos. Jazz is "modern and it is American … The Negro element is still important. But jazz has become a part of America. There are as many white musicians playing it as Negro.… We are all working together along

---

[21] Schuller notes that, later in his career, Young's style shows Sinatra's influence; *The Swing Era: The Development of Jazz, 1930–1945* (Oxford University Press, 1989), 556. Sinatra remarked in 1981 that Young and he were friends, influenced each other's styles, and had a "mutual admiration society"; in Will Friedwald, "Jazz: Forever Young – A Centennial Tribute," *The Wall Street Journal*, August 19, 2009, D9. On Sinatra crediting Holliday's influence, see Jody Rosen, "Frank Sinatra and Billie Holiday: They Did It Their Way," *The New York Times Magazine*, October 19, 2015, 132.

[22] Henry Louis Gates, Jr. and Cornel West, *The African-American Century: How Black Americans Have Shaped Our Country* (Simon & Schuster, 2002 [2000]). West invokes jazz as an element of his version of an American philosophy of pragmatism in many of his spoken and musical recordings and in lectures, including his 2023–2024 Gifford Lectures at the University of Edinburgh, "A Jazz-Soaked Philosophy for Our Catastrophic Times: From Socrates to Coltrane," www.cahss.ed.ac.uk/news-events/lectures/gifford-lectures/2023–2024-dr-cornel-west-gifford-lecture-series.

more or less the same lines. We learn from each other. Jazz is American now. *American* is the big word" (*Jazz*, 313; see 311–13). In 1947 at Town Hall in New York, Armstrong performed for the first time in an integrated ensemble, and it was such a hit he formed the first of his All Stars. He played with these groups for the remaining two decades of his life. He later noted with pride that, for white audiences, the experience was edifying: "while they're listening to our music, they don't think about" causing trouble for blacks. "What's more, they're watching Negro and white musicians play side by side. And we bring contentment and pleasure. I always say, 'Look at the nice taste we leave.' It's bound to mean something. That's what music is for" (*Jazz*, 340–41).[23] Ellington sought to close his life by endorsing the racial harmonizing jazz had achieved, and selected pianist Dave Brubeck (who led an integrated quartet) and drummer Louis Bellson (married to black jazz singer Pearl Bailey) for this signal. After Yale University "had given him an honorary degree" and established a fellowship in his name, he asked his son Mercer "to make sure Brubeck and his onetime drummer Louis Bellson were both made Ellington fellows. 'I don't want people to think I only had black friends,' he said" (*Jazz*, 380). In a younger generation, Miles Davis and arranger Gil Evans produced classic albums in the late 1950s in the "cool jazz" idiom; and Davis included pianist Bill Evans in his quintet for the successful album *Kind of Blue* in 1959 (*Jazz*, 407–08).

Ward and Burns also regularly trace the Jewish and philosemitic thread in the pluralism of jazz. They note that Armstrong wore a Star of David all his adult life given to him by his manager Joe Glaser, and in 1969 wrote an essay praising the Jewish family in New Orleans, the Karnofskys, who treated him like a son and paid for his first cornet (*Jazz*, 38, 40).[24] Ward and Burns note that Ellington credited his Jewish manager Irving Mills with launching and promoting his career as an artist and advocating black-white integration in both recording and performing (*Jazz*, 148–49, 178).[25] *Jazz* also makes a point of contrasting

---

[23] The contrast between Armstrong's 1956 up-tempo version of the murder-ballad *Mack the Knife* and his earnest 1967 *What a Wonderful World* might be bookends of his life; "the musical portrait of a fictional pimp and cutthroat who, but for having been born in London instead of Storyville [New Orleans], might have been a figure from Armstrong's own boyhood" versus the Christian-themed hope for social melioration, dignity, and happiness he had both achieved and fostered (*Jazz*, 394).

[24] See also Terry Teachout, "Satchmo and the Jews," *Commentary*, November 2009.

[25] See Edward Kennedy Ellington, *Music Is My Mistress* (Doubleday & Company, 1973) 77, 83, 89.

the Nazi criticism of the "mongrel" black-Jewish music with its achievement of a quintessentially American spirit of equality, liberty, and pluralism (*Jazz*, 216, 225).

David Tucker and Nathan Tucker, a professor of political theory and performing musician respectively, argue that jazz is civic-spirited without being "civic music" itself; the latter being anthems such as the *Star Spangled Banner* and *America the Beautiful*, or Aaron Copland's World War II compositions *Fanfare for the Common Man* and *Lincoln Portrait* as America fought for liberal democracy against fascism. It is jazz's mostly ensemble mode that makes its spirit of freedom more civic than the individualist, materialist connotation in F. Scott Fitzgerald's *Tales of the Jazz Age* (1922), about the post–World War I exuberance of the "Roaring Twenties."[26] The Tuckers see American music, across many genres but especially jazz, as perhaps "the most complete expression of American life" given "its capacity for renewal and surprise; its collaborative, competitive drive; its constant borrowing from the spirit and rhythm of its once most despised population; its amateur zeal and professional competence; [and] its beauty and crudeness" (188). They particularly find the "spontaneous, collaborative effort at the heart of jazz" as "intertwined with the American project of individualism and personal freedom, a 'rebellion' against the 'monarchical' ways of musical Europe" (179–80). The partnership between the Justice and the jazzman, O'Connor and Marsalis, affirms this view that America today needs not another Jazz Age but the unity-forging, civic-enabling spirit of jazz recounted here.

It is fitting to give Ellington the final note on this civic-forming spirit, and lessons we could draw. Ranked with Armstrong as a genius forming jazz itself, he composed and performed across its range, from short popular pieces to suites and Sacred Concerts.[27] Duke's 1973 memoir, *Music*

---

[26] "Music and Civic Life in America," in Gary J. Schmitt, ed., *The Professions and Civic Life* (Lexington Books, 2016), 175–89 at 175–76, 179–80. Here one must note the solo pianists who have shaped jazz, including James P. Johnson, Willie "The Lion" Smith, Fats Waller, and Art Tatum; but also later solo efforts from Bill Evans, McCoy Tyner, and Chick Corea to Keith Jarrett and Ahmad Jamal. See, for example, Schuller, *Early Jazz*, 214–25 and *The Swing Era*, 476–502.

[27] Sebastien Helary on his "jazz blog" *Nextbop*, celebrating jazz "as a contemporary art form," offers his "The 20 Most Famous Duke Ellington Songs" from across the eras of Duke's career, with recordings from across decades; www.nextbop.com/famous-duke-ellington-songs. Helary includes the astounding version of Ellington's 1935 *In A Sentimental Mood* that Duke and John Coltrane recorded in 1963, pulling together jazz's foundational and then-exploratory, post-bop eras.

is My Mistress, emphasizes his global travels as performer and teacher, mostly his own tours, some for the State Department; prodding thoughts on what was universal and what distinctive about the music which, from 1943 onward, he called "the American idiom" or "the Music of Freedom of Expression" (*Music*, 309).[28] Ellington includes in the memoir's final section "Jazz for Young People," his synopsis of its synthesizing spirit and historical development; with its variety of cultural and religious ingredients, its great performers, its global reach, and its "fascinating" focus on "the performer's freedom of expression" (*Music*, 415–23). These political overtones fit with his earlier depiction of "The City of Jazz," with its "heroes," including "those who built the walls" (trumpeters and band leaders Buddy Bolden and King Oliver of New Orleans) and "those who went down swinging" (trumpeter Bix Beiderbecke and drummer and band leader Chick Webb, dying young), to those "who long defended the walls" (saxophonists Sidney Bechet and Coleman Hawkins, Louis Armstrong), but also "those who just enjoy it," including "the daughter of W. E. B. Du Bois." The City of Jazz is "anywhere and everywhere" one can enjoy the music and it evokes a reaction; "the world digs this burg" (129–30). His one directly political note is pride in the 1941 musical *Jump for Joy* as an effort "to correct the race situation in the U.S.A. through a form of theatrical propaganda." It featured Ellington's music and band; with a main set of writers and lyricists but further lyrics by figures like Langston Hughes. The show would "take Uncle Tom out of the theater, eliminate the stereotyped image that had been exploited by Hollywood and Broadway, and say things that would make the audience think" (*Music*, 175). It premiered in summer 1941, but this "Sun-Tanned Revu-sical" was too provocative. Ward and Burns note *Jump for Joy* ran for only eleven weeks and never made it to Broadway (*Jazz*, 295–96).

Ellington seems to have concluded that his efforts for America's common good and justice had to be indirect, shaping culture. He devotes a

---

[28] Schuller's sequel, *The Swing Era*, looks back from 1989 to assess Ellington's kind of greatness. He praises Armstrong's "real greatness," concluding "our lives have all been touched by his genius and spirit, whether we realize it or not" (158–61, 196–97); and praises Billie Holiday for art embodying "the indestructible power and vitality of jazz itself," and her *Strange Fruit* "a powerful moving document and monument to Billie's artistry – and guts" (528–29, 532–33, 540–41, 543, 547); but reserves for Ellington that his artistic achievement and continual growth ranks with Bach, Mozart, Beethoven, Wagner, and Verdi, finding no later jazz figure yet whose "talent is of the magnitude of Ellington's," and concludes: "In jazz he was a giant among giants. And in twentieth-century music he may one day be recognized as one of the half-dozen greatest masters of our time" (156–57).

section "At the White House" to his multiple invitations there, meeting Presidents Truman, Eisenhower, Johnson, and Nixon, but emphasizes the human, cultural, nonpartisan spirit of these moments (*Music*, 424–33). He underlines culture in his 1969 White House remarks when Nixon awarded him the Presidential Medal of Freedom, the nation's highest civilian honor. Duke noted his band currently was invoking freedom in a Sacred Concert performance; and he cited the importance of freedom of expression. He then states "we would like very much to mention the four major freedoms that my friend and writing and arranging composer Billy Strayhorn lived by and enjoyed, and that was freedom from hate, unconditionally; freedom from self-pity; freedom from fear of possibly doing something that may help someone else more than it would him; and freedom from the kind of pride that can make a man feel that he is better than his brother."[29]

This strong linkage of freedom and high moral principle suggests Ellington's cultural teaching on justice rests upon, and expresses, religious principle. His memoir regularly notes the religious dimension of his life and music from boyhood onward (*Music*, 12, 15, 171–72). His first overtly religious composition seems to be *Come Sunday*, "the spiritual theme" of his 1943 *Black, Brown, and Beige* suite (*Music*, 143). On performing it with the gospel singer Mahalia Jackson in 1958, he notes "this encounter … had a strong influence on me and my sacred music" (*Music*, 256).[30] Ward and Burns note Ellington's steady interest in religious music; that he had worn a cross since his mother's death in 1935; and had read the Bible through at least seven times by his final decade. The *Jazz* documentary interviews Monsignor John Sanders, a trombonist with Ellington from 1954 until 1965 when he entered the Catholic seminary, praising Duke for his charity, humanity, and the spiritual dimension of his jazz. Ellington in his 1973 memoir praises Monsignor Sanders and includes the latter's statement that Duke "lived the Gospel message" (*Music*, 228–29).

Ellington composed a Sacred Concert in 1965, and a second in 1969. Ward and Burns note in his final years he "seemed consumed with the need to

---

[29] Ward and Burns, *Jazz*, 443–44. Strayhorn, so close a collaborator that he composed the band's theme song, *Take the 'A' Train*, had died in 1967; Duke recounts his grieving and prayers at Strayhorn's death, and recites there the four "most important and moral of freedoms," at *Music* 159–61; see also the New Sacred Concert program, 275.

[30] The Music Institute of Chicago provides an audio file of the Ellington and Mahalia Jackson *Come Sunday* from the 1958 Columbia album *Duke Ellington: Black, Brown, and Beige*, at www.musicinst.org/news/music-meditation-ellington-and-mahalia-jackson.

spell out his religious beliefs in music" – composing a Third Sacred Concert in 1973 (after publishing his memoir), to be performed at Westminster Abbey in London (*Jazz*, 453).[31] Ellington's memoir regularly invokes the Sacred Concerts, and Act Six (part six of the book) devotes several sections to religion. He states his Christian belief, and what he has learned from a lifetime of Bible reading, in sections on "Civilization" and "Seeing God" (*Music*, 259–60). He describes his commitment to the Sacred Concerts as his "response to a growing understanding of my own vocation" and to the encouragement of many clergy, mostly Protestant. He composed the first Concert at the invitation of Episcopal clergy in San Francisco, yet his account is ecumenical, noting Sacred performances in a reformed synagogue in Beverly Hills and in Catholic churches and cathedrals in France, Spain, and Jamaica. His vocation is "a messenger boy," mostly to remind people raised in any religious community but especially Christianity the importance of faith and the gratitude they should have ("Sacred Concerts," in *Music*, 261–85, at 266, 267; also 199). He reflects that the Sacred Concerts have been described as "deliver[ing] lyrical sermons, fire-and-brimstone sermonettes, reminders of the fact that we live in the promised land of milk and honey" – then adds: "I am sure we appreciate the blessings we enjoy in this country, but it wouldn't hurt if everyone expressed his appreciation more often. We shall keep this land if we all agree on the meaning of that unconditional word: LOVE" (*Music*, 268–69).

He declares his second Sacred Concert, premiered in 1969 in the Episcopal cathedral of St. John the Divine in New York, as "the most important thing I have ever done," thus "I am including here the routine and lyrics in full" (*Music*, 269; see 270–80).

5.1.2 The Declaration and Constitution as Achievements of Harmony

Plato and Aristotle saw music and politics linked given their view that music shapes the soul, not just in single performances but in educational formation through the musical modes dominant in a culture.[32] Aristotle further finds a strong musical analogy when arguing that pluralism and complexity in a political order could be a marker of its health and

---

[31] Ward and Burns also note saxophonist John Coltrane's turn to religion and spiritualism from the late 1950s, including in his famous 1965 album *A Love Supreme* (*Jazz*, 434–36).

[32] Plato, in *The Phaedo*, has Socrates state that "philosophy is the highest (noblest) music," at 61a; my thanks to Peter Minowitz for the reference.

durability. A polity with any degree of freedom is in fact complex, cannot be a complete unity, given the differing human types, views, and interests it comprises. It is "a many-voiced harmony" rather than a unison, a "rhythm" rather than one beat.[33] This is one reason Aristotle could propose a "mixed regime" as a just and durable political form, blending elements of monarchy, aristocracy, and democracy – what we would call today a constitutional monarchy, or complex constitutional republic.[34] The American Constitution, and the Declaration of Independence informing it, cannot be a mixed regime in this sense given our fundamental commitment to equal natural rights of all, thus consent of the governed; no element of monarchy or aristocracy could fit our basic principles. Yet an astute scholar of our founding, Herbert Storing, when considering whether the founders intended to establish a democracy or a complex republic that echoed the mixed-regime, argued for the latter.[35]

Regarding the Declaration, one argument for seeing it as informed by a plurality of philosophies or ultimate principles is the fact of a debate persisting across the past century over which intellectual influence on its main drafters and the Second Continental Congress was predominant: John Locke's philosophy of liberal rights, radical Whig philosophy advocating a modern English republic, civic republicanism stemming from the Renaissance, the Scottish Enlightenment, Protestant Covenant theology, or English common law.[36] I suggest Michael Zuckert's view is generally correct, seeing the Declaration as shaped by more than one school of thought, yet not therefore a confused mishmash; it achieves philosophical integrity, thus has been received as politically authoritative for our polity. Arguably he over-emphasizes Locke's dominance, seeing the several other influences as minor elements assimilated into a Lockean matrix. Zuckert's larger approach, that America's founding philosophy in the Declaration is an "amalgam" or alloy rather than one pure element, perhaps is more important than the ranking of differing traditions or schools of thought, as important as that debate is (see Zuckert, *Natural Rights Republic*, 7–8, 95–6, 208–19, 240–43). The amalgam view can readily be adapted to Aristotle's musical insight, to see our founding as a hard-earned harmony and rhythm not a unison on a single note. Strong

---

[33] *Politics*, book 2 Chapter 5, 1263b27ff.
[34] Aristotle, *Politics*, book 4 Chapter 9, 1294a30ff.
[35] Herbert Storing, "Foreword," in Paul Eidelberg, *The Philosophy of the American Constitution* (Free Press, 1968), xi–xii.
[36] See Michael P. Zuckert, *The Natural Rights Republic: Studies in the Foundation of the American Political Tradition* (University of Notre Dame Press, 1996), 1–8, 202–43.

warrant for this comes from the main drafter of the Declaration, Thomas Jefferson, in an 1825 letter reflecting upon the influences that shaped his effort. He recounted that he had sought to capture and express "the American mind" and "the harmonizing sentiments of the day," not reflect any particular philosophical source.[37]

Even brief consideration of the full text of the Declaration, not just the famous statements in its second paragraph, indicates the work needed to fit together quite distinct principles or views about politics, justice, and humanity. How does the famous statement of self-evident truths as to individual natural rights to life, liberty, and the pursuit of happiness fit with the closing phrase, that the signers mutually pledge not just their lives and fortunes but their "sacred Honor" to defend such rights? How do either of these large ideas fit with the opening invocation of a higher source for the principles of justice, "the Laws of Nature and of Nature's God"? Further, how to square any of these with the bulk of the document, the list of charges against the English king and parliament for violating specific principles of common law supposed to be observed by all Englishmen? Further, there is the clear presence of a God active in human affairs: Invocations of a "Creator" who endows rights, then the closing appeal "to the Supreme Judge of the world for the rectitude of our intentions" and "firm reliance on the protection of divine Providence." Danielle Allen, in her close analysis of the Declaration and defense of its intellectual integrity and persuasiveness, implies acceptance of the amalgam or harmony thesis.[38] Historian Hans Eicholz features Jefferson's emphasis on a harmonizing of several strains in American political thought, all the better to reconsider the influences on the Declaration and its enduring meaning.[39] Donald Lutz views the main harmonizing as that between Lockean philosophy and Protestant Covenant theology, while James Stoner argues the English common law must be seen as one of several important influences, not least given the common law's intellectual disposition to harmonize sources ranging from Christianity and natural law to modern Enlightenment philosophy.[40]

---

[37] Letter to Henry Lee, May 8, 1825, in *Thomas Jefferson, Writings*, ed. Merrill D. Peterson (The Library of America, 1984).

[38] Danielle Allen, *Our Declaration: A Reading of the Declaration of Independence in Defense of Equality* (Liveright/W.W. Norton and Co., 2014).

[39] Hans Eicholz, *Harmonizing Sentiments: The Declaration of Independence and the Jeffersonian Idea of Self-Government* (Peter Lang. 2001).

[40] Donald S. Lutz, "The Declaration of Independence as Part of an American National Compact," *Publius: The Journal of Federalism*, 19:1 (Winter 1989), 41–58; James R. Stoner, Jr., *Common Law and Liberal Theory: Coke, Hobbes, and the Origins of American Constitutionalism* (University Press of Kansas, 1992), 6–9, 177–96, 188–89.

It is easier to see the Constitution as harmonizing several strongly divergent views given that Americans long have studied James Madison's notes of the debates in Philadelphia during the Convention of 1787. We also know the ratification debate in 1787–88 featuring the often profound writings of both Federalists supporting the Constitution and Anti-Federalists opposing it, then the state convention debates, and finally discussions in Congress in 1789 forging the Bill of Rights (thereby accepting a major concern of the Anti-Federalists on the need for such explicit protection of individual rights). Two recent accounts of the 1787 Convention, by masters of their craft, provide ample grounds for seeing the process of our founding as a hard-earned harmony – beginning in 1785 with steps toward reforms of the Articles of Confederation (our initial proto constitution) and extending to ratification of the Bill of Rights in 1791 as the first ten Amendments to the new Constitution. Gordon Wood compresses his half-century of studies on the Constitution's framing and ratification into a chapter in his study of how ideas of constitutionalism percolated through the Revolutionary War, not only the middle years of the 1780s.[41] Biographer Richard Brookhiser, author of several studies of the intellectual, moral, and political character of leading founders from Washington through John Marshall – and extending to Lincoln as the Founder's Son – devotes a chapter in his Plutarchan study of Washington to the Constitutional Convention. He recounts the Founding Father's under-appreciated role in bringing about the convention itself, in its success through arduous debate in achieving a compromise document to replace the Articles, and in his quiet but crucial role in the ratification debate.[42]

This brief consideration that our two fundamental political documents are hard-won results of forging harmony recalls the idea suggested in the dialogue between Justice O'Connor and Wynton Marsalis that, long before New Orleans musicians forged jazz from multiple sources, the American framers were making a proto-jazz, and sketching jazz scores for us, from the 1770s.

---

[41] Wood, *Power and Liberty: Constitutionalism in the American Revolution* (Oxford University Press, 2021).

[42] Richard Brookhiser, *Founding Father: Rediscovering George Washington* (Free Press, 1996). In Chapter 4, when discussing a model university course in American civic thought and institutions, I noted the insight by scholar Herbert Storing that the full meaning of our constitutional order is found not in the Federalist views along but in the dialogue between the Anti-Federalist and Federalist views, and its continuing echoes down the centuries.

5.1.3 Religious Liberty and Pluralism as American Harmony

The editors of *What So Proudly We Hail* include religious liberty and pluralism among the pillars of our polity, listing an extraordinary Washington
document in the small set of texts defining The American Creed. Few
would quarrel with locating our fundamental ideals and principles in the
first four items they list – the Declaration, Gettysburg Address, *Federalist*
no. 10 on constitutionalism and liberty, and the Mayflower Compact. Not
nearly so renowned is their final item, Washington's 1790 letter to the
Hebrew Congregation in Newport, Rhode Island. Washington expresses
the American spirit that had produced the clause in Article VI of the
Constitution forbidding any religious test for federal office. Both that clause
and Washington's letter can inform our understanding of the more famous
protections in the First Amendment against an established federal religion
and restrictions on free exercise of religion. Amy and Leon Kass and Diana
Schaub conclude that this complex "separation" of church and state, if that
phrase is apt, "far from being indifferent to the religiosity of the people,
was intended to support liberty of conscience and freedom of worship"
(*Proudly We Hail*, 62). Washington's letter captures "the nation's vibrant
and peaceful religious pluralism." We should note that the Founding Father
also wrote letters in the first year of his presidency to Roman Catholics,
the Jewish congregation in Savannah, and Baptists among other religious
minorities. The letter to the Newport Jewish community declares:

The citizens of the United States of America have a right to applaud themselves
for having given to mankind examples of an enlarged and liberal policy – a policy worthy of imitation. All possess alike liberty of conscience and immunities of
citizenship.

It is now no more that toleration is spoken of as if it were the indulgence of
one class of people that another enjoyed the exercise of their inherent natural
rights, for, happily, the Government of the United States, which gives to bigotry
no sanction, to persecution no assistance, requires only that they who live under
its protection should demean themselves as good citizens in giving it on all occasions their effectual support.

May the children of the stock of Abraham who dwell in this land continue to
merit and enjoy the good will of the other inhabitants – while every one shall sit in
safety under his own vine and fig tree and there shall be none to make him afraid.[43]

---

[43] This final phrase is from the Book of Micah in the Old Testament or Hebrew Torah, 4:4.
The August 18, 1790, letter is also at www.contextus.org/George_Washington_to_the_
Hebrew_Congregation_in_Newport,_Rhode_Island_(Aug_18,_1790)?tab=contents.
I discuss these ideas further in "Religion and Liberty in America: The Moderate Spirit of
Montesquieu and Tocqueville," in *Democracy in Moderation*, 208–17, including recent
scholarship.

Journalist and historian Jon Meacham, in *American Gospel*, seeks to restore a consensus view of American religious liberty and pluralism. He, too, includes Washington's letter to the Newport Jewish community as a foundation of the novel American achievement, along with the 1796 Farewell Address with its exhortation to support religious belief: "Of all the dispositions and habits which lead to political prosperity, religion and morality are indispensable supports. In vain would that man claim the tribute of patriotism, who should labor to subvert these great pillars of human happiness, these firmest props of the duties of men and citizens." For Meacham the "sensible center" American tradition is that "[b]elief in God is central to the country's experience" yet faith is left to choice, not coercion. Here, "religion shapes the life of the nation without strangling it," and America avoids the fate of most polities – dominated by "excessive religious influence" or "excessive secularism." Religious belief along with liberty, in a mutually tempering accommodation, is a source of America's "finest hours – the Revolutionary War, abolition, the expansion of women's rights, fights against terror and tyranny, the battle against Jim Crow."[44] Washington's Farewell, attempting to capture the meaning of our founding and provide counsel about present and likely dangers, invokes religious belief from start to finish as a foundational, ameliorating, and unifying element of the American polity.[45]

America's other greatest president, Abraham Lincoln, endorses and extends this hard-won balance of religion and liberty in fruitful, dynamic tension, emphasizing this in three great presidential addresses: The First Inaugural, Gettysburg, and Second Inaugural. His statesmanship embraced America's founding principles and creed yet prudently worked to redress our tendency to majoritarian-democratic injustice and violence, evident in slavery and in political anger extending to mob violence. Although we have no evidence either Tocqueville or Lincoln knew of the other, this spirit accords with the analysis in *Democracy in America* of our great strengths yet weaknesses, including betrayals of our principles. As recounted in Chapter 1, three of the six elements of Tocqueville's concept of American reflective patriotism are religious, because we pervasively draw on our initial Christian political culture that prizes both political and religious liberty. When he analyzes the importance of basic schooling

---

[44] Jon Meacham, *American Gospel: God, The Founding Fathers, and the Making of a Nation* (Random House, 2006), xii, 5, 7, 15–16; see also 22–28 on "public religion."

[45] See Matthew Spalding and Patrick Garrity, *A Sacred Union of Citizens: George Washington's Farewell Address and the American Character* (Rowman and Littlefield, 1996).

and efforts to extend it to all classes of the citizenry, he is struck that the primary purpose for these efforts is religious. The Connecticut Code of 1650 intones: "It being one chief project of that old deluder, Satan, to keep men from knowledge of the scriptures ..." He concludes in America "it is religion that leads to enlightenment; it is the observance of divine laws that guides men to freedom" (*Democracy in America*, I.1.2, 41).

In Lincoln's First Inaugural in 1861, having devoted the bulk of his remarks to refuting any reasonable grounds for secession and rebellion, he closes with a gentle, quasi-religious appeal to shared principles and civic friendship that might motivate compromises rather than war. "I am loath to close. We are not enemies, but friends. We must not be enemies." The very final note appeals to finding and heeding "the better angels of our nature" as the source for repairing the Union. Later, amid the fire and horror of the war, at Gettysburg in 1863, Lincoln strikes several religious notes: The opening phrasing of scores and years would be grasped by a Bible-reading public as invoking Psalm 90, along with the references to consecrating the battlefield and "devotion" to the great work of justice the Union pursues. His direct appeal is that this "great task" entails "this nation, under God, shall have a new birth of freedom."[46]

Brookhiser's character study of Lincoln, *Founders' Son*, finds it striking that the Second Inaugural shifts entirely to a Biblical spirit and refers not once to America's political founding and principles, after Lincoln had devoted nearly every address of the preceding decades to expounding the Declaration, Constitution, or both. Theologian Ronald White emphasizes the unexpected spirit of the Address for the nation, which anticipated in March 1865 notes of triumph and vindication as the Confederacy neared collapse, perhaps also righteous vengeance toward the conquered who had brought this hell. Instead Lincoln argued that a just God, in a way and for purposes not penetrable by human reason, had brought this calamitous war on both sides to eradicate the evil of slavery which even the North in some way had supported for so long. Accepting that justice, the righteous path forward was healing, national unity, a reforging of

---

[46] In the voluminous literature on Lincoln, and the Gettysburg Address, works which resonate with this theme of renewing civic culture are Lord Godfrey Rathdorp Benson Charnwood, *Life of Abraham Lincoln* (Henry Holt, 1916); Richard Brookhiser, *Founders' Son: A Life of Abraham Lincoln* (Basic Books, 2014); Diana Schaub, *His Greatest Speeches: How Lincoln Moved the Nation* (St. Martin's Press, 2021). Leon R. Kass reveals the deeper religious dimension to the call for a new birth in "The Gettysburg Address and Lincoln's Reinterpretation of the American Founding," American Enterprise Institute, November 19, 2013.

the *e pluribus unum* in a spirit of Biblical love. White carefully reveals the deep theological meditation, and the study of Presbyterian theology, informing Lincoln's stunning effort.[47] The final charge to America and beyond, and for the good of all America both North and South:

With malice toward none; with charity for all; with firmness in the right as God gives us to see the right; let us stive on to finish the work we are in; to bind up the nation's wounds; to care for him who shall have borne the battle, and for his widow, and his orphan – to do all which may achieve and cherish a just, and a lasting peace, among ourselves, and with all nations.

White recounts that Frederick Douglass was in the crowd in Washington, DC that day; he remarked approvingly to a reporter afterward: "The address sounded more like a sermon than a state paper." Later that day Lincoln sought out Douglass's judgment of the Address, at a White House reception. Douglass offered: "Mr. Lincoln, that was a sacred effort."[48]

In 1963 Martin Luther King, Jr., and the organizers of the March on Washington chose the Lincoln Memorial as the site for remarks and addresses. King notes that all gathered stand in the "symbolic shadow" of this "great American" who secured the Emancipation Proclamation. While demanding justice, that America live up to the ideals in "the magnificent words of the Constitution and the Declaration," King promoted unity. All Americans, "all of God's children," should be able to sing together with full sincerity "My country 'tis of thee, sweet land of liberty, of thee I sing." His closing words emphasize "all of God's children" again, as encompassing black and white, also "Jews and Gentiles, Protestants and Catholics," being able to sing together the old spiritual "Free at last. Free at Last. Thank God Almighty, we are free at last."

Meacham rightly counsels that striking sound balances about religious liberty is a never-ending challenge. Controversies about religious holiday displays, religion in schools, government funding for abortion, or other controversial issues with religious resonances will always be present in the courts, legislatures, campaigns. Yet we are fortunate America's

---

[47] Ronald C. White, Jr., *Lincoln's Greatest Speech: The Second Inaugural* (Simon & Schuster, 2002); see especially pp. 22–28, 94, 101–20, 121–26, 131–36, 140–43, 159–63, 165–79, 184, 197–203.

[48] *Lincoln's Greatest Speech*, 184, 199. In the voluminous literature on this theme in Lincoln, and on the Second Inaugural, among other fine works to pursue are Allen C. Guelzo, *Abraham Lincoln: Redeemer President* (W.B. Eerdmans, 1999); Lucas Morel, *Lincoln's Sacred Effort: Defining Religion's Role in American Self-Government* (Lexington Book, 2000); Brookhiser, *Founders' Son*; and Schaub, *His Greatest Speeches*.

founders "left us a tradition in which we could talk and think about God without descending into discord and division" to the degree that has befallen many other countries. The spirit behind the complexity of our political forms matches the spirit of our complex balance between liberty and religion; it entails the "hard" work of republicanism, not founded on the "passion" of democracy but on "moderation," on "quiet, cool, judicious" arguments about negotiating and reconciling divergent views. Meacham urges us to be grateful for this foundation (*American Gospel*, 328, 16, 247).

This brief recounting of hopeful achievements in America's quest to build an *e pluribus unum*, from jazz to our traditions of principled republican constitutionalism and religious pluralism, might inform a renewal of efforts in civil society and civic culture and also in curricula and approaches to formal civics. It is a challenge today for educators and leaders in schools and colleges to appreciate the mutual reinforcement needed between a healthy civic culture and formal learning, because we have transformed higher education and schools toward narrower definitions of knowledge and learning. It also is a challenge to our prevailing intellectual culture of formal schooling, kindergarten to college, to perceive any advantages to adopting a less skeptical stance toward religious belief in its varied manifestations in American history and life. Perhaps these institutions might reconsider this issue if it is grasped as enlightened self-interest: The restoration of public confidence in K-12 public schools, and in higher education both public and private, will require evidence of real efforts toward rebuilding a healthy common civic culture and replenishing our common civic capital.

6

The Duty and Delight of Civics
and Civic Friendship

What renewed kind of jazz, what blend of confidence in and gratitude for the American idea along with humility and civic honesty about our country, can we negotiate and forge today in order to sustain real citizenship and our reflective patriotism?

I hope the questions posed in *Teaching America* provoke readers to accept or revise my answers, or develop alternatives and offer them for discussion. Readers might be inspired to join the national effort of civic renewal and a civics renaissance underway, especially as America begins in 2026 to commemorate A250, marking the semiquincentennial of our political founding in 1776. We owe this to America, and we need it for renewal of the civic health and strength upon which all of us rely. Indeed, we should sustain this educational effort across two decades – at least through 2041 to mark ratification of the Bill of Rights in 1791. (Can a reflective patriot dismiss the further call to commemorate in 2046 Washington's 1796 Farewell Address, a great American event and text, also of world-historical significance?) At this quarter-millennium mark of our history it is clear America has lost its swing, and is headed toward not meaning a thing. Regrettably, our educational and intellectual community is not doing enough to remedy the anger, babble, and apathy. It would do us good as human beings and citizens to join the civil society leaders, educators, and civic leaders already alert to these issues and committed to finding a consensus conception of the common good, at least as to civics in the K-16 system, then beyond. We must replenish the numbers of prepared citizens who are reflective, discursive patriots, interested in and capable of real self-government at all levels of our polity.

Reflecting on my own education, starting from a strong family as well as vibrant religious and local communities, to public schooling from kindergarten through 12th grade, then college and graduate study, I think of civic education as a duty and a delight. It has never been an onerous duty, though it has taken persistence and effort. An array of teachers introduced me to, and encouraged me to enjoy, a blend of classical liberal education and American civic education that speaks to the soul, to heart as well as mind, about the multiple meanings of human freedom and dignity. I was challenged to use my democratic-republican freedom to lead a life of meaning, of fulfillment or happiness. My parents were the children or grandchildren of recent immigrants, from Italy, Ireland, and Germany, and from my family as well as from my faith and local community I imbibed a love of America as an exceptional country, if a work in progress. I also imbibed the importance of, and a love for, education. In college and graduate studies I was absorbed in questioning, and became skeptical about faith and country. A blend of Socratic inquiry, extended international immersions (thanks in part to my wife Susan), and broader life experience brought me back to religious faith and a reflective patriotism about America. I am grateful for the college and university professors who sustained the serious yet joyous academic tradition stemming from the ancient Greeks and Romans, and that thrived in America until the last century: A blended liberal education and civic education, regarded as both a duty for any free person in a decent political order and an indispensable delight in an examined life. What the former president of the National Constitution Center, Jeffrey Rosen, recounts in his recent book *The Pursuit of Happiness* – his intense period during the COVID shutdowns studying the leading American founders and the classical works on moral and civic virtues that they studied in pursuit of personal and civic happiness – I had been helped to undertake across decades of education.[1] I've now continued it for three decades as a professor, learning from students, colleagues, fellow citizens and community members, and sources old and new.

Liberal education or liberal arts education means a tradition of free inquiry and dialogue about the most fundamental questions concerning humanity, nature and the cosmos, and the divine. Born in ancient Athens and continued across 2,400 years, it largely is study and discussion of enduringly important and insightful works from across millennia and

---

[1] Rosen, *The Pursuit of Happiness: How Classical Writers on Virtue Inspired the Lives of the Founders and Defined America* (Simon & Schuster, 2024).

civilizations if mostly from the West. It is liberal in a traditional or classical sense, from the same root word for liberty or freedom in English: The education befitting free people, in contrast to a more practical, necessitous education the Greeks called "technical." Several fine books in recent decades, by American scholars across a range of philosophical orientations or commitments, have articulated a conception of liberal education and why it very much matters for American life even, or especially, in our hyper-technical and hyper-dynamic era.[2] At its best such education also means awareness that "liberal" bespeaks a dual reality. Only among a free people, enjoying political liberty and the rule of law rather than rule by sheer power, can traditions and institutions of Socratic inquiry thrive and be perpetuated.

As discussed in the Introduction and Chapter 3, to define civics or civic education I invoke the recent national study for which I was a coauthor – along with educators from Harvard and Tufts universities, iCivics, and the Arizona department of education – entitled *Educating for American Democracy (EAD)*.[3] We gathered as a heterogenous group by design, holding progressive and liberal-to-conservative views; yet we shared a conviction that study of US history must be melded with the study of America's constitutional and political principles to prepare citizens for the great adventure of self-government. Such a civic education is indispensable for preparing informed and engaged participants in the American experiment. It requires instruction from kindergarten through

[2] A diverse set of views, sharing some basic ideas, includes Allan Bloom, *The Closing of the American Mind: How Higher Education Has Failed Democracy and Impoverished the Souls of Today's Students* (Simon & Schuster, 1987); Martha Nussbaum, *Cultivating Humanity: A Classical Defense of Reform in Liberal Education* (Harvard University Press, 1997); Andrew Delbanco, *College: What It Was, Is, and Should Be*, 2nd ed. (Princeton University Press, 2023 [2012]); Fareed Zakaria, *In Defense of a Liberal Education* (W.W. Norton & Co., 2015); and Roosevelt Montás, *Rescuing Socrates: How the Great Books Changed My Life and Why They Matter for a New Generation* (Princeton University Press, 2021). I have regularly assigned to undergraduates a 1959 address by the political philosopher Leo Strauss, "Liberal Education and Responsibility," which pulls together liberal and civic education for citizens of a constitutional republic such as America; in Strauss, *Liberalism Ancient and Modern* (Basic Books, 1968), 9–25.

[3] *Educating for American Democracy: Excellence in History and Civics for All Learners.* iCivics. www.educatingforamericandemocracy.org. I will refer to the report by its acronym, *EAD*. In June 2025, the host institution for ongoing *EAD* implementation efforts shifted from the national civics provider iCivics to the Adams Presidential Center in Quincy, Massachusetts; and *EAD* coauthor Jane Kamensky, who since has become president of Thomas Jefferson's Monticello, has made Monticello a partner with the Adams Center, iCivics, SCETL at ASU, and other institutions in this new phase of the *EAD* national project.

high school – and into higher education for those so fortunate – of the civic knowledge and civic virtues needed to contribute responsibly to civil society and political affairs. Contrary to what might be expected from a group of educators in our era, the *EAD* Report and its Roadmap of guidelines for K-12 educators and local educational authorities forthrightly declares our love for America, and defines a reflective patriotism as one of the civic virtues essential for an American civic education. It calls on teachers, educators, and serious citizens to endorse the further civic virtues of civil disagreement and civic friendship across philosophical, religious, and partisan views, pairing these with fundamental civic knowledge approached through inquiry and discussion along with mastery of foundational information.

A Tocquevillean discursive patriotism, paired with argument and study, incorporates love of people and place but elevates these sentiments given our country's foundations in universal principles and self-government. The *EAD* diagnosis is that our current deficit of such reflective patriotism and other civic virtues is intertwined with – both reflects and reinforces – our epidemic of civic ignorance. As should be evident, the *EAD* jazz makers basically incorporated classical liberal education into our conception of a reflective, patriotic civics for informed and committed American citizens. We also argued that civics renewal, a reprioritizing of the essential importance of a reflective civics, must occur in higher education for its own sake – and also so that academia can properly support the renewal of K-12 civics. Across two years of deliberation and argument, among ourselves and ultimately including over three hundred fellow-educators and civic practitioners, the *EAD* ensemble sought remedies to overcome the current extremes of civic apathy among too many Americans and a polarized, angry activism among an engaged few. These predominant extremes, passive and active, mean that a great many citizens repudiate a diversity of civic opinion and free civil discourse. A renewed civics can offer grounds for civic gratitude toward America's principles and achievements, regard for civil disputation, and the virtues needed to enjoy lively and respectful debate regarding America, civic knowledge, and current policy issues.

Former Harvard president Derek Bok, in his 2020 book *Higher Expectations*, independently confirmed that the *EAD* study was taking a sound approach in addressing the related deficits in civic knowledge and civic virtues, the latter including civic friendship and reflective patriotism. Bok argued that American higher education is failing students due to three grave deficiencies: The decline or absence of civic education, of ethics education, and of courses addressing meaning and the larger purposes of life. These subjects no longer are prioritized in the required curricula of most universities and colleges, and in some institutions aren't even elective offerings.[4] Bok is no curmudgeonly conservative disposed to criticize higher education. These serious concerns marked a shift toward recovery of a centrist view, a left-right consensus, that long had defined academia's mission. Indeed, it is heartening to realize in a time of such polarization across our academic and civic lives that Bok offers an insight on civics and character similar to that suggested in Richard Brookhiser's astute biography of George Washington, *Founding Father*: That the civic character and civility of this great statesman were mutually reinforcing. Here was a powerful and ambitious leader – as admirers of the musical *Hamilton!* might have recently rediscovered – who disciplined his soul as a boy and throughout his life according to "Rules of Civility" composed by French Jesuits in the sixteenth century about ethical regard for others. This education in other-regarding virtues, emphasizing the dignity of all persons including oneself, is a crucial reason Washington could discipline his immense ambition in order to found and serve a civic republican order. He twice relinquished near-absolute power (as victorious general and as our first president) to secure the new constitutional republic for posterity. The same ethical and political principles also led him to be the only slaveholding American president prior to the Civil War to emancipate all his slaves. Napoleon himself later remarked, in failure and exile after giving free rein to his ambition, that the French had wanted him to be a Washington – that is, to serve a common good and embody civility rather than ambition for one's own greatness. Amid all these lessons, Brookhiser helpfully instructs that Latin provides a common root for our English words citizen, civility, and civilization.[5]

The delight and the duty of undertaking such an education, in formal schooling and beyond, points to three final elements to be incorporated

[4] Bok, *Higher Expectations: Can Colleges Teach Students What They Need to Know in the 21st Century?* (Princeton University Press, 2020).
[5] Richard Brookhiser, *Founding Father: Rediscovering George Washington* (Free Press, 1996). Mount Vernon features The Rules, and explains their shaping of Washington's public and private character, at www.mountvernon.org/george-washington/rules-of-civility. As noted in the Introduction, Washington's exceptional decision to prepare to undertake manumission of hundreds of slaves is not so much qualified as confirmed by the fact that Grant had owned one slave, briefly, whom he emancipated before the Civil War.

in the civics renewal America needs. First, understanding of and emphasis upon the virtue of civic friendship would redress deficits in our current approach to civics, and remedy the cultural crisis we face of so many citizens alienated from community and from real citizenship. It is a duty and a delight to appreciate that our fellow citizens are friends, as Americans, without knowing their political views or even when aware of differences. We should enjoy a community of shared regard and gratitude for our polity while accepting the discipline and effort to sustain friendship irrespective of differences on important matters of principle and policy. The chapter then turns to my own profession, to reinforce the need for civics reform in higher education, highlighting that this now is in our enlightened self-interest. We need to restore core academic missions of inquiry achieved through robust discourse while also restoring the civic mission of higher learning – and by doing so we would redress declining public confidence in academia. That package of ideals and interest might inspire leaders to undertake the substantial reforms needed to fulfill our civic duty to America; to include restoring academia's proper responsibility to support K-12 civics and history education. The closing note suggests we measure ourselves against the standard set by Lincoln, the Founders' son and still widely admired as the common-citizen president. We seem to admire him in part because he embodies high American ideals and a demanding civic virtue. Amid our current crisis of civic apathy and polarized anger it is helpful to ask what civic knowledge, civic virtues, and civic culture we need in order to meet Lincoln's higher, hopeful call – after he had confronted a greater crisis and challenge than ours today – to reject malice, adopt charity for all, and strive to forge a just and lasting peace at home and internationally.

6.1 CIVIC FRIENDSHIP AND REPLENISHING AMERICA'S CIVIC CAPITAL

It is no accident that scholars who have urged academia to renew citizenship education also have renewed academic attention to civic friendship. Danielle Allen, a coauthor of the 2021 *EAD* study, argued two decades ago in *Talking to Strangers* that a healthy polity requires habits, and an ethos, of reciprocity and mutuality among citizens. We must view people with whom we don't obviously share beliefs and experiences as friends. Aristotle identified this as a crucial element of a healthy political community in the first political science, over

2,300 years ago, and it remains urgently important for modern liberal democracies.[6]

Josiah Ober, the founder of the Stanford Civics Initiative and the main energy behind launching the Alliance for Civics in the Academy, addresses civic friendship with coauthor Brook Manville as a crucial term of *The Civic Bargain* – the essential conditions for forging and sustaining a healthy democratic republic.[7] They define such friendship as the "mutual trust" among members of a political community who understand that fellow citizens care not only about the good of self but about each other and the common good. When this trust exists, civic friends have "good reason to believe" that those with whom they make compromises and bargains "are committed to keeping their promises because they regard the bargain as fair enough" and having "intrinsic value" simply because a civic bargain. Civic friends also believe the other is "deserving of *dignity*" just as oneself so deserves. Further, "the civic dignity that civic friends offer one another does not preclude vigorous debate and strongly expressed disagreement" (*Civic Bargain*, 36–37). Their four dimensions of civic friendship: "attitudes and behaviors of citizens or would-be citizens working together in good faith; not treating those of opposing beliefs as mortal enemies; following public norms that are reliable and predictable in a way that builds trust; and accepting that mutual respect for the common good may limit personal gains in various circumstances." If this civic virtue is strong in a polity, "deep enough," then "the distinction between gives and gets is blurred: doing the right thing as a citizen, because others will benefit, becomes a valued end in itself" (220). This is so demanding of citizens that civic friendship, the sixth of their crucial conditions of the civic bargain, points them to their seventh: The need for civic education.

Paul Ludwig connects the insights from Aristotle and Allen on civic friendship to the discussion Robert Putnam sparked a quarter-century ago in *Bowling Alone* on "social capital" in voluntary associations as being a crucial marker of our polity's health. Ludwig argues that the friendship shared among Americans at home or abroad is their admiration – and

---

[6] Danielle Allen, *Talking to Strangers: Anxieties of Citizenship since Brown v. Board of Education* (University of Chicago Press, 2004). Aristotle notes the importance of civic friendship early in Book 8 of the *Nicomachean Ethics*, the first of two books on friendship as the crown of the virtues; also in the sequel to the *Ethics*, his *Politics*, when discussing political education in the best regime (Books 7 and 8, or in the traditional/alternate ordering, Books 4 and 5).

[7] Brooke Manville and Josiah Ober, *The Civic Bargain: How Democracy Survives* (Princeton University Press, 2023).

gratitude – for our political order with its principles of freedom and equality. Yet the institutions don't generate these features of civic culture, and civic virtues, needed to sustain them; an insight with roots in Aristotle and affirmed by Tocqueville. Putnam, adapting Tocqueville as well as economist Glenn Loury, captures this in the metaphor of social capital: The reservoir of ideas and habits that modern liberal laws and markets rely upon but didn't invent, and don't replenish. The current moment suggests the need to extend Putnam's argument, and Ludwig's, to see civic friendship as an element of the *civic capital* we must renew. One dimension of this is to encourage voluntary associations in civil society, to include religious associations, as Putnam did in his initial work then in his sequel with David Campbell on religion, *American Grace*. Ludwig further notes that in America's current moment of deep polarization, featuring angry populism and narrow nationalism, civic friendship can engage with yet elevate and moderate these passions, while also pulling the apathetic and disconnected into the real life of citizenship.[8]

Ludwig confirms Tocqueville's insight (discussed in Chapter 2 on reflective patriotism) that while Americans might tell themselves they join and support voluntary associations out of enlightened self-interest – because of direct or indirect benefit gained for themselves or family – in fact, they also commit to these activities and friendships for higher, larger reasons. Americans know that "joining" is intrinsically good for others, for their community, and for themselves all at once. For example, "the desire to help" is "fundamentally different from self-interest, and this passion continues to play a role in citizen behavior" (*Political Friendship*, 17–19). We help others "even when the repercussions of doing so may damage our self-interest, a fact that is evidence that our passionate being-together with fellow citizens is not exhausted by considerations of interest." Thus Ludwig also affirms Tocqueville's insight that Americans invent and sustain a rich array of associations in civil society from an ethic of responsibility, even a sense of honor. Today we need civil society to understand itself as exemplifying this blend of the useful and the honorable, but especially the dignified reasons to be a civic friend, to invest in civic friendship, to see it as a civic virtue. We also need a civic education

---

[8] Paul W. Ludwig, *Rediscovering Political Friendship: Aristotle's Theory and Modern Identity, Community, and Equality* (Cambridge University Press, 2020), 1–2, xiv–xv, 7, 15. Robert D. Putnam, *Bowling Alone: The Collapse and Revival of American Community, Revised and Updated* (Simon & Schuster, 2020 [2000]); Robert D. Putnam and David E. Campbell, *American Grace: How Religion Divides and Unites Us* (Simon & Schuster, 2012 [2010]).

in schools and college that reinforces these truths (*Political Friendship*, 19, 154–61, 234–37, 242, 284, 267–68, 326).

Manville and Ober note the value of civic rituals in building and sustaining civic friendship, and Ludwig reinforces this element of a healthy civic culture. At a Fourth of July celebration, for example, the pleasure of the music and the crowd can reinforce civic principles: "Citizens contemplate their polity and themselves," and they "get together for the pleasure of it. But their pleasure is ennobled, in part, because citizenship is being celebrated. Taking pleasure in a [patriotic] parade is very different from the pleasure taken, e.g., in a trip to the beach or the casino" (*Political Friendship*, 119–20). Yet as Putnam's initial study showed, the civil society associations that organize such civic rituals, or generate the public spirit that encourages attendance and participation, need support – and this mostly can't be generated by new laws or government programs. What can help is to talk up civil society associations and other "intermediary institutions" (as Tocqueville calls them), standing between government and individuals, as being civic friendships (175–82).[9] We further should appreciate the nongovernmental civic function, and encouragement for civic friendship, provided by political parties beyond but adjacent to civil society (177).[10] This extended renewal in civil society, generating a sense of responsibility and agency in citizens, can in turn reanimate participation in town councils and county-level organizations (including political parties) that feature face-to-face citizen meetings – with the still further effect of inducing responsibility for America itself (181–82). These dimensions of civic friendship are related to patriotism, but not identical. This kind of "liberal patriotism" occupies "a middle ground between a nativist identity and having no patriotic identity at all" (*Political Friendship*, 253, 261–64, 270).

Ludwig's argument has been extended by Robert B. Talisse in warning that our current political culture is "overdoing democracy," thus harming democratic self-government. For Talisse, the "ubiquity of democratic

---

[9] This is also the spirit of Yuval Levin's diagnosis and proposed remedies in *The Fractured Republic: Renewing America's Social Contract in the Age of Individualism* (Basic Books 2016).

[10] Russell Muirhead argues in *The Promise of Party in a Polarized Age* (Harvard University Press, 2014) that America's current era of negative polarization and hyper-partisanship is, paradoxically, a consequence of weak national parties; we don't need less partisanship but rather better partisanship. Restoration of an older model of parties and of reasonable, constructive disagreement between them will require, however, civic education (see 168–72).

politics," the "saturation of social life" with categories and aims of politics, is not healthy for democratic politics. We should rediscover the maxim that "Thanksgiving dinner is more important than politics," relearn the need to "reserve spaces within our social lives for collaborative activities and projects in which politics is simply beside the point" – in part because these provide and sustain "the dispositions and habits that make democracy function properly." Further, we should tone down and tune out the politics in some parts of our lives because "there's more to life than the travails of democracy."[11] Thus, Talisse agrees with Ludwig on the need to revive places of activity traditionally above and beyond politics, which have withered in the past half-century: "neighborhoods, places of worship, households, shared public spaces." This points Talisse to the ideal, and practice, of civic friendship; to include a disposition that appreciates "civil political disagreement and a desire to cooperate across political divides" (*Overdoing Democracy*, 22, 36, 137). This virtue entails rising above "civic enmity" to restore an ethic of citizens "able to regard each other with a certain kind of *sympathy*." This means seeing "political opponents [as] mistaken or misguided" but not regarded as "unfit for citizenship." Given the current angry polarization, this is hard work. It requires recovering a sense of civic duty to "regard one's political rivals as one's equals" while also seeing "the humanity and civility of those whose politics are unknown to us" – the latter in civil society associations which teach us that civic friendship as Americans is more important than current political contestations (*Overdoing Democracy*, 147, 165).

The producer-writer team behind the *Jazz* documentary and its companion book, Ken Burns and Geoffrey Ward, recount a striking instance of civic friendship across racial and class lines in the 1920s when such divisions were stark. A group of white musicians in New York City who admired Louis Armstrong's genius but of course would face great social risk if they ever attempted to publicly join him in making music, organized a private dinner in his honor. They gave him a gold watch inscribed "from the Musicians on Broadway." This is a story about the peculiar power of jazz in American life, yet it also teaches about the power of civic friendship generally. Ward and Burns note: "In no other sphere of American life in 1929 would such a ceremony have been held for a black person, in none other would the tribute have been so heartfelt, the love and respect have been so palpable, the recognition of the black artist's

[11] Robert B. Talisse, *Overdoing Democracy: Why We Must Put Politics in Its Place* (Oxford University Press, 2019) 4–6.

supremacy so unquestioned." Armstrong was delighted, and suggested they all play in a jam session after dinner. He wrote years later: "And did we have a ball. My, my, my ...."[12]

The urgency of these concerns about decay of civil associations and civic friendship is compounded by the dramatic and accelerating effects of the digital-age transformation of civilization in recent decades. Its undeniable positive effects must be weighed against the erosion of face-to-face, embodied human community, from family and close personal friendships to civil society and its institutions – with cumulatively grave costs for American political life. These include self-sorting into information silos and single-minded communities or affinity groups, thus exacerbating angry polarization. We tend to overlook, however, the civic damage the digital revolution causes to our civic fabric at the other extreme: The individualism and self-isolation which pulls fellow citizens away from real human communities thus into amnesia about, or failure ever to develop, a genuine sense of their citizenship. Jonathan Haidt's recent work *The Anxious Generation* analyzes the crisis for younger people in terms of psychological development and personal health. Yet as a cofounder of the academic reform initiative Heterodox Academy, Haidt also is well aware of the civic costs of this digitally induced malformation.[13] Counteracting these deleterious effects requires us to double down on efforts to restore human-scale civic and political community from the ground up. Educators can play our part by restoring the ideals of citizenship education in both civic knowledge and civic virtues which once sustained a healthier and stronger American polity, the American experiment. While doing so we must work to revive, as argued in Chapter 5, the mutually reinforcing and enriching support between civic culture and formal schooling in our democratic republic.

6.2 A SPUTNIK MOMENT FOR ACADEMIA: RESTORING A HIGHER CIVICS

Harvard's Danielle Allen has argued that higher education could address some of its own shortcomings while also addressing the public's declining confidence by proposing a new social contract with America. In this

---

[12] Geoffrey C. Ward and Ken Burns, *Jazz: A History of America's Music* (Alfred A. Knopf, 2021 [2001]), 168–69). I discuss jazz as a model of American *e pluribus unum* in Chapter 5.

[13] Haidt, *The Anxious Generation: How the Great Rewiring of Childhood Is Causing an Epidemic of Mental Illness* (Penguin Press, 2024).

renewed bargain, a higher civics is restored as a primary mission of colleges and universities. As noted in the Preface and Introduction, this is a national-consensus call for reform that serves academia's enlightened self-interest. Doing the right thing to restore some of the delight of higher intellectual and civic discourse to higher education would simultaneously fulfill our civic duty and restore public standing. To paraphrase Johns Hopkins President Ronald Daniels, we would be offering the education to students that we owe to America's democratic republic, while renewing core academic missions of robust inquiry achieved through intellectual diversity. Yet such a significant reform is not easy. Educators might gain clarity about our real situation, and refocus on our civic duty, by considering the crisis-response analogy the *EAD* coauthors developed in our deliberations: that K-12 civics needs a Sputnik moment.

America has rallied against external threats across the past seventy-five years by reinvesting in both K-12 and higher education and by redesigning their priorities. This process occurred in response to the 1957 Sputnik crisis of the Cold War, then again in the economic-competitiveness crisis of the 1980s, with the educational beneficiary largely being science, technology, engineering and mathematical studies, or STEM, as well as pre-professional studies generally. America has forgotten, however, Lincoln's 1838 warning on the perpetuation of our political order: that if America were to fail, it would not be by foreign conquest but by suicide. Civic ignorance about our laws and Constitution would combine with decline in the civic virtues needed to sustain civil disagreement, as well as civic friendship, thus commitment to an ordered liberty amid the diverse views in our republic. The tendencies in a democratic political culture toward excesses, particularly the angry passions that can blaze in political disputes, would tend toward self-destruction if not moderated. Nearly two centuries later, this again is the greatest threat we face: our own failures of civic education and civic culture. That said, the failures in our era have manifested not only in anger and conflict but also in widespread civic apathy and alienation.

One reason a significant reform and renewal will be difficult for higher education is that among the small number of academics who have sustained an interest in citizenship education across the past half-century, the predominant approach is the progressive mode of democracy education. These colleagues can be expected to respond that the need now is to amplify their efforts promoting civic engagement, civic agency, democratic participation. As argued in Chapters 3 and 4 on schools and colleges, democracy education has been the increasingly dominant philosophy across the past century yet has proven itself inadequate to prepare citizens for our complex polity – a liberal, constitutional, democratic republic. Robert Talisse reinforces this judgment in arguing that, to remedy our civic culture of overdoing democracy to the detriment of democratic-republican self-government, we need to increase the nonpartisan space for civil associations and civic friendship. This kind of renewal and reform is needed for the sake of individual and collective happiness, and also to help "democracy" (in Talisse's phrasing) do what it can't do: Generate the civic virtues of civil disagreement and civic friendship which democracy needs. Many of us would recognize Talisse's description of the totalizing view of democratic politics, in which "our political divides have colonized the entirety of our social environment." It is harder to see that this excessive democratic commitment undermines a healthy politics, thus, is "politically reckless" (*Overdoing Democracy*, 5).

Talisse helpfully confronts a philosophical source of this self-defeating disposition. "To turn a famous maxim from Jane Addams and John Dewey on its head: the cure for some of democracy's ills is to do *less*, not *more*, democracy" (21). We need to revive places of activity that traditionally were above and beyond politics, which have withered in the past forty years: "neighborhoods, places of worship, households, shared public spaces" (22). This points Talisse to civic friendship, which fulfills one of democracy's aims in a way democracy itself cannot: "to foster valuable human relationships and lives that are devoted, collectively and individually, to meaningful projects that lie beyond the struggles of politics." Above the sustenance these give to sustaining a healthier politics, the larger point is that these relationships and associations are, ultimately, the "endeavors and aspirations that make life worthwhile" (36).

I would sharpen Talisse's point to apply it to the kind of civics renewal America now needs. The predominant approach of democracy education is not good for our constitutional democratic republic. Dewey's declaration that "the cure for the ailments of democracy is more democracy" meant, in his mind, an ambitious program of greater citizen participation and a refining, perhaps even replacing, of the "machinery" of government to empower all citizens more effectively.[14] Talisse rightly argues that "Dewey's principle overlooks the possibility that there are social means for enriching democracy that are *not democratic*, because they are

---

[14] John Dewey, *The Public and Its Problems* (1927), in *The Later Works of John Dewey, 1925–1953*, ed. Jo Ann Boydston (Southern Illinois University Press, 2008), vol. 2, 1925–27, at 325.

not political at all" (125). Dewey's democratic focus prevented him from seeing that "there are ways of failing at certain good pursuits that owe to the single-mindedness of our effort." Having tested Dewey's approach across nearly a century, we now need to see that the cure for the ailment of democracy we currently face "is to do something other than democracy" (126). I would add, we need to do something other than democracy education. This does not mean that civics is theoretical physics or mathematics; the teaching of civics must include the reality of a civic community and the citizen's way of thinking, thus debates and choices about how to act. The *EAD* report and Aristotle agree that developing political and civic knowledge, as with developing civic virtues, requires an orientation to practice and participation blended with formal learning and civic knowledge. The *EAD* argument, however, is that civic knowledge of our constitutional democratic republic must ground and guide civic participation, even if civic knowledge is itself developed through inquiry, discussion, civil debate and disagreement. Civic knowledge must precede, and partner with the development of, civic virtues.

Talisse's helpful critique mostly focuses on the reality of angry polarization that Dewey's democracy theory fails to anticipate (or, once it exists, to remedy). It now is obvious that our inadequate approach to and reduced priority for civics also has contributed to a problem Lincoln was not facing in 1838 and Talisse does not address: the widespread civic apathy across all ages but especially our younger citizenry. Tocqueville, however, does anticipate this problem, again proving an evergreen resource for America's constitutional democracy. Indeed, this is the closing theme of his two-volume study of America, diagnosing "what kind of despotism democratic nations have to fear" – unless they can remedy a rising culture of civic apathy, of citizens abandoning the delight and duty of self-government. He fears a soft or mild despotism that "reduces each nation to being nothing more than a herd of timid and industrious animals of which the [centralized] government is the shepherd."[15] Tocqueville foresees that modern rationalist and scientific thinking and the technology it produces, coupled with materialism and the quest for economic improvement, and also a related weakening of religious faith, altogether will yield increasing numbers of citizens-in-name-only lacking a genuine civic

---

[15] Alexis de Tocqueville, *Democracy in America*, ed. and tr. Mansfield and Winthrop (University of Chicago, 2000 [1835, 1840]), Vol. II, Part 4, ch. 6, 661, 663. See also the sequel chapter, II.4.7, "Continuation of the Preceding Chapters," and the closing chapter of the entire two volumes, II.4.8, "General View of the Subject."

spirit. Entering a solipsistic individualism, they willingly allow a centralized state to take care of them such that they descend, comfortably, from citizens to subjects. As subjects they willingly would "renounce the use of their wills" because the all-provident state "extinguishes their spirits" and "enervates their souls." Occasional participation in elections (if even that anymore) "will not prevent them from losing little by little the faculty of thinking, feeling, and acting by themselves, and thus from gradually falling below the level of humanity" (II.4.6, 665). Tocqueville foresaw this danger long before the digital revolution – to include smartphones and social media – facilitated and accelerated the path to individualism and isolation from community.

Across this closing Part of *Democracy*, Tocqueville urges efforts to restore the art and ability to organize and sustain voluntary associations. He deems these "secondary powers" located in between the centralized state and the citizen, and praises their capacity to kindle or rekindle a spirit of self-government and to provide lessons for undertaking its duties. He also champions participation in local government, and service on juries.[16] Long before the social and civic deterioration in our era, only partly caused by the digital revolution – declining mental health, self-sorting of opinions, self-isolation from human connections with friends, neighbors, fellow citizens – Tocqueville could see that the broader forces and tendencies he identified would produce citizens-turned-subjects each of whom is "withdrawn and apart ... like a stranger to the destiny of all the others." For this post-civic person, only "his children and his particular friends form the whole of the human species for him; as for dwelling with his fellow citizens, he is beside them, but he does not see them ... he exists only in himself and for himself alone, and if a family still remains for him, one can at least say that he no longer has a native country" (II.4.6, 663). Today it is clear we have difficulty even forming and sustaining marriages and families.

Many recent efforts in higher education to restore a priority for "civic learning" do not confront Tocqueville's diagnosis regarding the depth of the civic crisis we face – again, problems now amplified by our digital culture. Too many recent initiatives and programs offer retooled or re-energized versions of democracy education, focusing on democratic engagement and civic participation. While the renewed emphasis on civil discourse across differing views and "responsible" civic participation is

---

[16] See II.4.4, "Causes that Serve to Bring a Democratic People to Centralize Government or to Turn Away from That," and II.4 Chapters 6 to 8 generally.

welcome, it does not address the root issue that the *EAD* report addressed, and that academic leaders such as Derek Bok and Ron Daniels have identified: The need for required courses in civics, with a clear priority for constitutional civic knowledge as necessary to guide civic participation. As discussed in Chapter 4, the research culture of modern academia itself needs to be questioned, with its emphasis on narrow disciplinary knowledge and ever-new knowledge production. We need efforts to reweave the intellectual and civic missions of higher education precisely by restoring a commitment to truth-seeking and rigorous discourse across a genuine breadth of differing views, with civic and constitutional-democratic knowledge a top priority.[17]

The path being built by the Stanford Civics Initiative, by President Daniels at Johns Hopkins, and by the Civic Thought and Leadership renewal in public universities point us toward the needed remedies: required courses in civic knowledge of the American constitutional republic, and its origins, including our debates for 250 years about its meaning and how to abide by its ideals. This should include a discussion of the view now either actively or passively predominant on many campuses, that America is a sham and always was. Indeed, what we need to offer students – reflectiveness and civil disagreement – is just what we need in reasonable educators and reflective patriots from left to right, on particular campuses and in a national effort, in order to forge consensus plans on reforms to restore a robust nexus of liberal education and civic education. We can draw upon exemplars past and present showing it can be done, but now their work should spread to all universities and colleges, private and public, which claim to care about America and to educate leaders for civic life. The deep challenge is for institutional and curricular leaders to question some fundamental premises of academia which took hold in the past century and more, including that civic knowledge isn't a serious subject. We must question the prevailing view that civics about America's democratic republic is jingoism masked as patriotism, and is legitimate in K-12 schools (if there) but not in academia.

My discipline of political science could do its duty to academia and America by prioritizing serious study of the comprehensive kind of modern political philosophy undertaken by Tocqueville and his mentor

---

[17] Robert P. George and Cornel West connect the need for renewed liberal arts education in academia with a civic education in American principles of free speech and the First Amendment in *Truth Matters: A Dialogue on Fruitful Disagreement in an Age of Division* (Post Hill Press, 2025).

Montesquieu, striving to practice a political-intellectual virtue of moderation: Of avoiding extremes and single-mindedness in philosophy as well as action. Montesquieu identified this as the core principle of his political philosophy; and we largely have forgotten that his philosophy was the single greatest influence on the American founders from the 1760s to the 1790s, from declaring independence to forging state constitutions, the Constitution, and Bill of Rights. Tocqueville recommended, and practiced, moderation in his great study of America and modern democracy, advocating a careful balancing of principles about human liberty and its decent aims in modern circumstances.[18] Moderation is closely related to another classical virtue Montesquieu seeks to integrate into modern liberal philosophy, prudence, or practical wisdom. The leaders of curricular initiatives restoring the blend of liberal arts and civic education will need to not only study but also practice these virtues. One marker for self-assessment is to maintain intellectual diversity and robust discussion as features of courses, curricula and degrees, faculty hiring, and academic programs. There are few better places in the American academy today to study prudence or practical wisdom, from Aristotle and Aquinas to *The Federalist* and Lincoln, than the new field of civic thought and leadership discussed in Chapter 4; but leaders of the field must also practice this.

What partnerships can be built on a particular campus with the disciplines and departments that once offered a blend of liberal education and American civics but largely have turned against such research and teaching? Who are the best partners for showcasing Socratic dialogue across divergent views – within the faculty of a given campus, and with which guest speakers? What outreach to K-12 schools can be undertaken by professors with expertise in civics, and what other community-oriented civics programming with a liberal arts, reflective-patriotic spirit, might work best? An excellent option, perhaps the best for addressing our twinned academic and civic crises, is to establish civic thought and leadership as an interdisciplinary field, with its appropriate institutional autonomy; in departments and colleges with degrees, or in strong centers or institutes with control of tenure lines and curricula. From this new basis, however, we must invite Socratic debate with the transformed, now arguably anti-civic disciplines in the humanities and social sciences

---

[18] Sharon R. Krause, in *Montesquieu and the Politics of Liberty* (Bloomsbury Academic, 2025), emphasizes Montesquieu's balanced, comprehensive spirit in contrast to the single-mindedness of other moderns, and cites several recent works capturing the theme of moderation in his philosophy.

about the crucial issues of liberal education and citizenship preparation. This would be to the mutual benefit of fields that might discover a need to re-liberalize, and for ensuring civic thought and leadership resists narrowness and ideology.

Civic thought and leadership has further strong grounds for remaining Socratic given the argumentative, self-moderating character of America's civic order. We are a country grounded in ideals, with a Constitution designed to promote, as Yuval Levin helpfully argues, constructive disagreement on the premise that Americans always will disagree about what our ideals mean and how to live up to them.[19] American higher education understood itself for its first three hundred years as holding among its main missions the preparation of citizens and leaders to sustain our constitutional democracy. Leadership preparation is a role elite private and public institutions claim still today, but the genuine grounding for it has been lost or repudiated. Academia has the means and the motive today, through a proper civic education renewal, to show the broader public we serve not just economic-technological development, or individual student fulfillment, or our own narrow professional aims, but also our polity's common good. This need provides further grounds for restoring serious study of and scholarly debate about Montesquieu and Tocqueville in political science and related disciplines. Together these philosophers provide the comprehensive view of how America's complex constitutional order attempts to combine the rule of law, natural rights, liberty, religious belief, modern commerce, and capable but defensive military power to maintain national independence.

Montesquieu's 1748 *The Spirit of Laws* is the singular source of the "hardware" of our complex constitutional order, of a tripartite separation of powers and federalism; yet just as importantly, Montesquieu and Tocqueville together explain the "software" of civic and religious virtues indispensable for the functioning of a complex republic like America. These include the moderating of tendencies toward extremes of rationalism and materialism, and of partisan or sectarian fanaticism. Montesquieu's balanced, complex philosophy also was a greater influence on our Declaration of Independence – with its blending of classical, medieval, and modern elements – than most recent scholarship has recognized. The frequent references Montesquieu and Tocqueville make in their philosophy to classical and modern literature, history, custom,

---

[19] Yuval Levin, *American Covenant: How the Constitution Unified Our Nation – And Could Again* (Basic Books, 2024).

and religion reinforces the crucial need for sustaining the liberal arts spirit of a reflective, discursive patriotism if only to understand civics in a properly American way, and to help to maintain a moderation that avoids the pull toward a more polemical or tactical education. For example, a properly Socratic discussion of what is meant by the pursuit of happiness, how it might evoke larger realms and sources of meaning and purpose beyond politics – which also guides politics by keeping it in perspective – should prioritize moderation.

This reality also suggests the broader kinds of coursework and faculty expertise needed in a given college, department, curriculum, or initiative of civic thought and leadership, extending to literature, classics, theology, and philosophy. A blended liberal education and American civic education prepares not zealots or activists but committed citizens who also appreciate commitments to family, civil society, religion or spirituality, and other aims beyond and above politics. Such an education also yields greater appreciation for, and likelihood of practicing, civil disagreement and civic friendship. Still further, a Tocquevillean civic education prepares citizens to grapple with the hard realities of international affairs yet also the distinctive American effort to inject as much moral principle as possible into our strategies and policies. A civic education must include study of America's political and military leadership during the twentieth century in establishing the first global order safe for political, religious, and economic liberty. It should consider how this achievement might protect rather than betray our founding principles in the increasingly complex world of the twenty first century.

6.3 LINCOLN'S HIGHER CALL

In Chapter 2 I recommended the use of a Socratic kind of US Pocket Constitution, adding to the Declaration and Constitution as amended the 1863 Gettysburg Address and King's 1963 I Have a Dream Address. Teaching with such a reflective-patriotic device could include the exercise of considering what one or two other brief texts to add (within the practical limit of keeping this pocket-sized, not a backpack Constitution). Your candidates might be the Seneca Falls Declaration, a writing or address by Frederick Douglass, Susan B. Anthony, Calvin Coolidge, Langston Hughes, Franklin Roosevelt, Ronald Reagan, or others. Nonetheless it remains a civic fact still today that Abraham Lincoln is called upon often, and across a broad spectrum of American civic discourse, to help us understand our common ground – our founding documents and ideals – and our ongoing arguments about what they mean and how to live up to them. New national organizations on promoting civil disagreement and civic discourse in our angrily polarized era have invoked the call in his 1861 First Inaugural to find "the better angels of our nature," from the Bridge USA network of chapters on various college campuses to the Braver Angels association for citizens and aspiring citizens of all ages.[20]

The Gettysburg Address remains a touchstone of civic sacrifice and a call to undertake the work needed to achieve "under God ... a new birth of freedom" that would fully live up to our founding principles of 1776. My own international experience of studying and teaching in Britain, Africa, and India, and of living in our increasingly globalized era, has prodded me to consider the advantages of America even while a work in progress. These experiences also have led me to see America's enlightened self-interest in defending liberal principles in global affairs against the threat of advancing authoritarianism and totalitarianism. As Lincoln argued in his 1862 Annual Address to Congress, we may be the last best hope of humankind, even if imperfect.

Yet as noted in Chapter 5, perhaps Ronald White is correct to consider the Second Inaugural as Lincoln's greatest speech. Its capacious meaning and demanding call for charity not malice, to seek principles of right by divine standards rather than human ones, and "to do all which may achieve and cherish a just, and a lasting peace, among ourselves, and with all nations" – all of this calls us to high, other-regarding, and quintessentially American principles of political conduct at home and abroad. Lincoln could dare to call an exhausted nation to such high purposes, simultaneously thinking of them as practical and necessary for America to be America again, because he had done his civics homework and stood on a solid foundation. The self-educated Lincoln had the grasp of human nature, history, and politics to foresee the disaster of a civil war even as a young lawyer, in 1838. He dedicated the remaining quarter-century of his life to preventing it, without forsaking the minimum standards of justice existentially necessary to remain America while not thereby tipping the Union into being the instigator of such a war. Ultimately he accepted a war that the slave power started.

Lincoln's first great speech, the Lyceum Address, called for an education in the Constitution and laws. In subsequent decades he largely

---

[20] The American Council of Trustees and Alumni (ACTA) has pulled together these two institutions and their own work on civic discourse to form the College Debates and Discourse Alliance; see www.goacta.org/initiatives/college-debates/.

emphasized, and provided his fellow citizens an education in, the Declaration of Independence. In the final two years of his life he would lead the new birth of freedom he called for in 1863, to enact the full meaning of what the Laws of Nature and Nature's God required: the equal liberty of all people. We might hope that most Americans today would find common ground in admiration for Lincoln, and would seek his guidance on the meaning of the original common ground comprised by our founding documents. Yet our failing civic culture and system of civics raises doubts as to how many Americans have even a basic understanding of and regard for Lincoln. Our further need and aim today, therefore, is to ask what kind of civic education is required even to grasp the meaning of Lincoln's final, higher call in the Second Inaugural. What kind of American civics would adequately prepare us actually to "strive on to finish the work we are in," as he urges us in closing the address? Lincoln's call is, in effect, to make an *e pluribus unum* that is still more perfect. We must strive "to do all which may achieve and cherish a just and a lasting peace, among ourselves, and with all nations."

The study of such ideas and such statesmen should be as thrilling as it is necessary for a free people, for citizens who take themselves seriously. Have we done enough to ensure that every American citizen and aspiring citizen has been encouraged to study Lincoln, and all the works and ideas that Lincoln would urge us to study? That they also have been provided fair opportunity to undertake that duty and delight? The America250 commemorations provide a hopeful prospect for a broader citizenry to undertake such study themselves, and to help spread the opportunity to others. May such a broad-based, shared experience begin in 2026 and extend across two decades of observing and discussing the milestones of our founding and how we must invest in our civic culture and reflective American civics. This is not so onerous a burden as others in America have undertaken, Lincoln would note. The new Center for Civic Thought at Yale University, in 2025, chose for the main page of its website a picture of the statue of Nathan Hale which stands in the Old Campus quad. This Yale College alum of the class of 1773 – a schoolteacher – is famous for stating, before being executed by the British in September 1776 as a spy, "I only regret that I have but one life to lose for my country." The founding director of the center, Bryan Garsten, chose to display the view from the back side of the bronze statue – looking at Yale and America as Hale does – precisely to emphasize development of the perspective of a serious citizen: To understand the principles and prudence, the civic knowledge and civic virtues, necessary to participate reasonably and justly in civic life.

It is our duty to ourselves and our posterity to undertake such study and support it for others, and we are blessed that it also is a delight. This is our sacred honor. Invoking such examples as Lincoln and Hale, and such principles, seems not melodramatic but prudent given the extremes of anger and civic apathy in America today, including regular recourse to violent rhetoric and political violence. What should we do to redress these and other degradations and dysfunctions of our civic culture, including the low regard for our institutions, leading professions, and our country itself as well as the civic apathy and quiet despair of so many fellow citizens? Whether you are motivated more by self-interest, or by a reflective patriotism and a higher regard for America, or by some blend, this is a time for sober thinking. In America that means the blues, not animosity or despair – calling for jazz-like deliberation with each other about national-consensus efforts and reforms, to disagree better and act constructively before it is too late.

Index

For EU product safety concerns, contact us at Calle de José Abascal, 56–1°,
28003 Madrid, Spain or eugpsr@cambridge.org.

www.ingramcontent.com/pod-product-compliance
Ingram Content Group UK Ltd.
Pitfield, Milton Keynes, MK11 3LW, UK
UKHW022137120526
471007UK00012B/1099